The

EVERYTHING.
HISTORY
OF THE
BIBLE BOOK

Dear Reader:

Thank you for joining me in this exploration of the origin of the Bible and its modern-day discoveries. You won't need a doctoral degree to appreciate and learn from this book—only a willingness to investigate the historical, scientific, archaeological, and cultural evidence within these pages.

I get excited learning about the ancient world, whether it's about the Egyptians, the Greeks, or the Romans. The cultures of those times were incredibly advanced in their engineering, their architecture, and their understanding of science. Because of my interest, I have studied seventeen languages, searched for lost treasure, and been given this opportunity to share what I've learned with you. The information in this book is derived from many sources, including professors, books, and Internet Web sites. The credit for this information solely belongs to my sources. Almost every biblical passage is taken from the New International Version (NIV). In those few instances where the King James Version provides a better translation of the Hebrew, a notation is provided after the Scripture reference.

Whether or not you are a Christian, I hope this book gives you a deeper knowledge of the history of the Bible. This book is written for anyone interested in the topic. My allegiance is to whatever I am studying, researching, speaking about, or writing about.

Together, we are embarking on a scholarly investigation. Let's put on our Sherlock Holmes deerstalker caps and begin sleuthing.

Jeffery Donley

The EVERYTHING Series

Editorial

Publishing Director	Gary M. Krebs
Associate Managing Editor	Laura M. Daly
Associate Copy Chief	Brett Palana-Shanahan
Acquisitions Editor	Gina Chaimanis
Development Editor	Katie McDonough
Associate Production Editor	Casey Ebert

Production

Director of Manufacturing	Susan Beale
Associate Director of Production	Michelle Roy Kelly
Cover Design	Paul Beatrice
	Matt LeBlanc
	Erick DaCosta
Design and Layout	Colleen Cunningham
	Holly Curtis
	Sorae Lee
Series Cover Artist	Barry Littmann

Visit the entire Everything® Series at *www.everything.com*

THE
EVERYTHING®
HISTORY
OF THE
BIBLE BOOK

From divine inspiration to modern-day discoveries—
a complete reference

Jeffery Donley, Ph.D.

Adams Media
Avon, Massachusetts

This work is dedicated to my mother, Donna Donley, for her unwavering belief in me. Thanks also go to my dad, Rex Donley, for all his help.

An Everything® Series Book.
Everything® and everything.com® are registered trademarks of F+W Publications, Inc.

Published by Adams Media, an F+W Publications Company
57 Littlefield Street, Avon, MA 02322 U.S.A.
www.adamsmedia.com

ISBN: 1-59337-556-5
Printed in the United States of America.

J   I   H   G   F   E   D   C   B   A

Library of Congress Cataloging-in-Publication Data
Donley, Jeffery.
The everything history of the Bible book: from divine inspiration to
modern-day discoveries—a complete reference / Jeffery Donley.
p. cm.
Includes bibliographical references
ISBN 1-59337-556-5
1. Bible—Introductions. I. Title.

BS445.D66 2006
220.09—dc22

2005026050

*This book is available at quantity discounts for bulk purchases.
For information, please call 1-800-872-5627.*

Contents

Acknowledgments

Many people have helped me over the course of this project's inception and development. First, my heartfelt gratitude goes to my wife, Johnnie Alexander Donley, for her contributions to the writing process. I owe her more than thanks because without her this project would not have been completed on time. Second, I acknowledge and express gratitude to my editor, Gina Chaimanis, for her constructive criticism and encouragement. She gave me crucial advice and assistance at various points and in many ways. I also enjoyed my spirited discussions with editor Katie McDonough. And finally, I'd like to tell my children, Bethany and her husband Justin, Jill, and Nathaniel: You enrich my life more than you'll ever know. I thank God every day for giving each of you to your mom and me.

Top Ten Archaeological Discoveries
Pertaining to the Bible

1. The Dead Sea Scrolls
2. The John Rylands Papyrus
3. The House of David Inscription
4. The Pilate Inscription
5. The Jesus/Galilee Boat
6. The Ossuary of Caiaphas
7. The Baruch Bulla
8. The Ekron Inscription
9. Peter's Home
10. The Ruins of Sodom and Gomorrah

Introduction

▶ The history of the Bible is invaluable in explaining the present. Many questions that puzzle over 1,000 Protestant, Roman Catholic, Greek Orthodox, and Russian Orthodox groups can be answered by studying the history of this one book. Differing beliefs and practices become more understandable when examined in the light of past events.

For Christians, the value is even greater. By studying the history of the Bible, they discover their spiritual legacy. An intellectual foundation for a Christian's faith and belief comes from knowing the origins of the Bible and discovering the archaeological, historic, and scientific discoveries that suggest the true events of that era. Understanding varying viewpoints, and knowing why one holds particular beliefs, leads to personal enrichment.

The apostle Paul, a renowned scholar, believed that knowledge of the past gave hope to the Christian life (Romans 15:4). The depth of this hope motivated preachers such as John Wesley, who preached over 10,000 sermons during his lifetime while traveling thousands of miles on horseback. The inspirational Billy Graham devoted his life to preaching the gospel to an estimated 200 million people during his lifetime. Studying the history of the Bible both inspires and challenges the curious student.

Exciting archaeological discoveries provide evidence that substantiates some of the biblical writers' many claims. Excavations of ancient cities, the discovery of ancient manuscripts such as the celebrated Dead Sea Scrolls, and mysterious artifacts such as the Shroud of Turin—there's so much more to the study of the Bible than a lot of "thou shalt not's."

As you read this book, your first task will be to use sound principles of exegesis, or proper interpretation, to discover the identity of the wise men from the East who followed the star to Bethlehem. You will also investigate the Bible's own claim of divine inspiration, which includes reviewing why certain writings were included in the biblical canon and others were not. You'll have fun exploring the archaeological discoveries that many believe support the history of the Bible. For example, did you know that the greatest buried treasure map was found in a cave near Qumran? Countless questions will come to your mind. What can we learn from the remains of a man (and we don't mean Jesus) who was crucified in the first century? Have we really found the bone boxes of Caiaphas, the first-century high priest, and James, the half-brother of Jesus?

Toward the end of the book, you will also spend some time learning about the founders of modern scientific disciplines and how their studies relate to the Bible. Finally, you will examine the propositions put forth in Dan Brown's bestseller *The Da Vinci Code* through the lens of history, and you'll take a close look at other modern works of literature and film that bring the Bible into our present-day experiences.

There's only one way to find out the answers to your questions. Turn the page and begin your journey through the history of the Bible.

chapter 1

Getting Started

Adventure. Intrigue. Poetry. Whatever you enjoy reading, the Bible has something for you. Interested in a love story? Check out Ruth or Esther. Do wars and adventures grab your attention? Start at Judges and keep on going. You can read any of these books for pleasure, but understanding the history and culture behind them brings these historical accounts to life. In this chapter, you'll learn the basic principles of interpretation and come to understand the Bible's relevance in the twenty-first century.

In the Beginning

Early cultures respected their pasts by valuing oral tradition. These preliterate cultures told stories of their ancestors' heroic exploits and passed these from one generation to the next. Their primitive cave drawings tell of dangerous hunting expeditions and provide a small glimpse into their daily activities. Today, people are still curious about the past. They want to know where their ancestors lived and who they were. Their imaginations take them to earlier times and places as they wonder what it was like to live in the days of the Egyptian Pharaohs. Could Noah actually have built an ark to hold all those animals? Did the walls of Jericho really come tumbling down? What is the earliest mention of Israel outside of the Bible?

These questions and many others can be answered by exploring the remains of abandoned cities, examining the artifacts of past cultures, and deciphering the manuscripts of long-dead scribes. To put together the various pieces of the biblical puzzle, this book will travel to the ancient Middle East at the dawn of civilization. From there, it will move forward through the centuries, pausing to examine pertinent events along the way.

Timeless Truth

Mesopotamia was the site of one of the earliest known civilizations. This fertile region, which lies between the Tigris and Euphrates rivers, includes a territory nearly 660 miles in length and 250 miles in width. The Sumerian civilization, with its capital city of Sumer, is believed to be the first civilization that originated here.

Archaeology—the very word conjures up images of Indiana Jones searching for the Ark of the Covenant. However, few archaeologists share in such hair-raising adventures. Instead they sweat for hours in the hot sun as they painstakingly excavate their digs for the tiniest clue to a long-ago society. But that tedium has been rewarded with some spectacular finds, such as the discovery of Pharaoh Tut's tomb with all its treasures.

Using scientific methods, professionals can date an artifact and either verify or refute its authenticity. Historians and researchers examine these artifacts so that they can understand the culture of a specific society. The search for ancient civilizations and lost cities is a search for meaning. What did these people eat? How did they make their clothing? How did they govern themselves? What did they value? Similarly, your journey through this book is a search for the meaning of the Bible's divine inspiration, coded themes, and historical discoveries.

Fantastic Find

The Merneptah Stele is a six-foot stone monument inscribed with a poetic eulogy of the Pharaoh Merneptah. One line of the eulogy states, "Israel is laid waste, its seed is not." It was discovered in the mortuary temple of Pharaoh Merneptah who reigned in Thebes from 1212 to 1202 B.C. This is the only Egyptian record that archaeologists have found that mentions Israel, and, except for the Bible, the earliest mention of Israel in any ancient record. The stele, now kept in the Cairo Museum, was found by Flinders Petrie in 1896.

The Clarity of Scripture

With so many versions of the Bible, how is it possible to know which one is right? With scholars disagreeing on what the Bible says, is it possible for the ordinary layperson to figure it out? These are legitimate concerns. After all, many passages in the Bible are difficult to understand and trace back to real occurrences.

Luckily, one of the primary messages the Bible puts forth—that of redemption and salvation—is fairly clear. This message begins in Genesis and is emphasized throughout both the Old and New Testaments. Christians believe that God has revealed himself to mankind and given them the intellect to understand his revelation. The prophet Isaiah says that God's "word that goes out from my mouth: It will not return to me empty, but will accomplish what I desire and achieve the purpose for which I sent it" (Isaiah 55:11).

Above all, the Bible is primarily a historical document and should be treated no differently than any other historical work. But the Biblical texts also fall under other literary genres, each with its own specific rules of interpretation that apply to all the texts of that genre. The Bible is not exempt from these rules. It doesn't get any special treatment.

Bible Lesson

Someone once said that the Bible is like a mysterious pool—shallow enough for a child to wade in, yet deep enough for an elephant to swim in. In other words, the surface meaning of passages may be easily understood, but deeper insights are gained by additional research and careful study.

The Author's Meaning

An author's intended meaning is determined by following established hermeneutical principles. Objective scholars interpret or explain as clearly as possible what the writer meant in his text. Scientific interpretation does not allow you to come up with your own individual opinions. For example, when you write a book, you want your readers to understand your meaning. A reader shouldn't insist that your meaning is something you never intended, nor should a reader change someone else's meaning. The same courtesy extends to the biblical writers. The goal is to discover their intended meanings, not to make up your own. Of course, in a work that has undergone numerous translations and been recreated in various versions, it's sometimes difficult to determine exactly what was intended by each of the biblical writers.

Timeless Truth

Hermeneutics is the science of interpreting a written text. Rules of interpretation must be followed for each literary genre. The meaning of words is decided by the custom and the usage that existed in the author's time. For instance, you need to know the meanings of words as they were used at the time it was written, not in the year 2006, to properly understand the book of Revelation.

Everyone has the right to interpret the Bible as he searches for its meaning, but misinterpretation should be avoided. If you read into a text what you want it to say, you are guilty of *eisegesis*, a Greek word that means "to put into." Instead, you want to practice *exegesis*.

Exegesis

The Greek word *exegesis* literally means "to lead out of" and suggests a narration or explanation. In John 1:18, for example, it says that Jesus, "the One and Only, who is at the Father's side, has made him known," or exegeted (explained) God to mankind. The verse means that Jesus himself is the explanation or meaning of the Father. Likewise, after Jesus' resurrection, Luke wrote in his Gospel that the two men on the road to Emmaus exegeted, or explained the meaning of, seeing Jesus alive to the other disciples (Luke 24:35). More examples of this word being used in Scripture include the following:

- Luke 24:27 declares that Jesus began with Moses and all the prophets to exegete all the things concerning his own person and mission.
- Cornelius, the first gentile convert to Christianity, exegeted to others the vision he had (Acts 10:8).
- Paul and Barnabas exegeted the "miraculous signs and wonders God had done among the Gentiles through them" (Acts 15:12).
- Peter exegeted how God first visited the gentiles (Acts 15:14).
- Paul exegeted what God had achieved through his ministry to the gentiles (Acts 21:19).

In each of these instances, the word *exegete* means "to explain." When you exegete a biblical passage, or any other historical document, you are explaining the intended meaning through responsible interpretation.

Look in the Book

Cornelius, a Roman military officer called a *centurion*, converted to Christianity in A.D. 40, about ten years after the church was established (Acts 10:1–48). Many believe that a centurion commanded 100 men; however, a centurion actually commanded a battalion made up of ten groups of eight soldiers—i.e., eighty men. These eight soldiers lived and ate together on their military campaigns.

Exegesis also means "translation." The Gospel of Matthew gives its readers the translation of the Hebrew word *Immanuel* as meaning "'God with us'" (Matthew 1:23). The Gospel of Mark says that the Aramaic phrase *talitha koum* translates to "'Little girl, I say to you, get up'" (Mark 5:41). These verses demonstrate that proper translation, or exegesis, provides the meaning of the text in its original context. This strongly supports the claim that interpretation is the search for the author's intended meaning, not the search for a subjective twenty-first century opinion.

Background Studies

To properly investigate the Bible, or any other piece of literature, it is essential to understand its authors and their cultural and historical backgrounds. Since the Bible was written over a period of 1,546 years by approximately forty different authors, this is a tremendous task. Studying the Bible means studying higher criticism—i.e., a book's author, culture, date, literary genre, politics, social conditions, and language. It also involves lower criticism, the study of the text and canon. Yes, this is a difficult undertaking, but not an impossible one. As a scholar of hermeneutics, you are prepared to meet this challenge with curiosity and excitement.

Bible Lesson

Job was the first biblical book to be written. It is asserted that Moses wrote it in 1450 B.C. The last book to be written was Revelation, supposedly written in A.D. 96. Many believe the apostle John wrote this book while he was exiled on the island of Patmos by the Roman emperor Domitian. At this time, John was the sole surviving apostle. An alternative viewpoint from a minority group of scholars is that the dates for the Biblical books cannot be determined.

To illustrate how to use the historical background of an event, take a look at the Bible's account of Moses. First Kings 6:1 states that King Solomon began building the Temple 480 years after the Exodus of the Israelites from Egypt. Solomon began building the Temple in 967 B.C. That dates the Exodus at 1447 B.C. Exodus 7:7 states that Moses was eighty years old when he went to Pharaoh and demanded that the Israelites be set free from their bondage. Subtracting eighty from 1447 B.C. means that Moses was born in 1527 B.C.

Moses' Birth and Delivery

In the year of Moses' birth, Pharaoh Thutmose I (1540–1504 B.C.) ruled Egypt. Exodus 1:22–2:10 says that Thutmose I decreed that every son born of the Hebrews was to be thrown in the river. Moses' mother hid her son in a basket (ark/box) and he floated down the reeds along the bank of the Nile River. Pharaoh's daughter was walking along the riverside and found the box with the baby inside. Pharaoh's daughter's name was Hatshepsut and she was married to Thutmose II. She named the baby Moses and raised him in the very household palace of her father, the ruler who decreed the death of all Hebrew boy babies. Rather ironic, isn't it?

Hatshepsut: Daughter of Pharaoh

Why would Hatshepsut's father, the Pharaoh, agree to raise a baby from the river as a prince of Egypt, especially one, like Moses, who was to have been murdered? Look at history. The Egyptians believed the Nile River was a god called Nilus. Hopi was the fertility god of the Nile River. When Hatshepsut found Moses, she was at the river performing rituals and praying for a son. When the Nile (Nilus) floated a little ark to her, she believed that the child was from Hopi and guided by Nilus. Her father, the Pharaoh, also believed that Nilus and Hopi had answered his daughter's prayer. This is the only explanation for Moses being accepted and raised in the Pharaoh's household.

After Hatshepsut's father died, her husband Thutmose II became Pharaoh. However, she was the real power of Egypt and became one of its greatest rulers. She co-reigned with her husband from 1504–1490 B.C. In 1487 B.C., Moses killed an Egyptian taskmaster for beating an Israelite slave and fled Egypt. He was forty years old (Acts 7:23–30).

Thutmose III: The Napoleon of Ancient Egypt

When Thutmose II died, his son from another woman, Thutmose III, became Pharaoh. He co-reigned with Hatshepsut until 1482 B.C. when she suddenly disappears from the historical record. It's possible she was murdered by the envious Thutmose III. Thutmose III was the greatest warrior and conqueror in Egyptian history. Forty years after Moses left Egypt in 1487 B.C., he returned to deliver his people Israel from Pharaoh Thutmose III.

Exodus 14:23–28 says that Moses parted the Red Sea and when the waters closed again, Thutmose III and his charioteers drowned. But critics state that Thutmose III couldn't have been the Pharaoh of the Exodus because his tomb has been excavated. However, in Exodus 14:30, it very clearly says, "That day the Lord saved Israel from the hands of the Egyptians, and Israel saw the Egyptians lying dead on the shore." Pharaoh Thutmose III was found dead on the seashore and was buried. A man named Victor Loret discovered his mummy in February 1898.

Literary Context

To read a document within its literary context is to understand that specific words have specific meanings in the context of a specific sentence. The sentence is understood in the context of the sentences preceding it and coming after it—in its surroundings. This is similar to the way the simple phrase "How are you?" means one thing when you're greeting a friend at the grocery store and quite another when you're visiting that friend in the hospital.

The reader must ask, "What is the author saying?" and "Why is he saying it right here?" She also must have knowledge of the text's literary genre. By answering these questions, she gains an understanding of the author's intended meaning and practices responsible exegesis.

Finding Relevance

Once a reader understands the meaning of a text in its original context, she can then relate this knowledge to her own experience. For example, suppose a reader of the Bible exegetes the well-known passage of Psalm 23:1: "The Lord is my shepherd, I shall not be in want." She wonders how God is like a shepherd. Understanding that the role of a shepherd is to be sure his sheep are protected from danger, she concludes that the message of this passage is that God similarly protects his people from danger. The shepherd ensures that his sheep have enough to eat and drink; they are not in want. Similarly, God provides for his people.

Bible Lesson

Determining the biblical authors' intended meaning has never been easier. You have so many resources at your disposal, including Bible dictionaries, encyclopedias, and atlases full of maps. Bible commentaries provide information on the meanings of verses. With a concordance, a reader can look up a word and find every verse it appears in.

What is the relevance of this analogy for the reader? In truth, that is up to her. Chances are she is not literally in danger from wolves or other wild animals. She has a pantry full of food and bottled water in her fridge. But it's possible that this passage has a deeper meaning for her than care for her physical well-being. She may believe that as the shepherd cares for the physical needs of his sheep, God cares for the spiritual well-being of his people. This leap from a physical explanation to a spiritual explanation is supported further in the psalm. For instance, verse 3 refers to "paths of righteousness" and verse 4 says, "I will fear no evil, for you are with me." Perhaps this reader finds comfort in the promise of God's protection, giving the passage relevance for her as she faces various trials in life.

Though this is a simplistic example, the point is crucial: The reader can't apply the passage to her life without understanding its original meaning. She can learn the meaning by using various resources, and then she must assess its relevance to her life.

The Author's Outline

In order to understand a biblical book, you must discern the author's outline or structure. Many individuals do not even bother searching for the outline, or they invent one. But how an author structures his work is critical to understanding both the big picture and its individual components. The following example illustrates this point.

The power behind the early Christian church and its outreach was God the Holy Spirit. In the book of Acts, you can find the record of how the gospel moved from its beginning in Jerusalem to the ends of the known world—the great city of Rome. The advancement of the gospel is organized by Luke (the author of Acts) into six movements, which are earmarked by the repetitious phrase, "And the Word of God spread." This outline of the book of Acts follows.

Movement 1: Acts 1:1–6:7

Christianity began in Jerusalem on the day of Pentecost, A.D. 30. This movement focuses on the Jews and the preaching in Jerusalem. The pause, found in Acts 6:7, allows the reader to "catch his breath" before the next movement begins. The verse says, "So the word of God spread. The number of disciples in Jerusalem increased rapidly, and a large number of priests became obedient to the faith."

Movement 2: Acts 6:8–9:31

This second movement of God the Holy Spirit centers on the gospel being preached outside of Jerusalem, namely in Judea, Samaria, and Galilee (i.e., Israel). The preaching of Stephen and Philip are highlighted in this movement. Acts 9:31, the pause in the action, says, "Then the church throughout Judea, Galilee and Samaria enjoyed a time of peace. It was strengthened; and encouraged by the Holy Spirit, it grew in numbers, living in the fear of the Lord."

Movement 3: Acts 9:32–12:24

The third movement of God the Holy Spirit advances the gospel into the gentile world with the conversion of Cornelius (Acts 10). The gospel has now moved out of the confines of Israel into Antioch of Syria. The Church in Antioch became the home base of Paul's missionary work. Acts 13:2 says that God the Holy Spirit set apart Barnabas and Paul to go to the gentiles. It was their practice to go to the Jews first, then to gentiles. Acts 12:24, the pause, says, "But the word of God continued to increase and spread."

Movement 4: Acts 12:25–16:5

The fourth movement takes the gospel into southern and central Asia Minor. Some of the Jewish brethren were demanding that the gentiles become Jews in practice before accepting them as Christians. God the Holy Spirit and the apostles said that gentiles didn't have to become Jews in practice (Acts 15:28). Acts 16:5 is the Holy Spirit's pause. The verse says, "So the churches were strengthened in the faith and grew daily in numbers."

Movement 5: Acts 16:6–19:20

The fifth movement of the Holy Spirit advances the gospel into Europe with Lydia as its first convert (Acts 16:15). God the Holy Spirit did not permit Paul, Silas, and Timothy to go into Asia or Bithynia (Acts 16:6–7). He wanted them to go to Macedonia instead (Acts 16:10). The pause in the narrative is Acts 19:20, "In this way the word of the Lord spread widely and grew in power."

Movement 6: Acts 19:21–28:31

This is the sixth and final movement as recorded by Luke in the book of Acts. It was the will of God the Holy Spirit to advance the gospel to Rome (Acts 19:21), which was also Paul's desire. Little did he expect to go as a prisoner, but that is what happened (Acts 28:16). Once in Rome, Paul wrote some of his letters while "under house arrest" (Acts 28:30). During his two-year imprisonment (A.D. 61–63), the gospel made its way into the household of Caesar, winning converts (Philippians 4:22). Now that the gospel had reached Rome, the overall purpose of Luke's narrative came to a close. The gospel message was heard in Jerusalem to the ends of the earth—i.e., Rome.

Transitional Outline

With the writing of the book of Colossians during Paul's Roman imprisonment, the gospel had been preached to every creature in the known world (Colossians 1:23). The book of Acts ends: "For two whole years Paul stayed there in his own rented house and welcomed all who came to see him. Boldly and without hindrance he preached the kingdom of God and taught about the Lord Jesus Christ" (Acts 28:30–31).

Four Transitions

During the six movements of God the Holy Spirit, four groups of people made the transition from the old covenant of death into the new covenant of life (2 Corinthians 3:6; Hebrews 8:7–13). The early church went to the nations in stages or transitions because of prejudice and racial bigotry.

1. In the first transition, 3,000 Jews became Christians on the day of Pentecost (Acts 2:41).
2. The second transition involved the Samaritans, who were considered to be half-breeds by the Jews. Primarily through the gospel preaching of Philip, the despised half-breeds made the transition into new life (Acts 8:12).
3. The third transition was with the gentiles and a Roman centurion named Cornelius (Acts 10). From the first transition to the third, ten years passed (A.D. 30–40). When the apostles didn't take the Great Commission to the gentiles in that time, God the Holy Spirit directly intervened. God wanted the gentiles in his family and no racial bigotry was going to stop God.
4. The fourth and final transition has to do with some disciples of John the Baptist (Acts 19:1–7) who did not know that the Holy Spirit had been given to believers. Paul baptized them into Christ and they received forgiveness and the gift of the Holy Spirit. Paul then laid hands on them to impart outward manifestations of the Spirit for the purpose of communicating God's word to their community.

chapter 2
Biblical Inspiration

𝔍magine that the Bible is on trial and you are a member of
the jury charged with deciding whether or not it is God's
word. Like any defendant, the Bible must be allowed to testify
on its own behalf. You must examine its claims, together with
other internal and external evidence, before rendering your verdict. Inspiration is a big piece of this puzzle. This chapter defines
inspiration and its various aspects.

What Is Inspiration?

Ten people can witness the same bank robbery and give police investigators ten different accounts of what happened. Why, then, should you believe that common shepherds, fishermen, and tax collectors—the biblical authors—can get all the details right?

The Greek word *theopneustia*, which means "God-breathed out," appears in 2 Timothy 3:16. This is a great starting point for understanding the concept of biblical inspiration as God breathing his message into his messenger. Some Christians believe that whether God's prophet is speaking or writing, he is guided by God the Holy Spirit, making his message infallible. This supernatural process is called inspiration.

Look in the Book

There are those who do not believe that the Bible is inspired by God. They believe there are historical and scientific errors within the text that disprove this assertion. Whatever your beliefs, the Bible itself does hold that the words therein are inspired, or "breathed," by God.

The word *inspiration* may cause you to think of a great work of art or a moving symphony. Of course, this kind of emotional and intellectual inspiration happens to most people. However, Biblical inspiration is the supernatural guidance of God's prophets and apostles to ensure that no errors or omissions occurred in the Biblical writings.

Revelation and Inspiration

It is supposed that Moses, the author of Genesis, knew the origins of the universe and of mankind because God revealed to him the mysteries of creation. He could not have known about Adam and Eve and the Garden of Eden in such detail through any other means. Similar examples of this kind of revelation from God to his messengers, though perhaps not always as dramatic, occur throughout most of the Bible. Some writings, however, were based on other existing documents, personal investigations, or the writer's individual experience.

The warrior Joshua, for example, referred to the unknown book of Jasher when he spoke of the sun not giving forth its light (Joshua 10:13). Before writing his Gospel account, the physician Luke "carefully investigated everything from the beginning" (Luke 1:3). Because he traveled with Paul on one of the missionary trips, Luke had firsthand knowledge of some of the events he recorded in the book of Acts (Acts 20:6–7, 13–15). Paul often included greetings and messages for specific individuals in his letters (Romans 16:1–23). When Paul addressed the Athenians on Mars Hill, he quoted a Greek poet (Acts 17:28). Of course, Joshua, Luke, and Paul were willing messengers, eager to record their remarkable experiences.

Timeless Truth

An autograph, called an *autographa*, is the original book or scroll. The author or a secretary would put ink to papyrus or parchment to produce an original document. Professional scribes could copy this document, or autographa. These copies are called manuscripts.

For Christians, whether the information in the Bible came to its writers through revelation or personal knowledge or experience is not as important as the fact that they were writing under the divine guidance of God the Holy Spirit. What they spoke and what they wrote as messengers of God were thought to be inspired. The original writings of the Bible, known as the autographs, are thought by some to be of divine origin.

Verbal Inspiration

Inspiration applies to the very words of Scripture; however, verbal inspiration does not mean that God dictated every word of the Bible. This is an important point. It is believed that the writers used their own writing styles and vocabularies; God is thought to have guided and confirmed each word.

Bible Lesson

In the ancient world, no one could read to himself; this is a modern phenomenon. People listened as small children, and then they read out loud until they learned to "read in their heads." Every written document in the ancient world was read out loud—even a personal letter from a wife to a husband. The biblical books were no different. Rhetoric, the art of persuasive speaking, was one of the most important and valued areas of learning.

It is believed that God assured Moses before sending him to Pharaoh, "I will help you speak and will teach you what to say" (Exodus 4:12). When Moses brought the Ten Commandments down from Mount Sinai, he said to the Hebrews, "And God spoke all these words" (Exodus 20:1). God told Jeremiah, "Now, I have put my words in your mouth" (Jeremiah 1:9). Along with most of the other prophets, Jeremiah wrote that his messages were from God (for one example, see Jeremiah 36:2). King David steps up to our witness stand and says, "The Spirit of the Lord spoke through me, his word was on my tongue" (2 Samuel 23:2).

The apostle Paul claimed to speak "in words taught by the Spirit" (1 Corinthians 2:13). He writes to the Thessalonians: "And we also thank God continually because, when you received the word of God, which you heard from us, you accepted it not as the word of men, but as it actually is, the word of God" (1 Thessalonians 2:13). Like the Old Testament writers mentioned above, Paul recognized that his message came from God and he made sure his readers knew that, too.

Aspects of Inspiration

Some people picture the biblical writers as robotic stenographers, carefully taking down God's dictation. This view ignores the variety of writing styles found in the Scriptures. These differing writing styles reflect differing backgrounds, cultures, personalities, and vocabularies. The writers were believed to be inspired, but this doesn't mean that they weren't actively engaged in the writing process. It's unclear exactly how this process worked. The Bible emphasizes the fact of inspiration, but not its method.

Bible Lesson

Plenary is defined as that which is complete and extends to every part. The Bible can be considered plenary, as it is believed to be entirely inspired. Those who believed what the Bible said gave evidence of how prophetic writings were given by the Spirit of Christ (1 Peter 1:10–11; 2 Peter 1:20–21). They quoted from other biblical books and referred to them as Scripture. They claimed the New Testament was as inspired as the Old.

Most Christians hold that the process of inspiration is not as important as the product of inspiration—the Bible. Because it is considered an inspired work, it is a trusted work. It was written in ancient times in ancient languages for a people inhabiting an ancient world. Incredibly, its message is one that seems to transcend time and culture.

Based on all the biblical evidence, most Christians trust that the entire Bible is inspired, including its historical, geographical, scientific, and personal accounts. However, the verbal, plenary inspiration of the Bible applies directly only to the original text as it was first written down. The inspired originals of the biblical books, known as autographs, were written on papyrus. None of them exist today. Copies or translations are accurate only if they are accurate reproductions of the originals. Accurate reproductions, however, carry the same authority as the inspired autographs.

Timeless Truth

Papyrus sheets were made from the papyrus plant. They could not be preserved unless found in a very dry climate—e.g., in Egypt. But the New Testament has close to 25,000 manuscripts in existence today, the most of any ancient document. The second most belongs to the singer-poet Homer's *Iliad* with 687 copies. The more manuscripts of a document that exist, the easier it is to reconstruct the original.

Through the science of textual criticism and with a multitude of copies, an original document can be almost entirely reproduced. This is how we determine the texts of Virgil, Julius Caesar, and even the letters of more recent writers, such as Thomas Jefferson and Abraham Lincoln. With 687 manuscripts, all scholars agree that Homer's *Iliad* is 95 percent accurate; the remaining 5 percent concerns differences in word order. With nearly 25,000 copies of the New Testament, we have close to a 99 percent reconstruction. Textual criticism is not concerned with particular beliefs or the accuracy of the text's content, but only with the accurate reconstruction of ancient manuscripts. The more manuscripts of a particular document you have, the closer to the original you can come.

Truth, Belief, and Trust

Christians believe that all of the Bible's claims will one day be fulfilled. Jesus stated, "[N]ot the smallest letter, not the least stroke of a pen, will by any means disappear from the Law until everything is accomplished" (Matthew 5:18; see also Luke 16:17). He also said, "Everything must be fulfilled that is written about me in the Law of Moses, the Prophets and the Psalms" (Luke 24:44). In that one verse, Jesus divided the entire Old Testament into three sections that record prophecies about him. The apostle Peter proclaimed, "Brothers, the Scripture had to be fulfilled which the Holy Spirit spoke long ago" (Acts 1:16).

Look in the Book

In the Bible, Jesus makes the statement that he cannot be trusted in heavenly matters if he cannot be believed in earthly (historical) ones. He told his nighttime visitor Nicodemus, "I have spoken to you of earthly things and you do not believe; how then will you believe if I speak of heavenly things?" (John 3:12). The Bible must be similarly trusted in order to be believed. The biblical writers emphatically stated that the Bible could be trusted.

Belief is a facet of trust. Here's an example: A young boy watched in awe as a French tightrope walker slowly made his way across Niagara Falls. Taking hold of a wheelbarrow, the Frenchman asked the young boy if he believed that he could make it across the Falls pushing the wheelbarrow. "Oh, yes," the boy eagerly agreed. "Great!" said the Frenchman. "Get in!" The boy refused. Though the little boy believed the tightrope walker could successfully push the wheelbarrow across the rope over the Falls, he didn't trust him enough to get in and go along for the ride. This is the difference between belief and trust.

Scripture itself claims to be completely true and without error. Jesus said, "[Y]our word is truth" (John 17:17). To people who denied the truth of Scripture, Jesus said, "You are in error because you do not know the Scriptures" (Matthew 22:29). The psalmist stated, "The law of the Lord is perfect" (Psalms 19:7) and "All your words are truth" (Psalms 119:160). "Every word of God is flawless," writes Solomon (Proverbs 30:5). The Bible claims to be God's word and God cannot make mistakes (Titus 1:2; Hebrews 6:18), therefore the Bible contains no errors. It is the inerrant, infallible word of God.

The Bible claims to be the final authority in matters of faith and Godly behavior. When facing temptation after a forty-day fast in the wilderness, Jesus quoted Old Testament Scripture to combat Satan's wiles (Matthew 4:1–11). It worked. Later, he used Old Testament authority as justification for clearing the Temple of the moneychangers (Mark 11:17). Jesus used the Old Testament to prove the resurrection to the Pharisees (Matthew 21:42).

Bible Lesson

According to the Bible, the apostles also understood the authority of the Scriptures. Paul, the scholarly apostle, used Old Testament passages to reason with the Jews (Acts 17:2). Peter stated, "[I]gnorant and unstable people distort" Scriptures "to their own destruction" (2 Peter 3:16). Since it is thought to be God-breathed, the Bible is considered indisputable.

The Bible writers were supposedly under the supernatural guidance of God the Holy Spirit. They wrote and even verified the prophetic books (Mark, Luke, James, and Jude) as New Testament books. The early church did not create the Bible, but it was responsible for properly translating and interpreting the Scriptures.

God's Word

Christians believe the Bible is the word of God because it claims to be the word of God. However, any text or author could make a similar claim. This belief and acceptance must be based on more than the claim. It's easy to fall into the trap of circular reasoning: "I believe what the Bible says because it is God's word and I believe the Bible is God's word because it says it is." Instead, it helps to look for solid evidence to support such a claim.

The Unity of the Bible

As previously stated, the Bible consists of sixty-six separate books written by approximately forty different authors in three distinct languages over a time span of more than 1,500 years. Additionally, the books are of different literary genres, including law, history, poetry and songs, prophecy, biography, letters, and apocalyptic writings. Despite such a wide variety of writing styles and personalities, a common theme weaves its way from Genesis to Revelation.

The promise of a Redeemer first appears in the third chapter of Genesis and continues throughout the Old Testament (Genesis 3:15). The promise is fulfilled with the birth, death, and resurrection of Jesus as narrated in the New Testament. Like any good story, this one has a beginning, a middle, and an end (which is yet to be). However, it is believed that this drama played out in history with real people and actual events.

Fantastic Find

Cover the state of Texas with 100 million billion silver dollars and the pile would be two feet high. Mark one of the silver dollars and toss it into the pile. Blindfold a friend and give him one chance to pick up the marked silver dollar. The odds of your friend selecting the one marked silver dollar are the same as one person fulfilling only eight of the numerous prophecies. Mathematicians calculate the probability of fulfilling forty-eight prophecies as the number one followed by 157 zeros.

Fulfilled Prophecy

What are the odds that all the Old Testament prophecies could be fulfilled in one man? Nigh impossible. And yet Christians believe they were. Mathematicians have calculated the odds of just one man fulfilling only eight prophecies at 100 million billion. Yet, Jesus has supposedly fulfilled a few hundred prophecies—with more expected in the future.

For Christians, these fulfilled prophecies confirm the divine origin of the Bible. Christians have long believed that prophecies can only be fulfilled with a God who knows the future before it happens, especially when many prophecies are predicted hundreds of years before they actually occur.

During the Last Supper, Jesus said to his apostles, "'I am telling you now before it happens, so that when it does happen you will believe that I am He'" (John 13:19). He then foretold Judas's betrayal, his own death, and other events, including the coming of the Holy Spirit and the apocalypse. Because all of the Old and New Testament prophecies are believed to have come true, except those involving the second coming, Christians have confidence that the Bible is truly God's word.

Look in the Book

The prophet Daniel predicted the very year that the Messiah (Jesus) would come (Daniel 9:24–27). Daniel's countdown begins in 457 B.C. He predicts that the Messiah will make himself known 487 years later. That brings us to A.D. 26, the year that Jesus was baptized and began his public ministry.

Historical Accuracy

The Bible is a historical document that mentions specific people, specific places, and specific events. During the nineteenth century, critics delighted in pointing out what they considered to be historical mistakes they supposedly found in the Bible. However, other historical documents, scientific evidence, and archaeological discoveries, to be discussed later in this book, have confirmed that the Bible is accurate and reliable in its historical references. Since the Bible is trusted to be historically accurate in even minor details, Christians trust its accuracy in spiritual matters.

Some of those of Christian faith believe that no one person could have orchestrated the combining of so many books written over a millennia and a half and come up with such a cohesive storyline. They hold that only a divine and eternal mind, the mind of God, could have moved through his people to provide humanity with his written word. Others find the Bible to be testimony to the mystery of humanity and that prophecy has to do with the need to trust God, not to predict the future.

chapter 3

Biblical Testimony

The New Testament refers to God as the author of the Old Testament more than fifty times. If a court were convened to determine the truth of inspiration, Jesus and the New Testament writers would top the witness list. In addition to the New Testament's claims on behalf of the Old Testament, it also claims divine inspiration for itself. The biblical phrases "prophecy of scripture" and "the prophetic word" refer to both the Old and the New Testaments. This chapter presents the biblical testimony supporting its claim of divine inspiration.

Jesus' Testimony: Old Testament

Again and again, Jesus' teachings and admonitions prove that he believed both the Old Testament and his own words to be from God. Examine his testimony. He often used the phrase "It is written" when quoting from the Old Testament (see Matthew 4:4, 7, 10). The very words of the entire Old Testament, Jesus claimed, spoke of him (Luke 24:27, 44; Hebrews 10:7).

Jesus also said that not even the smallest part of a Hebrew word or letter could be broken (Matthew 5:18). This is arguably the strongest declaration for the claim that every word of Scripture is inspired.

The Law of Moses

Jesus referred to the Law of Moses, specifically Exodus 20:12 and 21:17 and Leviticus 20:9, as the word of God (Matthew 15:6; Mark 7:13). God spoke his law through Moses, revealing it to him and also guiding his written record of it (compare Matthew 15:4 with Mark 7:10). Thus, Moses' Law is the word of God as Jesus claimed.

When Jesus was tempted by Satan to turn stones into bread, he quoted Deuteronomy 8:3, saying, "It is written: 'Man does not live on bread alone, but on every word that comes from the mouth of God'" (Matthew 4:4). The words that came from God were supposedly inspired, and Jesus used them to combat Satan's temptations.

Timeless Truth

In the ancient world, if something was written down (inscripturated), it was as good as if the deed was already accomplished. The 1956 movie *The Ten Commandments*, starring Charlton Heston as Moses and Yul Brynner as the Pharaoh Ramses, includes a scene that illustrates inscripturation. Condemning Moses to exile, the Pharaoh proclaims, "So shall it be written; so shall it be done."

Once, while teaching in the synagogue, Jesus quoted Psalm 110:1 and said that the author, King David, was "speaking by the Holy Spirit" when he wrote it (Mark 12:36; Matthew 22:44; Luke 20:42). Jesus reproved those who valued tradition more than the word of God (Matthew 15:1–3). He emphasized the authority of his message by often proclaiming, "You have heard that it was said . . . but I tell you" (see also Matthew 5:21–22, 27–28, 31–32, 33–34, 38–39, 43–44). By using the phrase "but I tell you," Jesus is claiming his words are of equal authority as those of the Old Testament. The phrase is from the Greek *ego lego* ("I, I tell") which means "I and no one else tell you." The language is emphatic—in other words, "Pay attention! God is speaking!"

Genesis

In responding to a question about divorce, Jesus replied, "[A]t the beginning the Creator 'made them male and female,' and said, 'For this reason . . . the two will become one flesh'" (Matthew 19:4–5). Jesus quoted Genesis 2:24 as being said by God, even though the account does not say that God said these words. Here is proof that the book of Genesis is of divine origin.

The Old Testament

Further, Jesus speaks of the testimony of the Old Testament as equal with the testimony of God. "There is another who testifies in my favor," Jesus said, "and I know that his testimony about me is valid" (John 5:32). Jesus said this testimony is not from man, but from "the Father who sent me" (John 5:37) and that the Scriptures "testify about me" (John 5:39).

The Truth Shall Set You Free

Nicodemus, a member of the Jewish supreme high court, came to Jesus under the cover of darkness. He was a secret disciple and didn't want the other members to know about the visit. Jesus admonished him for not understanding that the new birth was a spiritual birth, not a physical one (John 3:10). On another occasion, Jesus flatly told the priestly Sadducees, who prided themselves on their wisdom, that they were mistaken (Matthew 22:29). He said, "If you hold to my teaching, you are my disciples. Then you will know the truth, and the truth will set you free" (John 8:31-32).

Even Jesus' enemies recognized the authority of his teachings. "'Teacher,' they said, 'we know that you are a man of integrity and that you teach the way of God in accordance with the truth. You aren't swayed by men'" (Matthew 22:16). It is quite evident that Jesus was concerned with the truth.

Timeless Truth

The Sanhedrin was a council of Jewish elders and chief priests that made up the Jewish Supreme Court (Acts 4:5–22). The Pharisees, meaning "separated ones," were legislative scribes of the people and believed in the resurrection. The Sadducees were mainly wealthy, aristocratic priests who rejected belief in angels and the resurrection.

Paul's Testimony: Old Testament

The apostle Paul began life as Saul, the son of a Hellenistic Jewish family who were also Roman citizens. After becoming a Christian in A.D. 34, Paul made several missionary trips throughout Asia Minor to establish churches among the gentiles. The majority of the New Testament Epistles are letters he wrote to churches and individuals to encourage them and to teach them. In his writings, there is an unquestioned belief in the Old Testament as God's inspired word.

Bible Lesson

Saul of Tarsus was an intellectual Jewish scholar who had a promising future in the Jewish religious leadership. He was determined to destroy Christianity, which he considered a vile heresy. But after seeing the risen Lord on the road to Damascus, he became the early church's most influential and determined missionary.

In Romans 3:1–2, Paul says that the Jews were "entrusted with the very words of God" (Romans 9:6). He writes that "the Scripture says to Pharaoh" and then quoted Exodus 9:16 as Scripture (Romans 9:17). Similarly, he writes that the Scripture "announced the gospel in advance to Abraham" and quoted Genesis 12:3 (Galatians 3:8). These examples indicate that Paul considered Scripture to be intertwined with the very breath of God.

Yet Paul's strongest claim concerning the Bible's inspiration is found in a letter he wrote to his young protégé, Timothy. "All Scripture is God-breathed," he said, "and is useful for teaching, rebuking, correcting and training in righteousness" (2 Timothy 3:16). Paul was referring to both the Old and New Testament canons. He believed God the Holy Spirit guarded the minds and the hands of his spokesmen so that their message came from the actual mind and hand of God. Their words, written on common papyrus sheets, were considered as unerring and reliable as the very breath of God.

Timeless Truth

The Christians of Berea, a southern Macedonian town, did not accept even what the apostle Paul said without first investigating the Scriptures. They thought for themselves. The Bereans are an example for Christians of the importance of diligently searching the Scriptures to find the truth. Paul encourages the Christian to be a workman "who correctly handles the word of truth" (2 Timothy 2:15).

Here are some additional examples of Paul's belief:

- The apostle Paul reasoned with the Jews from the Scriptures (Acts 17:2). He also states, "[E]verything that was written in the past was written to teach us" (Romans 15:4).
- The Bereans "examined the Scriptures every day" (Acts 17:11).
- Apollos, who was called "a learned man, with a thorough knowledge of the Scriptures," debated with the Jews, "proving from the Scriptures that Jesus was the Christ" (Acts 18:24, 28).

Additionally, there are references in the New Testament to "the prophetic writings" (Romans 16:26), that Jesus died and had risen "according to the Scriptures" (1 Corinthians 15:3–4), that Scripture foresaw that God would justify the gentiles (Galatians 3:8), that "the Scripture declares that the whole world is a prisoner of sin" (Galatians 3:22), and to the question, "But what does the Scripture say?" (Galatians 4:30).

Peter's Testimony: Old Testament

The apostle Peter, as a leader of the early church, was a prominent figure in the first several chapters of the book of Acts. Luke quoted him in Acts 1:16, saying that "the Scripture had to be fulfilled, which the Holy Spirit spoke long ago through the mouth of David" (Acts 4:25). Like Paul, Peter had a fundamental belief in the inspiration of the Old Testament Scripture.

Look in the Book

As further proof of Peter's confidence in the Old Testament canon, he stated that what "God says" in Joel 2:28–32 was spoken "by the prophet Joel" (Acts 2:16–17). He is also quoted as proclaiming that the sufferings of Jesus were "foretold through all the prophets" (Acts 3:18).

Peter wrote two of the letters of the New Testament. In his first, he wrote that the ancient prophets "who spoke of the grace that was to come" had "the Spirit of Christ in them" (1 Peter 1:10–11). His second letter, however, contains his strongest statement regarding inspiration. He writes that "no prophecy of Scripture came about by the prophet's own interpretation. For prophecy never had its origin in the will of man, but men spoke from God" (2 Peter 1:20–21). This passage clearly states that the writers did not create their own messages, but were guided by God the Holy Spirit.

Others' Testimony: Old Testament

The testimony of Jesus and the two major apostles, Paul and Peter, is overwhelming. Even so, it makes sense to call a few more witnesses to the stand. First is the apostle Matthew, a former tax collector. In his Gospel, it is written that an angel appeared to Joseph in a dream to tell him of Jesus' birth. This was "to fulfill what the Lord had said through the prophet" (Matthew 1:22; 2:15), referring to Isaiah. Next is Zechariah, a Jewish priest and the father of John the Baptist, who said that God spoke "through his holy prophets of long ago" (Luke 1:70). Finally, the author of the letter to the Hebrews repeatedly attributed Old Testament prophecies to God the Holy Spirit (Hebrews 3:7; 10:15; see also 1:5–13; 4:4–7; 7:21; 8:8).

Bible Lesson

Zechariah, of a priestly family, "belonged to the priestly division of Abijah" (Luke 1:5). One of 24,000 priests, he was chosen to burn incense in the Temple (Luke 1:9), a once-in-a-lifetime honor for a Jewish priest. He was struck mute after the angel Gabriel foretold John the Baptist's birth (Luke 1:19–22).

Jesus' Promise: Supernatural Guidance

Jesus promised to teach his apostles and he promised they would remember what he taught them (John 14:26; 16:13). "Do not worry about what to say or how to say it," he told them. "At that time you will be given what to say, for it will not be you speaking, but the Spirit of your Father speaking through you" (Matthew 10:19–20; cf. Mark 13:11; Luke 12:11–12). During stressful situations, Jesus promised, God the Holy Spirit would guide their words.

The promise was also meant for those apostles who participated in the writing of the New Testament. During the Last Supper, Jesus told them, "But the Counselor, the Holy Spirit, whom the Father will send in my name, will teach you all things and will remind you of everything I have said to you" (John 14:26). Later he said, "But when he, the Spirit of truth, comes, he will guide you into all truth" (John 16:13). Jesus was reassuring his apostles that their written accounts would be God-breathed—i.e., inspired. Thus, according to the text, the apostles were promised the presence of God when they spoke or wrote God's message. Whatever they said or wrote, the apostles were inspired. This promise was made only to the apostles, not to all Christians (Acts 2:43; 5:12). Only the apostles, and those upon whom they laid hands, performed miracles. These confirmed and proved that their message was from God. Some modern-day Christians, such as Pentecostalists and charismatics, believe the power to perform miracles is still available.

These apostles, along with their prophetic associates (e.g., Luke, Jude, and James), became the writers of the New Testament. There were also prophets, such as Agabus, who spoke their prophecies (Acts 11:28). The apostle John referred to himself as a prophet (Revelation 22:9).

Paul's Testimony: New Testament

The apostle Paul now takes the stand to testify for the inspiration of the New Testament. He told the Thessalonians that his spoken message was "the word of God" (1 Thessalonians 2:13). Then he claimed that his writings had the same authority as his spoken message (2 Thessalonians 2:15; Galatians 1:11–12; Ephesians 3:1–5; 1 Timothy 2:7; 4:1). He said, "[W]hat I am writing to you is the Lord's command" (1 Corinthians 14:37; 2 Corinthians 13:3).

Revealed to the Apostles and Prophets

Writing to Timothy, Paul quotes Deuteronomy 25:4 and Luke 10:7 and he referred to both as Scripture (1 Timothy 5:18). The divine message was "revealed by the Spirit to God's holy apostles and prophets" whether they were writing the Old or the New Testament (Ephesians 3:5; 2:20; 4:11). This also demonstrates that Paul was familiar with other New Testament books—e.g., the Gospel of Luke.

Bible Lesson

Peter had a collection of Paul's New Testament books (2 Peter 3:15–16). Paul told the Colossian Christians to read and circulate their Epistle (Colossians 4:16). The Thessalonians were charged to read their own letter (1 Thessalonians 5:27). Each New Testament church would copy Scriptures and keep them for their congregations.

In his first letter to the church at Corinth, Paul referred to the divine mysteries revealed "to us [the apostles and prophets] by his Spirit" (1 Corinthians 2:10). Then he spoke of revelation: "We have not received the spirit of the world, but the Spirit who is from God, that we may understand what God has freely given us" (1 Corinthians 2:12). Immediately, Paul testified that the revealed messages of the apostles and prophets were God-breathed: "This is what we speak, not in words taught us by human wisdom but in words taught by the Spirit, expressing spiritual truths in spiritual words." The apostles and prophets spoke and wrote God's very words—the church was built upon this foundation (Ephesians 2:20).

Look in the Book

In Matthew 16:16–19, Jesus called Peter a rock (*petros*, meaning a small pebble). He then said that "on this rock" (*petra*, a feminine form for rock which refers to the underlying rock of the earth's surface), he would build his church. The church is built upon the confession that Jesus is the Christ (Messiah) and God the Son. Peter used the "keys to the kingdom" (Matthew 16:19) to provide salvation to the Jews (Acts 2:14–41) and to the gentiles (Acts 10:1–48).

Examining Scripture

Earlier, 2 Timothy 3:16 was submitted as evidence for inspiration. Now, take a closer look at this passage: "All Scripture is God-breathed and is useful for teaching, rebuking, correcting and training in righteousness, so that the man of God may be thoroughly equipped for every good work." There are four points in this passage that deserve examination:

1. The word *all* (*pasa*) means the entire Bible, Old and New Testaments.
2. The word *Scripture* (*graphe*) refers to the writings themselves.
3. The word *God-breathed* (*theopneustos*) refers to all Scripture being breathed out of God's mouth (inspiration).
4. The word *useful*, sometimes translated *profitable* (*ophelimos*), means that the Scriptures are beneficial because they are inspired.

Peter's Testimony: New Testament

Now it's Peter's turn to take the stand a second time. Like Paul, Peter viewed the New Testament writings as equal to the Old Testament books. In his second letter, he affirms Paul's apostolic status and the inspired nature of his letters. He reminds his readers of what "our dear brother Paul also wrote you with the wisdom that God gave him" and he writes that some people distorted Paul's letters, "as they do the other Scriptures" (2 Peter 3:16–17).

Bible Lesson

In 2 Peter 3:17, Peter very clearly states that it is possible to distort Scripture if it is not *exegeted* or explained correctly. Distortion of Scripture or any written document must be avoided at all costs. Hard work and diligence must be part of a scholar's life.

In this same letter, Peter writes that all prophecy was spoken by those "carried along by the Holy Spirit" (2 Peter 1:21). He also asked his readers to "recall the words spoken in the past by the holy prophets and the command given by our Lord and Savior through your apostles" (2 Peter 3:2). This is clear testimony that the apostles, as Jesus' messengers, had the same authority as the Old Testament prophets.

chapter 4

Books in the Biblical Canon

The Old Testament begins with the Book of Genesis, but why doesn't it include the Book of Adam and Eve? Why does your New Testament include the Gospels of Matthew, Mark, Luke, and John, but not the Gospel of Thomas? Who determined which writings belong in both the Old and New Testaments? In this chapter, you'll discover the standard for including certain books in the biblical canon. You'll also take a brief look at the biblical languages.

What Is the Biblical Canon?

The word *canon* means "standard" or "rule." Before becoming the central personality of the New Testament canon, Jesus used a *kanon* in his earthly father's workshop. This Greek word means a carpenter's rule. In turn, the Greek word originated from *kaneh*, the Hebrew word for reed or a measuring rod (Ezekiel 40:3; 42:16). From the time of A.D. 170, the Church Fathers spoke about the canon of Christian teaching, the canon of truth, the canon of faith, and the canon of the church. Athanasius (A.D. 295–373), one of the Church Fathers, used the word *canon* in referring to the Scriptures in A.D. 350.

Fantastic Find

The cherished Old Testament scrolls were stored in the holy Ark of the Covenant (Deuteronomy 31:24–26). Once the building of the Jerusalem Temple was completed in 959 B.C., the scrolls were kept in this holy place (2 Kings 22:8).

The ancient Jews did not refer to the Scriptures as the Old Testament canon, but as sacred writings. After handling the Scriptures, the Jewish priest washed his hands before touching anything else. Touching the sacred writings made his hands impure inasmuch as it was his unclean hands touching the clean. This belief protected the scrolls from irresponsible and irreverent handling. It also emphasized the holy nature of the writings.

When Joshua assumed leadership of the Israelites after Moses' death, God told him to meditate on the Law "day and night" (Joshua 1:8). Joshua needed to know the Law so that he could be an effective leader. The authority of the Law didn't end with the settling of the Promised Land, however. Whenever a new king claimed the throne of Israel, he took on the long and laborious task of copying the Law. The sacred Law instructed that the king read his copy "all the days of his life so that he may learn to revere the Lord his God" (Deuteronomy 17:18–19).

The apostle Paul, who wrote most of the New Testament, referred to the Old Testament as sacred writings in a letter to his young friend Timothy (2 Timothy 3:15). The Hebrews and the apostles considered these writings as authoritative Scripture that came from God.

Bible Lesson

The first five books of the Old Testament are known collectively as either the Law, the Pentateuch, or the Torah. The Old Testament was called the *Tanak*. The T corresponds to the Torah (Law), the N to *Nevi'im* (Prophets), and the K to the *Ke'tuvim* (other writings). The two As were added to aid pronunciation.

The Thirty-Nine Old Testament Sacred Books

Although there are a number of writings dating from as far back as the time of Moses, only thirty-nine compose the sacred and authoritative Old Testament canon. Moses penned the first five books, with the exception of the last few chapters of Deuteronomy that recount his death and burial. Other books were written by kings and prophets. The prophet Malachi wrote the final book of the Old Testament during the Persian domination in 430 B.C. After this time, no additional prophets brought messages from God to the Israelites. The Old Testament canon was complete and closed.

The Twenty-Seven New Testament Sacred Books

While instructing his disciples and his followers, Jesus affirmed the inspiration of the Old Testament canon. He also promised that God the Holy Spirit would guide his chosen apostles and prophets in writing the books that would become the New Testament canon. Only twenty-seven books of the writings from this time period were determined to be part of the canon. Just as the Old Testament Hebrews accepted God's authority in the sacred writings of the prophets, the early Christians accepted his divine authority in the apostles' and prophets' New Testament writings. A book was not the word of God because it was consented to by God's people, but it was consented to by God's people because it was the word of God.

Look in the Book

Roughly 400 years passed, known as the Intertestamental Period (from 430 B.C. to A.D. 26), before the Old Testament prophecies of Jesus' birth and ministry were fulfilled. These 400 years of silence were broken by a "voice of one calling (*boontos*) in the desert" (Luke 3:4 quoting Isaiah 40:3–5). That voice belonged to the last of the Old Testament prophets—John the Baptist. Christians believe that John was the herald who prepared the way for the Messiah—i.e., Jesus.

Prophets and Apostles

A prophet was considered to be God's spokesman and law enforcer. He was known by many names. A prophet was a servant of the Lord (1 Kings 14:18) and a "watchman" (Ezekiel 3:17; Hosea 9:7). Being a "seer" (Isaiah 30:10), he was recognized as a "man of God" (1 Kings 12:22) and as a "messenger" (Isaiah 42:19). These various titles distinguished a prophet from all other vocations.

God's prophets were to speak only what he commanded them to speak. He said of the prophet Moses, "I will put my words in his mouth, and he will tell them everything I command him" (Deuteronomy 18:18). Moses was also given miraculous powers as proof that his calling came from God (Exodus 4:1–9). True prophets did not consult witches or mediums (Deuteronomy 18:10–11), nor did they follow false gods (Exodus 20:3–4; Deuteronomy 13:1–3). A true New Testament prophet did not deny that Jesus is God (Colossians 2:9) and attested to Jesus' full humanity (1 John 4:1–2).

"The Sovereign Lord has spoken," wrote Amos; "who can but prophesy?" (Amos 3:8). This intimates that God's prophets were compelled to speak on his behalf. In fact, when the prophet Balaam tried to avoid speaking God's message, he got a message from his donkey (Numbers 22:21–39). Balaam's error, and the reprimand he received from his donkey, are corroborated by the apostle Peter (2 Peter 3:16). Is it any wonder that there isn't an Old Testament book called Balaam? God's prophets had the authority to speak God's message and the Old Testament books are their written narratives.

God's New Testament Apostles

According to Acts 1:21–22, the qualifications for being an apostle of Christ were threefold: he was personally chosen by Jesus; he was an eyewitness of the ministry of John the Baptist through Jesus' three-and-a-half year ministry; and he saw the resurrected Jesus.

Bible Lesson

How did Paul get to be an apostle? Well, he saw the risen Christ on the road to Damascus (Acts 9:3–9), and it is believed by Christians that he then spent three years in Arabia receiving revelation from the time of John the Baptist's ministry through Jesus' ministry (Galatians 1:16–17). Paul said that he was "an apostle sent not from men nor by man, but by Jesus Christ and God the Father" (Galatians 1:1).

The apostles performed many miracles (Acts 3:1–10; 28:8–9), even raising the dead (Acts 20:10–12). The apostle Paul said, "[T]he things that mark an apostle—signs, wonders and miracles—were done among you with great perseverance" (2 Corinthians 12:12). Because they were chosen as apostles, their books have divine authority. As in Old Testament days, miracles once again confirmed God's message. Without a miraculous confirmation, a work was not accepted in the biblical canon.

Nicodemus confirmed that Jesus was performing miracles. As a skeptic, he secretly came to Jesus. "'Rabbi,' he said, 'we know you are a teacher who has come from God. For no one could perform the miraculous signs you are doing if God were not with him'" (John 3:2). It's noteworthy that Jesus' enemies never state that he didn't perform miracles.The apostles wrote most of the New Testament books. Matthew's Gospel, written primarily to the Jewish people, emphasizes that Jesus was the promised King and Messiah. John wrote his Gospel, three letters, and Revelation. His Gospel emphasizes Jesus' deity to a world audience. The fisherman Peter wrote two letters as he faced the persecution of the Roman emperor Nero. And Paul, the apostle to the gentiles, wrote at least thirteen letters: Romans; 1 and 2 Corinthians; Galatians; Ephesians; Philippians; Colossians; 1 and 2 Thessalonians; 1 and 2 Timothy; Titus; and Philemon.

Timeless Truth

It is believed that there are two possible authors of the book of Hebrews: the apostle Paul or the physician Luke. Both men had the educational background to write such an in-depth treatise. The author did not sign his letter, perhaps to avoid prejudicing his readers, which was written to Jewish Christians who were contemplating leaving Christianity. If Luke wrote Hebrews, then he, by sheer number of words, wrote most of the New Testament.

God's New Testament Prophets

Nonapostles wrote the other books of the New Testament. So what authority do their writings have? Why would their books be included in the biblical canon? Even though these writers were not apostles, they were prophets, and the apostles accepted their books as being authoritative Scripture.

In their writings, the apostles confirmed that Luke, Mark, James, and Jude had the gift of prophecy. The following passages are submitted as evidence on their behalf:

- Luke was a physician who accompanied Paul on one of his missionary trips. He wrote a gospel and the book of Acts. His prophetic gift is attested to by Colossians 4:14 and Philemon 1:24.
- Mark was another of Paul's companions. His Gospel was written for a Roman audience and is known as Peter's Gospel because Mark recorded what Peter preached. His prophetic gift is attested to by Acts 12:25; 2 Timothy 4:11; and 1 Peter 5:13.
- James, a half-brother of Jesus and a leader in the Christian church in Jerusalem (Galatians 1:19; James 1:1), wrote the book of James. His prophetic gift is attested to by Acts 15:13 and Galatians 2:9.
- Jude, also a half-brother of Jesus, speaks on his own behalf in the book he wrote. His prophetic gift is attested to by Jude 1:3, 5, and 20ff.

Not everything that an apostle or a prophet said was included in the biblical canon. For example, Paul referred to a third letter to the Corinthians that is not part of the New Testament canon. The twenty-seven books of the apostles and prophets were copied and distributed among the churches during the first century A.D. They were public documents, not private records, and were God's instructions to the church leaders and their followers.

If everything that Jesus did had been written down, "I suppose that even the whole world would not have room for the books that would be written," writes the apostle John (John 21:25). The New Testament canon closed when he wrote the book of Revelation in A.D. 96. By this time, he was the only apostle still living. He died four years later in the city of Ephesus in Asia Minor. As no one else had the miraculous or prophetic gifts needed to confirm their message, no more books were considered to be inspired by God.

Passing the Tests

Prior to acceptance into the canon, a book had to pass two essential tests. First, it had to articulate the truth about God. Second, it could not contradict previously accepted canonical books. These two tests were of paramount importance because, as the Bible says, God cannot speak what is false (Hebrews 6:18), nor can he contradict himself (2 Corinthians 1:17–18). A book that failed either of these tests could not be considered the word of God. Such writings were not accepted in the biblical canon.

The Bible itself talks about both these tests. To falsely claim to be a prophet was both foolhardy and reckless. "But a prophet who presumes to speak in my name anything I have not commanded him to say, or a prophet who speaks in the name of other gods, must be put to death" (Deuteronomy 18:20). The passage continues: "You may say to yourselves, 'How can we know when a message has not been spoken by the Lord?' If what a prophet proclaims in the name of the Lord does not take place or come true, that is a message the Lord has not spoken. That prophet has spoken presumptuously. Do not be afraid of him" (Deuteronomy 18:21–23).

Fantastic Find

The oldest surviving document that lists the contents of the Old Testament canon comes from a Christian scholar named Melito of Sardis and is dated at A.D. 170.

The apostle Paul commended the Berean Christians because they did not accept his teachings at face value. Instead they diligently searched the Scriptures to be sure his teachings were consistent with other Scriptures (Acts 17:11). He also praised the Thessalonian Christians because they accepted his teachings as coming from God (1 Thessalonians 2:13). The apostle John commanded that his readers test the truth he proclaimed by the known standard (the Old and New Testament writings) before they accepted it as a message from God (1 John 4:1–6).

Passing these tests, the books of the Old and New Testament were accepted as being the word of God. Look at the evidence:

- When Moses wrote, his books were immediately placed in the Ark of the Covenant (Deuteronomy 31:26).
- Joshua's book and the books of Samuel were also immediately accepted (Joshua 24:26; 1 Samuel 10:25).
- Daniel had a copy of Moses and the Prophets, which included the book of Jeremiah (Daniel 9:2, 10).
- Paul quoted the Gospel of Luke as Scripture (1 Timothy 5:18; Luke 10:7).
- Peter had copies of Paul's letters (2 Peter 3:16), proof that the New Testament books were being compiled early in the first century A.D.
- The apostles commanded that their letters be read aloud and dispersed among the churches (Colossians 4:16; 1 Thessalonians 5:27; Revelation 1:3).

Who then determined the biblical canon? Christians believe God did, by inspiring certain men to write down, without error or omission, what he deemed necessary for mankind's salvation and service. People simply recognized the Scriptures that were inspired by the prophets and apostles.

The Councils of Jamnia and Nicaea

Some believe that the Council of Jamnia, which met in A.D. 90, was a community of Jewish scholars who determined what books belonged in the Old Testament canon. Actually, the council was a teaching and legal academy. The

Jewish scholars assembled as a polemic or assault against Christianity and its canon of New Testament writings. They discussed whether or not they thought the books of Ecclesiastes and Song of Songs were inspired, but they did not decide the Old Testament canon. That had been done long before the council met.

Many scholars believed that the Council of Nicaea, convened in A.D. 325, determined the New Testament canon just as it was believed that the Council of Jamnia determined the Old Testament canon. This has been found to be untrue. From records of the event, it is clear that the Council of Nicaea did not even discuss the New Testament canon.

In fact, the first council to discuss the biblical canon was held at Carthage in A.D. 397. This council decreed that only the canonical writings were divine Scriptures. In essence, their findings recognized what was already a fact: the sixty-six books written by the prophets and apostles were unquestionably authentic.

The Great Persecutions

The persecution of Christians began almost immediately after Jesus' resurrection and ascension. The Jewish leaders persecuted the Christians because they claimed Jesus was God the Messiah. The leaders refused to accept that a carpenter from Nazareth was their long-awaited King. A young Jewish scholar known as Saul of Tarsus orchestrated one of the most severe persecutions of Christians. He held the cloaks of those who stoned Stephen, the first Christian martyr (Acts 7:54–60). Saul of Tarsus later became known as the apostle Paul who was converted to Christianity while traveling to Damascus to persecute the Christians who were hiding there.

Look in the Book

Saul of Tarsus held the cloaks of those who stoned Stephen because he was the instigator of this murder. Stephen was stoned to death for preaching an international Jesus—i.e., a Jesus for both the Jews *and* gentiles. Little did the unbelieving Saul know at that time that God planned for him to replace Stephen as the Christian missionary to the gentiles.

From Nero to Domitian

Nero's persecution of the early Christians pales in comparison to what they experienced during the reign of the Roman emperor Domitian (ca. A.D. 95). Then, for more than a century, the Roman emperors committed heinous acts against the Christians, ranging from the cruel to the horrific. They burned their biblical books; exiled and imprisoned them; confiscated their property; sentenced them to work in the mines (which meant almost certain death); pitched them in tar and set them on fire; butchered them and fed them to wild beasts; and crucified them.

Bible Lesson

In the second century A.D., Christians were given three opportunities to renounce Jesus as Lord and God. If they did not recant, their property and possessions were confiscated and they were murdered.

The early Christians knew that they could be put to death for possessing Scripture. This didn't frighten them, but they obviously had an interest in hiding the biblical books. Because of this, the early church researched and investigated the Bible canon once again.

Persecutions Ended by Constantine

The persecution finally ended when the Roman Emperor Constantine became a Christian. He issued the Edict of Milan in A.D. 313, which allowed the church to collect and reaffirm their Scriptures once again. With the persecutions behind them, the church, through councils, debates, and writings, concentrated on the authenticity of their biblical canon.

Destructive Heresies

During the second and third centuries A.D., a number of destructive heresies crept into the churches that threatened to corrupt the biblical canon. False gospels and letters appeared that claimed to have been written by the first-century apostles. Remember the tests that a book had to pass to be accepted into the biblical canon? These books did not pass the tests because they invented stories, disregarded history, and contradicted earlier canonical writings.

The Gnostics of the second century onward believed that all physical matter is inherently evil; therefore, Jesus did not have a physical body. This heresy must have had an early beginning, because the apostle John condemns an early form of Gnosticism as false teaching. The apostle says that he and others saw a physical Jesus, and touched him, after the resurrection (John 1:14; 1 John 1:1).

Timeless Truth

Docetism denied that Jesus had a physical body, but believed that he seemed to appear in one as a human. The heretical beliefs of Adoptionism stated that Jesus was a mere man whom God adopted and promoted to sonship. Apollinarianism taught that Jesus had a physical body but no human soul or mind. This heretical group said that Jesus' human flesh was made up of some kind of divine matter instead of bone, flesh, and blood (Luke 24:38–39).

Gatherings of scholars, called councils, met to debate theological issues. In every one, Gnosticism, Docetism, Adoptionism, and Apollinarianism were clearly demonstrated as false and condemned as heresy. Proponents of these teachings were allowed to debate the issue. But in every instance, they contradicted the existing books of the biblical canon. It was very clear that these teachings, and their teachers, were false and dangerous. The false teachings of these and other heretical groups compelled the church to once again confirm the biblical canon.

The Chosen Languages

A permanent written record of God's message to mankind has several advantages. First, language is precise. For thought to be fully expressed in writing, it must be clearly understood. The accurate use of words requires a very precise understanding of them, and expression requires precision. Mankind's most treasured knowledge is in the form of written records and books.

A written work can be precisely copied so that the copy is an accurate reproduction of the original. The accuracy of an oral communication is more difficult to determine. Failing memories were an obvious problem. To transmit revealed truth accurately, written records were created and copied by hand until the invention of movable type. The advantage of the printed page and the ability to reproduce accurate copies on a mass scale became readily apparent.

Hebrew

The Old Testament canon is primarily the biography of the people of Israel and God's dealings with them. Hebrew is a pictorial language that presents pictures of narrated events. Utilizing vivid, bold metaphors, the Hebrew language challenges and dramatizes the narrative. God's supposed acts among the Israelites became examples or illustrations for future generations. Since the Old Testament is a biography of a people, it is fitting that the record is written in a "picture-language."

The Hebrew language is also a personal language that addresses the heart and emotions of the reader. The message is felt rather than thought, yet the language expresses the facts of experience.

Aramaic

Aramaic is used in only a few occasions in the Old Testament (Genesis 10:22; 31:47; 2 Kings 18:26; Ezra 4:7–6:1; Isaiah 36:11; Jeremiah 10:11; and Daniel 2:4–7:28). It was the local language of the people of Israel and much of Syria. Jesus and his disciples spoke Aramaic on a daily basis.

Koine Greek

The New Testament was written almost entirely in *Koine* Greek with a few verses in Aramaic. *Koine* means "common," and was the Greek used from the time of Alexander the Great (355–323 B.C.) through the first century A.D. It was the lingua franca of the first-century world. This meant that Greek was the "language of the world" and widely spoken and read.

In contrast to Hebrew, Greek is more a language of the mind than of the heart. It is an intellectual and technically precise language that was perfect for communicating propositional truths to other cultures and future generations.

Chapter and Verse

Ancient writers did not separate their words from one another; neither did they divide their sentences into verses, paragraphs, or chapters. These divisions occurred at a later date. Sometime before 586 B.C., the Torah was divided into 154 sections to assist in teaching lessons from these books. About 586 B.C., the Torah was further divided into 669 section-chapters. The Prophetic books were divided into fifty-four section-chapters around 165 B.C.

Timeless Truth

Prior to the invention of movable type, Stephen Langton, a professor at the University of Paris, divided the Bible into our modern chapter divisions (A.D. 1227). The Wycliffe Bible of A.D. 1382, the first handwritten English translation of the Latin Vulgate, followed Professor Langton's divisions. These divisions are the basis still followed today.

The first indications of verses were mere spaces between words; until then the words ran together throughout the book. Sometime after 586 B.C., space stops were used to assist in public reading and interpretation. Additional markings were added later, but because these were not regulated, they differed from place to place. The markings were standardized about A.D. 916.

The autographs of the New Testament books, like the Old Testament books, were written without spaces between the words. However, an early division into paragraphs, which differs from our modern chapter divisions, appeared before A.D. 325. Eusebius, a fourth-century historian, developed his own system for sectioning the New Testament into shorter paragraphs. A fifth-century Greek manuscript known as the Codex Alexandrinus had yet another system of division.

The Vulgate New Testament was printed by Johann Gutenburg in A.D. 1456. Also known as the Mazarin Bible, it was the earliest book, and the most important one, printed by Gutenburg from movable types. It, too, followed Professor Langton's divisions. This work paved the way for the Rheims-Douay Version (A.D. 1581–1609) which became the official Bible for Roman Catholics. The first Greek New Testament was printed in A.D. 1516 by the Christian humanist, Desiderius Erasmus (A.D. 1466–1536). He also followed the chapter divisions of the Mazarin Bible.

The numbering of verses was later added to help in cross-referencing and to make public reading easier. Verses first occurred in the fourth edition of the Greek New Testament by Robert Stephanus, a printer from Paris, in 1551. These verses were introduced into the English New Testament by William Whittingham of Oxford in 1557.

Timeless Truth

Erasmus emphasized the study of classical history and languages in order to explain the Bible. This kind of study is called the grammatical-historical method, a model for Christians to follow. The Christian humanists paved the way for the Reformation to begin. They were also instrumental in the development of the Renaissance and the scientific revolution of the seventeenth century.

The first Bible to use both the modern chapter and verse divisions was the Latin Vulgate edition of Robert Stephanus (1551). The first English Bible to incorporate both the modern chapter and verse divisions was the Geneva Bible (1560).

chapter 5

Disputed and Rejected Books

Are there writings that aren't in the biblical canon that should be? This is a legitimate question and it's true that some people have thought so. Some ancient texts that were considered for the canon didn't meet the exacting standard. Other texts were immediately rejected despite their claims of having been written by apostles or prophets. In this chapter, you'll learn why these rejected books were excluded from both the Old and New Testaments.

Classifying the Ancient Texts

Before investigating the rejected books, return to the canon for a moment. These books can be divided into two groups. The books that were immediately and universally accepted are known as the *homologoumena*, which means "one in agreement." Their place in the canon has never been disputed. The *antilegomena* books were "spoken against" or disputed by a few rabbis. A few rabbinical scholars initially had questions about the Old Testament books of the Song of Songs, Ecclesiastes, Esther, Ezekiel, and Proverbs, but their skepticism was quickly resolved.

Timeless Truth

There are generally two schools of thought when it comes to who wrote the four Gospels. Some people believe that the Gospels were actually written by four individuals named Matthew, Mark, Luke, and John. However, others hold that the authors are unknown and the four names were attributed to the Gospels after the fact, as it was common practice in the ancient world to attribute written works to famous people.

A few in the third century A.D. had questions about the New Testament books of Hebrews, 2 Peter, and Jude even though these were accepted in the first century A.D. However, each of these Old and New Testament books had already been included in the Bible canon before any questions about them were asked. The skeptics' questions were soon withdrawn.

The homologoumena and antilegomena books are the books that are in our Bibles. The reasons for their acceptance into the biblical canon were discussed in Chapter 2.

The books that were accepted and later rejected are known as the *apocrypha*, a word that means "hidden" or "secret." The group of books that were universally rejected is known as the *pseudepigrapha*. This term means "false writings" or "spurious." Now you're ready to examine the writings in these two groups.

Bible Lesson

Why did the scholars have questions about some books? Here are just a few reasons: Song of Songs talks about sex; Esther is about a Jewish girl marrying a pagan ruler; Hebrews was not signed by the writer; and Jude is about apostasy.

Books Rejected by All: Old Testament Period

The pseudepigrapha books were not seriously considered as authoritative or sacred. Though they claimed biblical authorship, the texts include the religious fantasy and sorcery more commonly found from 200 B.C. to A.D. 200, centuries after the Old Testament was completed. Most of these books comprise dreams and visions written in an apocalyptic style—i.e., depicting God's people in need of his rescue. None of these books can claim the authority of God, nor did the early Hebrews consider them sacred. Eighteen works are classified as follows:

- **Legend:** the Book of Jubilee, the Letter of Aristeas, the Book of Adam and Eve, and the Martyrdom of Isaiah
- **Apocalyptic writings:** 1 Enoch, the Testament of the Twelve Patriarchs, the Sibylline Oracle, the Assumption of Moses, 2 Enoch (the Book of the Secrets of Enoch), 2 Baruch (the Syriac Apocalypse of Baruch), and 3 Baruch (the Greek Apocalypse of Baruch)
- **Teaching:** 3 Maccabees, 4 Maccabees, Pirke Aboth, and the Story of Ahikar
- **Poetry:** the Psalms of Solomon and Psalm 151
- **History:** the fragment of a Zadokite (Zadokite refers to a priestly family)

Books Accepted by Some: Old Testament Period

The books of the apocrypha, unlike the pseudepigrapha, never claim to be the word of God. Even though they were post-biblical, they were erroneously included in the Old Testament canon. However, each one includes errors, contradictions, and false teachings and was eventually removed from the canon. The apocrypha books are classified into the following six categories:

- **Teaching:** the Wisdom of Solomon and Ecclesiasticus (Sirach; not to be confused with the Old Testament book of Ecclesiastes)
- **Religious:** the Tobit
- **Romance:** the Book of Judith
- **History:** 1 Esdras, 1 Maccabees, and 2 Maccabees
- **Prophecy:** Baruch, the Letter of Jeremiah, and 2 Esdras
- **Legend:** the Additions to Esther, the Prayer of Azariah, Susanna, Bel and the Dragon, and the Prayer of Manasseh

As stated earlier, these books contain teachings that are contrary to the books of the biblical canon. For example, 2 Maccabees 12:45–46 teaches prayers for the dead. This is in direct conflict with prohibitions against praying for the dead found in 2 Samuel 12:19; Luke 16:25–26; and Hebrews 9:27. Tobit 12:9 teaches salvation by works that contradict Genesis 15:6; Romans 4:5; and Galatians 3:11. Some of the apocryphal books are extrabiblical, such as Bel and the Dragon, Additions to Esther, Prayer of Azariah, Susanna, Tobit, and Judith.

Timeless Truth

The term postbiblical means that such texts were written after the Old Testament canon closed in 430 B.C. Extrabiblical means anything that entered the writer's imaginative mind, but not found in any of the books of the Bible canon.

Incredibly, much of the teachings in the apocryphal books are viewed as downright immoral. In the book of Judith, it claims God assisted in committing a falsehood (Judith 9:10, 13). Both Ecclesiasticus and Wisdom teach a morality based on one's personal experience instead of God's teachings. In addition, geographical, chronological, and historical mistakes are found in these books. Tobit's book claims he lived in 722 B.C. *and* in 931 B.C. Judith 1:1 says that Nebuchadnezzar reigned in Nineveh, but he was the ruler of Babylon.

As evidence that these books do not belong in the canon, consider that neither the Alexandrian Jewish philosopher Philo (A.D. 30–100) nor the renowned Jewish historian Josephus (A.D 37–101) accepted any of these apocryphal books as Scripture. Furthermore, the great linguist Jerome (A.D. 340–420) rejected the apocryphal works as Scriptures.

Bible Lesson

Though Jesus and the New Testament writers often quoted the Old Testament canon (and called it Scripture), they never quoted from any of the apocrypha. Neither did the Jewish scholars at Jamnia (A.D. 90), nor the scholarly Church Fathers from A.D. 170–595.

Books Rejected by All: New Testament Period

In the centuries following the first century A.D., numerous books of a fanciful and heretical nature were written that were universally rejected. An English translation quotes the historian Eusebius of Caesarea (A.D. 263–339) as calling these pseudepigraphal books "totally absurd and impious." No orthodox scholar or council accepted these writings into the biblical canon. By the ninth century A.D., there were 280 such books in existence.

A number of pseudepigraphal gospels exist, so this discussion will only focus on the more prominent ones. The majority of these date from the second century A.D. onward. Notice the obvious falsehoods. For example, the Gospel of Thomas contains imaginative stories of Jesus' childhood, including an account of a five-year-old Jesus creating twelve living sparrows out of soft clay (2:1–4). In another passage, Jesus cursed and murdered another boy by making him wither like a tree (3:2–3).

The Gospel of the Ebionites stresses the Law of Moses, thus denying the New Testament's teaching of salvation by grace alone (Ephesians 2:8). It also denies Jesus' deity by claiming he was just a man whom God adopted when he was baptized. Further, it says that the Ebionites were vegetarians and denies that John the Baptist ate locusts.

The Gospel of Peter, though found only in fragments, denies the humanity of Jesus and teaches that Pilate was guiltless in Jesus' death. It says that Jesus' crucifixion was painless, and claims that Jesus' half-brothers and sisters came from a former marriage of Joseph's. The Protevangelium of James teaches that Mary, miraculously, was born six months after conception and that she was a perpetual virgin who was sixteen years old when Jesus was conceived.

The Gospel of the Hebrews claims that the apostle Paul was a false teacher, that Jesus' half-brother James was present at the Last Supper, that

God the Holy Spirit is our "Mother," and that Mary was pregnant for only seven months before Jesus was born. Here are a few more rejected texts:

- The Gospel of the Egyptians teaches asceticism, contempt for Jesus' physical body, and that childbearing is evil, and it also denies the Holy Trinity.
- The Gospel of the Nazaraeans contradicts the biblical Gospel accounts by teaching that Jesus did not spend three days in the tomb and that thousands of Jews were converted at his crucifixion.
- The Gospel of Philip teaches that the soul goes through seven successive spheres of hostile powers.
- The Gospel of Thomas the Athlete condemns the physical body, women, and sexuality.
- The Gospel of Judas teaches that Judas' betrayal made the salvation of all mankind possible.
- The Epistle of an Apostle claims that Jesus was the angel Gabriel who appeared to his disciples.
- The Apocryphon of John teaches that God eternally exists as Father, Mother, and Son.
- The Gospel of Truth speaks of the Father and the Mother. It says that the Father revealed his breast, the Holy Spirit.

Look in the Book

Mark 1:6 tells us that John the Baptist did eat locusts and honey. Because he had a Nazarite vow, John could not cut his hair; he could not drink wine or grape juice (no fruit of the vine); and he could not touch anything that was dead. His hair was divided into seven locks (long braids), two on each side and three in the back. Samson also had a Nazarite vow and was under the same restrictions. Unlike John, Samson broke his vow.

Books Accepted by Some: New Testament Period

A few churches and individuals in the first century A.D. accepted some writings as part of the New Testament canon that were rejected in later centuries. Known as the New Testament apocrypha, these books include the following:

- Epistle of Pseudo-Barnabas (A.D. 79)
- Epistle to the Corinthians (A.D. 96; not to be confused with 1 and 2 Corinthians written by Paul)
- Second Epistle of Clement (A.D. 140; also called Ancient Homily)
- Shepherd of Hermas (A.D. 140)
- Didache (A.D. 120; also called The Teaching of the Twelve)
- Apocalypse of Peter (A.D. 155)
- Acts of Paul and Thecla (A.D. 170)
- Epistle to the Laodiceans (fourth century A.D.)
- Gospel According to the Hebrews (A.D. 100; not to be confused with the letter to the Hebrews)
- Epistle of Polycarp to the Philippians (A.D. 108, not to be confused with Paul's letter to the Philippians)
- Seven Epistles of Ignatius

The biblical Gospel writers do not offer many details about Jesus' childhood. Some writers, living hundreds of years later, told imaginative stories of Jesus both as a baby and as a young boy. Others fabricated events in the three days between Jesus' death and his resurrection. To give credibility to their tales, these writers claimed that the stories were written by first-century A.D. apostles and prophets. Two dozen of the gospels written during the early centuries of Christianity were written either about Jesus' childhood or his fictitious descent into hell between his death and his resurrection.

The Jesus described in these works is not compatible with the Jesus described in the New Testament. For example, one of the apocryphal gospels says that when the boy Jesus was bumped as he was walking through a crowd, he struck the offending person dead.

The fourth-century Gospel of Nicodemus (also called the Acts of Pilate) and the fifth-century Gospel of Bartholomew are apocryphal accounts of Jesus' fictitious descent into hell.

Bible Lesson

The second-century infancy gospels known as the Protoevangelium of James and the Infancy Gospel of Thomas claimed to describe the miracles that supposedly occurred involving Jesus' clothing and even his bathwater. Over the following centuries, these two works and other similar texts evolved into the History of Joseph the Carpenter and the Arabic Gospel of the Infancy.

Apocryphal Acts

The book of Acts in the biblical canon recorded the activities of only a few of the apostles. The Apocryphal Acts, written centuries later, erroneously claimed to fill in the gaps. However, they include deviant teachings of cults and emphasize sexual asceticism and martyrdom. For example, the Acts of Peter (A.D. 190) describes a rivalry between Simon Peter, the apostle, and Simon Magnus, the magician. It also includes a miraculous talking dog, the resurrection of a dried fish, Peter's crucifixion, and a story about Simon Magnus attempting to fly to heaven from the Roman forum.

The Acts of Thomas (third century A.D.) is the only book in this group that is preserved in its entirety. It erroneously tells of this apostle's missionary journey to India where he was murdered. The Acts of Paul falsely describe the apostle Paul as a short, bald man with crooked legs and eyebrows that met above his hooked nose. It also says that the apostle preached the gospel to a lion in the amphitheater at Ephesus and later baptized the animal.

Apocryphal Letters

Though few writings claimed to be biblical letters, those that did taught a theology that contradicted the biblical canonical letters. The spurious Third Letter of Paul to the Corinthians tells about predictions of the future, creation, Jesus' humanity, and the bodily resurrection. Paul's Letter to the Laodiceans is a make-believe correspondence between Paul and the Roman Stoic philosopher Seneca (who both died in the first century A.D.) that consists of more than 300 manuscripts. Other apocryphal letters are the Epistle of Titus and the Epistle of Christ and Abgar.

Apocryphal Apocalypses

The earliest of this kind of writing is the Apocalypse of Peter (A.D. 150). It has more in common with the view of the afterlife found in Homer's *Odyssey* and Virgil's *Aeneid* than with the biblical account of heaven in the book of Revelation.

The Apocalypse of Paul falsely claims that Paul was taken to paradise and then through hell. While there, he interceded for the inhabitants so that they were relieved from their torment on Sundays. In heaven, he met Adam, the Old Testament patriarchs, and the major prophets.

The Nag Hammadi Library

Nag Hammadi is a modern Egyptian town on the Nile River north of Luxor. Not too far from the town, a library with forty previously unknown documents and several known texts was discovered in 1945. Among the findings was a copy of Plato's *Republic*, a portion of the Hermetic tractate Asclepius, the Teachings of Silvanus, and part of the work called Sentences of Sextus.

However, most of the works are Gnostic in origin. A fanatical religious movement of the early centuries A.D., Gnosticism taught a radical dualism that rejected the physical world. In this view, the physical body was a prison that the soul desired to escape. The Gnostics distinguished between the God of the Old Testament and a creator they called the Demiurge who holds mankind in bondage. Humanity, which they defined as God, was a spark of the divine heavenly light imprisoned in a physical body. They emphasized asceticism and taught that commandments of morality should be disobeyed. According to their belief, salvation occurred when one woke from the nightmare of this world to their own divinity and heavenly origin.

The Gnostic gospels did not talk about Jesus' ministry, nor his death and resurrection. Instead, the library's Gnostic works claimed to present the revelations Jesus made to his disciples after his resurrection and before his ascension. According to these apocryphal writings, Jesus and his disciples discussed the origin of the universe, the Genesis creation narratives as explained by the Gnostics, and the destiny of the incompatible divisions of mankind. These books include:

- The Gospel of Truth, a contemplation of Jesus' philosophy of life
- The Gospel of Philip, a rambling discussion
- The Gospel of Thomas, a compendium of pronouncements ascribed to Jesus

The biblical Gospels stated that Jesus ascended forty days after his resurrection, but the Gnostic writings stretched it to 550 days.

chapter 6
Uncovering Genesis

Once Charles Darwin's theory of evolution became popularized, many refuted the belief that the Book of Genesis was anything other than a collection of myths. The Garden of Eden and the Great Flood were thought impossible. Instead, many people insisted that the stories were written simply to provide a heritage for the Hebrews and as morality tales to encourage good behavior. This chapter examines archaeological discoveries that clarify possible answers to these age-old questions.

The Garden of Eden

Did the Garden of Eden really exist? This question is a big point of debate; however, some people think the Bible provides possible clues. Moses, the writer of Genesis, says that the headwaters of four rivers are located in the Garden of Eden and names them as the Euphrates, Tigris, Gihon, and Pishon (Genesis 2:10–14). The Tigris and Euphrates Rivers are known by those names still. The other two have been identified as today's Araxes and Uizhun, respectively. The Pishon River is identified with gold in Genesis. The Uizhun, known to present-day locals as the Golden River, meanders between ancient gold mines and lodes of lapis lazuli. For many, these facts are enough to prove that the Garden of Eden is a real place.

Nod, Cherubs, and Cush

The land of Nod, said in Genesis to be east of Eden, was where Cain spent the remainder of his life in exile after murdering his brother Abel. Today, the area is known as Noqdi. A few miles south is the town of Helabad, formerly known as Kheruabad or the "settlement of the Kheru people." Kheru is a permutation of the Hebrew word *keruvium*, which translates as "cherubs." People often think of cherubs as chubby, winged babies, such as those found in Renaissance paintings. But the Kheru people, fierce warriors whose symbol was the eagle or falcon, considered themselves protectors in the tradition of the cherubs who stood guard in front of the Garden of Eden and refused to allow anyone to enter its gates. Biblical cherubs are also powerful guardians of God's throne.

Fantastic Find

Critics said that the teraphim, or household gods, that Rachel stole from her father Laban didn't exist (Genesis 31:19). But archaeological studies in the 1920s uncovered more than 20,000 tablets in northern Iraq. Known as the Nuzi Tablets, they refer to the teraphim as property deeds used to determine the inheritance and titles of the sons of a family.

Scholars believed for many years that the land of Cush was in Egypt. However, recent discoveries place it north of Kusheh Daugh, the mountain of Kush.

Sumerian Tablets

Istanbul's Museum of the Orient houses ancient Sumerian cuneiform clay tablets that provide possible clues to the Garden of Eden's location. Reginald Walker, a British scholar specializing in these documents, says that an emissary of Enmerkar, the Sumerian priest-king of Uruk, traveled to Eden. One of the ancient tablets, titled *Enmerkar and the Lord of Aratta*, describes the 5,000-year-old route to Eden, which took three months to complete.

Look in the Book

Sargon, king of Assyria, is mentioned in Isaiah 20:1. But skeptics doubted Isaiah's accuracy since no other evidence verifying Sargon's existence had been found. However, some archaeologists believe that Sargon's palace has been found in Khorsabad, Iraq. Some also believe that Sargon's capture of the city of Ashdod, predicted in Isaiah 20, is depicted on the palace walls in Khorsabad.

According to the narrative, the Sumerian emissary was sent to Aratta, located on the plain of Edin, to get gold and lapis lazuli. Enmerkar wanted these riches for a temple he was building in Uruk. The emissary apparently traveled through seven mountain passes, or gates, through the Zagros Mountains to the "seventh heaven," the foothills of Mt. Sahand at the southern edge of Eden.

A Walled Garden

The biblical word *gan* means "walled garden" (Genesis 2:8). This indicates that the Garden of Eden was enclosed, though not necessarily by walls. Some believe the Garden of Eden was an alpine valley walled in by towering mountains and reached by a narrow mountain path. It has been said that the Garden is located ten miles from Tabriz, a city northwest of Tehran, Iran. Mount Sahand, an extinct volcano covered with snow, is the tallest of the mountains there.

Red Clay and Adam

Genesis says that God made Adam from the ground. The Hebrew name *Adam* derives from the Hebrew word for ground or red clay, *adama*.

Interestingly, reddish clay covers the foothills of Tabriz. Adam's skin color was probably reddish in appearance, similar to that of a Native American. It is believed his genes had all the variations of skin pigment found today.

The Ebla Tablets

The ancient kingdom of Ebla boasted a population of 260,000 at the height of its power circa 2300 B.C. The grandson of Sargon the Great, Naram-Sin, destroyed Ebla in 2250 B.C. University of Rome professors Dr. Giavanni Pettinato, an epigrapher, and Dr. Paolo Matthiae, an archaeologist, discovered almost 17,000 tablets in 1975 and 1976 at Tell Mardikh, the ancient Ebla. These tablets are a scholar's treasure trove.

The Ebla tablets are court records and copies of records taken from the royal archives. Dating from around 2300 B.C. to the city's destruction circa 2250 B.C., the tablets name names and places and false deities that are named in the book of Genesis. For example, Adam, Eve, Noah, and the false god Baal are mentioned and so is Abraham's city of Ur. One single text provides 260 geographic names. Others list animals, fish, birds, possessions, and the names of officials.

Fantastic Find

Critics said that the Hebrew name of Canaan wasn't used at the time of Ebla's existence, nor was it used in Genesis 11:31. But the Ebla tablets supposedly contain the name Canaan, possibly proving those critics wrong.

Most of the tablets are economic records concerning tariffs, receipts, and other commercial and legal matters. Treaties and trade records made with the Hittites were also found. These treaties and agreements are similar in form to treaties recorded in the Old Testament book of Exodus, but they record transactions that occurred long before Abraham bought the Cave of Machpelah from the Hittites of his day. Others are literary texts that include mythology, incantations, rituals, and hymns to false gods. A creation account found among the texts mirrors the Genesis creation narrative.

The vocabulary of the Ebla tablets and the Hebrew language are both Semitic and thus closely related. Many cities mentioned in the Old Testament are also mentioned in the Ebla tablets. These include Salilm (the city of Mechizedec), Hazor, Lachich, Megiddo, Gaza, Dor, Sinai, Ashtaroth, Joppa, and Damascus. The tablets refer to Urusalima, or Jerusalem, and are the earliest known reference to this important city.

Look in the Book

Critics of the book of Genesis say that the Hebrew word *tehom*, meaning "the deep," was a later word that didn't exist until long after Genesis was written. But the Ebla tablets supposedly prove that the word was part of the Ebla kingdom's vocabulary and in use an amazing 800 years before Moses wrote Genesis.

The tablets refer to Carchemish, a town mentioned by Isaiah the prophet (Isaiah 10:9), and the King's Highway, a major road leading to Damascus. They also refer to the five "cities of the Plain": Admah, Zeboiim, Zoar, and the infamous Sodom and Gomorrah (Genesis 14:2).

Sodom and Gomorrah

Biblical critics claim that the destruction of Sodom and Gomorrah is a morality myth. The Old Testament prophets, Jesus, and the apostles refer to the devastation of Sodom on several occasions (Deuteronomy 29:23; Isaiah 13:19; Jeremiah 49:18; Matthew 10:15; 2 Peter 2:6; and Jude 1:7).

Genesis 14:3 says that the two cities were located in the Valley of Siddim, known both as the Salt Sea and the Dead Sea. The ruins of ancient cities were found alongside five of six *wadis*, or river valleys, that flow into the eastern side of the Dead Sea. The northernmost, Bab edh-Drha, was excavated in 1924 by Dr. William Albright, the renowned archaeologist. Though he believed that this heavily fortified city was one of the five cities of the plain, he couldn't find evidence to support his belief.

Archaeologists continued excavating this area in 1965, 1967, and 1973. They found a large temple and houses surrounded by a twenty-three-inch thick wall that dated to the Bronze Age—which is also when Abraham lived.

Thousands of skeletons in huge gravesites were uncovered outside the city, which indicates that it had a large population.

Timeless Truth

Joseph, the one with the coat of many colors, was sold in Egypt as a slave. Through a divine turn of events, the Bible says he became Pharaoh's second-in-command. Critics scoff at the story, unable to believe that Pharaoh gave Joseph his signet ring, fine linen garments, and a gold chain, and allowed him to ride in a chariot behind the Egyptian ruler. Many Christians believe that an engraving found in an Egyptian royal tomb portrays the investiture ceremony of a new prime minister, and that the details are portrayed exactly as recorded in the Genesis account (Genesis 41:41–45).

A layer of ash, several feet thick, covered the city of Bab edh-Drha. Archaeologists also found the charred remains of roofs and bricks. The researchers believe burning roofs collapsed and then the fire spread throughout the structures. Did the massive fire rain down from heaven, as described in Genesis 19:24?

Traveling south from Bab edh-Drha, you come first to a city called Numeria and then to a city called es-Safi. Continuing on, you find the ancient cities Feifa and Khanazir. Excavations of these cities indicate that they were abandoned circa 2450–2350 B.C. If, as some archaeologists surmise, Bab edh Drha is Sodom, then Numeria is Gomorrah, and es-Safi is Zoar, another of the five cities.

Fantastic Find

Haran, the home of the patriarchs, has supposedly been discovered in Turkey. It is said to stand on top of the ancient city named in the Old Testament. Nearby villages reportedly still bear the names of Abraham's grandfather and great-grandfather, Nahor and Serug (cf. Genesis 11:22–26). The man Haran, the third son of Terah and Abraham's youngest brother, was the father of Lot whose wife turned into a pillar of salt (Genesis 11:27; 19:26). The city of Haran, most likely named for Abraham's brother, is where Abraham and his family went after leaving Ur of the Chaldees.

With the exception of Zoar, these other cities were buried in ash just like Bab edh-Drha. The ash covering Numeria measured seven feet in some places. Because the ash deposits transformed the soil into spongy charcoal, the sites could not be rebuilt. In the Genesis account, four of the five cities of the plain were destroyed by fire, and Lot fled to Zoar. Though it was not burnt, it was abandoned close to the same time that the other four cities were destroyed (Genesis 19:18–29).

Ancient Clay Seals

In ancient times, official documents were written on papyrus, which was then rolled up and tied with a string. To validate the document, the document's owner or writer pressed a signet ring into a lump of clay placed on the string's knot. Similarly, other clay seals were decorated and worn as amulets. The clay survived conditions, such as fire, that destroyed other ancient artifacts. Archaeologists have uncovered literally hundreds of these clay seals. Some are more than 5,000 years old and provide significant insight into an ancient culture's beliefs. Many discovered seals are reminiscent of those described in several biblical accounts, including some in Genesis.

The Adam and Eve Temptation Seal

The familiar story of the creation and the temptation of Adam and Eve, found in the first chapters of Genesis, is considered a myth by biblical critics. Yet in Sumer, the site of the most ancient known civilization, archaeologists made an important discovery—a clay seal, known as the Adam and Eve Temptation seal, depicting a man and woman who are both reaching for the fruit of a tree. A serpent is shown behind the woman. Now kept in the famed British Museum, this 5,000-year-old seal pictures an event that wasn't written about until circa 1440 B.C. Some say this is a coincidence, while others believe the item proves that the seal's artist somehow knew about the temptation story of Adam and Eve before there was a written record. Many Christians take this to mean that the story of Adam and Eve is a real, historical account and therefore not simply a morality tale, as biblical critics often assert.

The Adam and Eve Seal

Another Sumerian seal shows a naked man and woman bowing in humiliation and followed by a serpent, or Adam and Eve's expulsion from the Garden of Eden (Genesis 3:23). This seal dates to about 3500 B.C. and is kept in the museum at the University of Pennsylvania. Again, many people believe that this seal is sufficient proof that the story of Adam and Eve, as related in the Bible, actually happened.

The Gilgamesh Epic

Though the Great Flood narrative has its many critics, others believe that 100 years of archaeology have come to its defense. These supporters cite the earliest civilizations attesting to a worldwide flood. Clay tablets known as the Gilgamesh Epic, translated by the British Museum's George Smith in 1872, are the ancient Babylonians' telling of the Flood. The Genesis and Gilgamesh accounts are believed too different for one text to have borrowed from the other. The Babylonian's ark is cube-shaped and it only rains for fourteen days. Ancient Sumerian tablets, the earliest written texts we have, provide another account.

Fantastic Find

The Eleventh Tablet of the Gilgamesh Epic describes an ark, the animals taken onto the ark, and the birds that were released. It also tells about the ark landing on a mountain and that a sacrifice was offered after the ark landed. Many believe that the Tablet is an amazing confirmation that the Genesis Flood was not an isolated local event, but a worldwide catastrophe.

Historian Aaron Smith has found 80,000 works in seventy-two languages regarding the Flood. With this amount of plausible evidence, it is hard to believe that Noah's Flood was just a regional event—so many different peoples around the world have recalled it.

Abraham's City of Ur

According to the Bible, at God's bidding, Abraham left his home of Ur and journeyed to Canaan. However, many skeptics don't believe that either Abraham or the city of Ur ever existed. Leonard Woolley supposedly proved the critics wrong when he excavated the city of Ur in 1922. The city was found in southern Iraq. At the time Abraham lived, around 2000 B.C., Ur was a thriving metropolis. Woolley drew a map of the city and blueprints of some of the spacious dwellings. Based on his findings, it seems that Ur's streets were well-kept boulevards and the homes had indoor baths. Lessons on grammar and arithmetic were found on the tablets of schoolchildren in excavated classrooms. Excavators even reportedly found variations of the name of Abraham that dated to the century of his death.

Bible Lesson

The Bible reports that Abraham bought the Cave of Machpelah as a burial place. Both he and his wife Sarah apparently were buried there and so were Isaac and Rebekah, and Jacob and Leah. Though critics claimed that the cave didn't exist, it was believed to be found in the city of Heron below the Haram el-khalil, which means "sacred precinct of the friend of the merciful One, God." The bones of several people were found in the cave. Their identities are unknown.

The Bible describes the city of Ur as more sophisticated than one might think. Abraham was a wealthy man who owned large herds of cattle and flocks of sheep (Genesis 12:16). He had weapons and musical instruments (Genesis 27:3; 31:27). In royal tombs south of Cairo, Egypt, a painting of Semites entering Egypt was found that dates to about 1900 B.C. In the painting, the women and children wore multicolored garments similar to Joseph's (cf. Genesis 37:3). Goats and donkeys are also present in the painting, as are other implements that appear as described in Genesis.

The Tower of Babel

According to the Bible, the Tower of Babel was a building project designed to reach heaven. Not wanting the builders to succeed, God confused their language so they couldn't communicate with each other (Genesis 11:1–9). While many skeptics hold that the Tower of Babel never existed, excavations begun a century ago in Iraq have supposedly uncovered the royal seat of Nebuchadnezzar, his Hanging Gardens, and the legendary Tower of Babel.

For many, these findings confirmed the biblical account of the tower's construction. For example, only asphalted bricks were used in the construction of the foundation. The asphalt worked to waterproof the stone. The tower was made from seven squares that stacked on top of one another. Archaeologists apparently found an architect's tablet that indicates that the length, width, and height of each section of the tower were equal measurements. The base's measurement was given at slightly over 290 feet and archaeologists measured it at 295 feet. That meant the tower was almost 300 feet tall—the height of a thirty-story building.

Fantastic Find

Sumerian tablets support the biblical account of how language became confused at the Tower of Babel. The tablets talk of a golden age when all mankind spoke the same language. They even say that God, lord of wisdom, confused the language. In a Babylonian record, the gods destroyed a temple tower, scattering the people and, again, confusing their language.

At some point, the original tower was destroyed, but archaeologists believe a similar tower was built on the same site during the reign of Nebuchadnezzar (605–562 B.C.). After this tower was severely damaged during a war (652–648 B.C.), it was reportedly restored by Nebuchadnezzar. The Greek historian Herodotus described his visit to this tower in 460 B.C. Each side of this tower's base measured ninety meters and it was thirty-three meters high. Xerxes, the Persian king, demolished it in 472 B.C. The local residents eventually removed the bricks and today the site, Etemenanki, is a deep pit, the same distance as the original length of the Tower of Babel.

Chapter 7
The Significance of Water

Hydrology, the study of water, is an ancient and universal science. All cultures need to manage water for their personal use, for their livestock, and for irrigation. Dams, irrigation canals, water conduits, and other hydraulic structures have been found in the ruins of the oldest civilizations. In this chapter, you'll review the biblical and scientific cycle of evaporation and condensation. Then you'll take a look at the ancient world both before and during the global flood that reportedly destroyed all except the passengers sheltered inside a large rectangular box.

The Basics of Water

To understand the significance of the relationship between biblical history and plain, ordinary water, it helps to review the science of water. There's much more to a raindrop than meets the eye.

The hydrologic cycle is the fancy name for the earth's circular rainmaking process. Like a magnet, the hot sun pulls ocean water into the skies. Clouds take their shifting shapes from these evaporated drops and are blown by winds over the land. When the clouds condense, water falls as rain or snow, hail or sleet. The precipitation soaks into the earth and fills the riverbeds, slowly making its way to the oceans once more. The cycle is so commonplace that people tend to forget how vital it is to survival. Though it is simple enough for a child to understand, it is also a very sophisticated process.

Timeless Truth

Oceanography, as the name suggests, is the study of the oceans. Meteorology is the study of the atmospheric phases of the weather cycle—evaporation, cloud formation, and precipitation. Here are some more pertinent -ologies: potamology, the study of river flow; limnology, the study of lakes; and geohydrology, the study of groundwater.

So, tons and tons of water defy gravity because of the immense power of our faraway sun. The water particles cling to dust or other foreign particles and—voilà!—a cloud is born. The air currents that move the clouds also purify the particles of the ocean water of its heavy salt.

The Bible writers understood this amazing cycle. God "brings out the wind from his storehouses," writes the prophet (Jeremiah 10:13). "The wind blows to the south and turns to the north," King Solomon says, "round and round it goes, ever returning on its course" (Ecclesiastes 1:6). In Proverbs 8:26, Solomon refers to the "dust of the world."

Rain, from the Biblical Perspective

As water evaporates and forms clouds, enough smaller particles eventually become large enough that they overcome gravity and clouds fall apart. "He loads the clouds with moisture," said Job, "he scatters his lightning through them" (Job 37:11). Solomon says, "If clouds are full of water, they pour rain upon the earth" (Ecclesiastes 11:3).

Imagine what would happen if all the water particles in a large cloud mass fell together. What a destructive mess! But even a heavy rainfall is the gradual falling apart of the cloud. "Do you know how the clouds hang poised," asks Job, "those wonders of him who is perfect in knowledge?" (Job 37:16) "He wraps up the waters in his clouds, yet the clouds do not burst under their weight" (Job 26:8).

When rain seeps into the ground, it becomes groundwater. Some water bubbles up into springs and the rest continues seeping deeper and deeper into the ground. Wells must be dug for this water and plants extend their roots deep into the soil for the moisture they need. The rain that falls into creeks and streams heads back to the seas and oceans.

Look in the Book

Here's Job: "For he views the ends of the earth and sees everything under the heavens. When he established the force of the wind and measured out the waters, when he made a decree for the rain and a path for the thunderstorm, then he looked at wisdom and appraised it; he confirmed it and tested it" (Job 28:24–27). Now Solomon: "All streams flow into the sea, yet the sea is never full. To the place the streams come from, there they return again" (Ecclesiastes 1:7).

Geology, climate, the landscape—so much affects the hydrologic cycle. "Who has measured the waters in the hollow of his hand," asks the prophet Isaiah, "or with the breadth of his hand marked off the heavens? Who has held the dust of the earth in a basket, or weighed the mountains on the scales and the hills in a balance?" (Isaiah 40:12).

The Hydrologic Cycle in Scripture

As part of the cycle, an electrical field generates within a cloud and acts as a kind of magnetic glue that causes the water particles to adhere to one another. The same field also produces lightning. "He makes clouds rise from the ends of the earth," writes the psalmist, "he sends lightning with the rain and brings out the wind from his storehouses" (Psalms 135:7). This one verse clearly outlines four aspects of the hydrologic cycle: evaporation, wind, electricity, and rain. God "sends lightning with the rain," Jeremiah says on two separate occasions (Jeremiah 10:13; 51:16). The important emphasis in each case is that rain and electricity are linked.

Bible Lesson

The ancients didn't know that wind or air has weight, and yet the biblical writers seem to have expressed this and other scientific concepts. The writer of Job says, "To make the weight for the winds" (Job 28:25; King James Version, or KJV). The natural philosopher Empedocles (500– 435 B.C.) used a clepsydras, or water-thief, to discover air. ("Natural philosopher" is a title equivalent to our modern term "scientist.") Even though air can't be seen, he believed it exerted a pressure. He is the one who said that the fundamental "stuff" of the universe is earth, air, water, and fire.

The waters that were stored above the expanse, or sky, at creation joined the water "under the expanse" at the time of Noah's Flood and filled the great ocean beds (Genesis 1:7). These ample "storehouses" are essential for our sun-controlled water cycle (Psalms 33:7). Each step is acknowledged in Scripture:

- Water evaporates from the oceans (Psalms 135:7).
- Water is carried inland by the winds (Ecclesiastes 1:6).
- Water encounters particles of dust and sea salt that serve as nuclei for condensation (Proverbs 8:26).
- Water condenses into liquid droplets to form clouds (Job 26:8).
- Water coalesces and falls, under the right conditions, as rain (Job 36:27–28).
- Water provides needed sustenance for life on earth (Isaiah 55:10).
- And, finally, water returns to the oceans whence it came (Ecclesiastes 1:7).

A Different World

The modern hydrologic cycle, as explained earlier, is controlled by the sun. In contrast, according to the Bible, the hydrologic cycle that was occurring before Noah's global Flood was earth-controlled. You are investigating the available evidence for ancient events. To understand the world before the Flood, take a look at the testimony of Genesis.

Ocean above the Earth

The Bible says that after the earth was created, it was cloaked in darkness (Genesis 1:2). God commanded light to shine through this darkness and divided the day from the night. On the second day of creation, the waters were divided into great reservoirs. One was set on the earth below the sky and the other was set above the sky (Genesis 1:6–10). The sky divided the waters on the earth from the waters above the sky. The water above the earth was a canopy of water vapor that surrounded the entire earth.

Fantastic Find

The canopy was not considered a giant cloud. Though there are six different Hebrew words for *cloud*, not one of them is used in Genesis 1:7. Rockets fired at great altitudes turned up evidence that water-cluster ions were found at 85 kilometers in the D layer of the ionosphere. This shows that the water canopy described in the Bible once existed because its water-ion remnants are still in our present-day atmosphere.

How was such an ocean kept in place? The gases of the lower atmosphere must have held it up. Because the world was no longer in perpetual darkness, the light of the sun, moon, and stars must have shone through (Genesis 1:14–16). This suggests that the upper ocean was a type of canopy, a vast thermal blanket extending far out into space. Though it was believed to be an invisible vapor, it exerted a profound influence on the earth's climate and living conditions.

A Giant Shield

According to the Bible, rain as we know it did not exist before the Flood (Genesis 2:5–6). Rivers and seas were nourished by the water confined beneath the land (Genesis 1:10; 2:10–14). A daily evaporation/condensation cycle occurred with the low-lying vapors (Genesis 2:6). These rivers, especially the ones that emerged from a great artesian spring in the Garden of Eden (Genesis 2:10), were the main sources of water for Adam and his descendants.

Bible Lesson

The canopy is described as creating a greenhouse effect over the entire earth, resulting in a tropical paradise with lush vegetation. The temperatures would have been almost uniform no matter how far one traveled from the equator.

The canopy also was a highly effective deflector shield against the sun's powerful rays. Our present atmosphere only partially filters this radiation and it is now known that some of the rays are harmful. They cause physical damages to our genetic systems and a general biological deterioration.

No Seasons Prior to the Flood

The canopy supposedly absorbed much of the sun's energy and dispersed it uniformly throughout the earth. Because of the consistent temperatures, the air masses remained at the same density and pressure. Violent winds were nonexistent. This early earth was not tilted on an axis as it is today (at twenty-three and one-half degrees) so the world's climate was spring-like every day. Christians believe the modern four distinct seasons exist because of the earth's post-Flood tilt.

The Bible reports that before the Flood, the earth enjoyed a mild climate, without storms, and was watered by a mist. This was due to the effects of the vapor canopy. The seasonal variations—summer, winter, cold, and heat—are mentioned in Genesis 1:14, but did not come into effect until after the Flood.

Ocean below the Earth

The two sources of water for the Flood were the "floodgates of the heavens" and the "springs of the great deep" (Genesis 7:11). Moses saw the waters above (Genesis 1:6–8) as the source of the water that came through heaven's floodgates. It is believed that before the Flood, the canopy God created provided such perfect climate control that "the Lord God had not sent rain on the earth" (Genesis 2:5). The groundwater evaporated each day and condensed each night, appearing as "streams [that] came up from the earth and watered the whole surface of the ground" (Genesis 2:6).

Look in the Book

The various seas of the world were all "gathered to one place" (Genesis 1:9). This means they interconnected and had a common sea level. Four rivers are named in Genesis 2:10–14 and, even though they all had a common source, each was evidently a large and important river covering a broad geographical area.

The tremendous amount of water flowing through these four rivers came from deep springs that were like artesian wells. Imagine how immense these deep reservoirs must be, and how great their pressure, to supply four major rivers. The pressures in the subterranean deep were sustained by the earth's own internal heat. The "fountains of the deep" were "fixed securely" (Proverbs 8:28) to withstand these pressures and temperatures. The Bible says that the outlet for these pressurized reservoirs was in Eden where the rivers provided water for the lush garden (Genesis 2:10). This one earth-controlled, hydrologic system served the entire globe.

The Flood

The canopy was large enough that, once it began to collapse, it sustained a forty-day continuous rainfall of about half an inch an hour. This calculates to approximately forty feet of water, or an atmospheric pressure measurement of 2.18 pounds per square inch on the pre-Flood earth. The post-Flood, sun-controlled hydrologic cycle has reduced the atmospheric pressure on the surface of the earth from the pre-Flood 2.18 measurement to its present level.

The cataclysmic events preceding the Flood included ash being hurled into the air by erupting volcanoes. These dust particles adhered to water droplets in the atmosphere, which then became heavy enough to fall as drenching rain (Genesis 7:11; Psalms 18:7–15).

Timeless Truth

Atmospheric pressure is the force that is exerted on an individual by the weight of particles of air. It presses against an individual with a force of one kilogram per square centimeter, which calculates to 14.7 pounds per square inch.

The Bible says that God determined to "bring floodwaters on the earth to destroy all life under the heavens, every creature that has the breath of life in it. Everything on earth will perish" (Genesis 6:17). To destroy life, God used the natural element that sustains life. The ocean above the sky condensed and fell to the earth at full intensity for forty days and forty nights (Genesis 7:12). This gigantic washing cleansed and purified God's beautiful creation.

The old world order, maintained by the ocean above and the ocean below, was destroyed (*kataklustheis*) by the merger of these waters (2 Peter 3:6). Psalm 33:6–9 clearly states that God gathered the seas together in a heap and laid them up in heavenly storehouses (*osar*). This word, *storehouse*, always refers to heavenly reservoirs. Nowhere is it used to refer to the earth's oceans.

Look in the Book

The word translated "rain" (*geshem*) means a "pouring rain" (1 Kings 18:41). The rain is so drenching, it's impossible to see through the drops. This kind of rambunctious torrential downpour was what the Bible says Noah and his family experienced during the forty days and nights of the Flood.

When the condensing vapor canopy began to fall, it became a great mass of a single dark cloud that could scarcely be penetrated by sunlight. The worst and fiercest rains and upheavals lasted forty days, but rain continued to fall and the earth churned until "closed" after 150 days (Genesis 7:24–8:2). The subterranean waters burst through the earth's crust as "all the springs of the great deep burst forth" (Genesis 7:11). This upheaval was followed by the eruption of subterranean magmas and tsunami-like waves in the seas.

Noah's Ark

The Minoans from the island of Crete, the Egyptians, and the Chaldeans traveled far and wide in the ancient seas. Ancient India and Malaysia traded by sea with the Babylonians. The Phoenicians, with their great seaports at Tyre and Sidon on the eastern shore of the Mediterranean and their far-flung colonies at Carthage in North Africa, Cadiz in Spain, were the most famous navigators of the ancient world. During Job's time, around 1800 B.C., there were swift boats (Job 9:26). And King Solomon had a great navy around 950 B.C. (1 Kings 9:26), and so did Hiram of Tyre (1 Kings 10:22).

Timeless Truth

Matthew Maury (1806–1873), the father of modern-day oceanography, read about the "paths of the sea" in Psalm 8:8. Maury then searched for and found the ocean currents that make navigation possible. Maury was a devout Christian who believed in creation by a Creator God of the Bible.

But the Bible reveals that the first and greatest of all ancient vessels was the one built on dry land to protect a family from a rainy catastrophe, a phenomenon that was unheard of at that time. Noah's ark measured 450 feet long, 75 feet wide, and 45 feet tall, giving it a capacity of 1,396,000 cubic feet. Imagine a giant box, taller than a three-story building and as long as one and a half football fields, with the capacity of about 522 standard railroad stockcars (each one could hold 240 sheep). This also equals eight freight trains of sixty-five stockcars each. Such dimensions might not work for traveling across the ocean, but the ark was perfectly designed to float and to hold its animal cargo.

Genesis 6:14 (KJV) says that the ark was made from gopher wood and covered with pitch. It is suggested that the pitch was used to make the ark waterproof. But what exactly is gopher wood? This is the only time in the Bible when the word translated "gopher wood" is used. Perhaps the word isn't translated correctly or perhaps these trees didn't survive the Flood. From a practical standpoint, it's clear that the wood was strong enough to provide stability and shelter. But it couldn't be too dense or Noah, his sons, and hired carpenters wouldn't be able to saw through it with the tools available to them.

Fantastic Find

The ark was built for only one purpose—to stay afloat. It could not capsize under the impact of the great waves and winds that might beat against it. Simulations of a scaled-down ark model could not be capsized by 300-foot tidal waves. The dimensions of Noah's ark were the basis for the design of more modern luxury liners such as the Queen Mary.

The ark was built with three levels. Noah and his family lived in the top level. The animals were kept in the middle level. The bottom level was used for storage. It's possible that many of the animals went through a time of hibernation while they were in the ark. Many explorers throughout history have claimed they found the ark, even Marco Polo. NASA has also gotten involved with searching for the ark.

Though the torrential rain lasted only forty days and nights, Noah's cruise lasted 377 days. It took that long for the water to subside from the mountains and land. The flood waters rose at least thirty-seven feet above the highest mountains (Genesis 7:20). Eventually, the ark came to rest in the mountain range of Ararat. This mountain range, with an elevation of 17,000 feet, is one of the world's most majestic.

The waters receded and Noah and his family, for the first time in over a year, once again walked on dry land. Leaving the ark perched upon the mountaintop, they descended to lower ground. The time had come to plant and rebuild.

As previously stated, the loss of the canopy caused climate changes. Imagine feeling winter's icy cold and seeing snow for the first time. A permanent ice cap eventually covered the summit of Mount Ararat and the ark that had protected Noah, his family, and the surviving animals.

The Rainbow

The Bible says that God set the rainbow in the sky for the first time after the Flood as a fitting symbol of his promise not to destroy the earth by water again (Genesis 9:8–17). As usual, this creative phenomenon has a scientific rationale. Rainbows form only when water droplets greater than 0.30 millimeters gather in the atmosphere. This is the size of falling rain, not cloud droplets.

Bible Lesson

According to the Bible, God said he set his rainbow in the sky (Genesis 9:13). The Hebrew word *rainbow* is the military word for "battle-bow"—in other words, a warrior's weapon. But there is no string or arrow in God's bow. His weapon points away from the earth, as if God had hung his weapon in the sky. His promise not to flood the earth again is symbolized by the powerlessness of his weapon.

The rainbow's colors, in order, are red, orange, yellow, green, blue, indigo, and violet. The rainbow is a half arc from one point of the earth to another point. But this is not the whole picture, according to Christians. They believe that the rainbow is actually a full circle that can only be seen once Christians are in heaven. John writes in Revelation 4:3 that a rainbow encircled God's throne. It is believed that people only see half of this rainbow in the earthly world.

chapter 8

A Whole New World

This chapter reveals what the Bible says happened when Noah left the ark and describes the many changes to the earth. The accounts of this chapter describe a young universe, most likely aged only a few thousand years. A differing view is that the worldwide flood occurred when a comet or small asteroid hit the Yucatan Peninsula seventy million years ago, causing the canopy to collapse, the Mid-Oceanic Ridge to form, and the dinosaurs to become extinct. A third view, theistic evolution, holds that God created the universe over a long period of time using an evolutionary method.

After the Flood

By the time the ark rested on Mount Ararat, the thermal-vapor canopy was gone and so was the worldwide temperate climate. Great winds soon began to blow, causing massive ocean waves and currents (Genesis 8:1, 3). These may have triggered the tectonic forces that caused the waters to flee (the mountains rose, the valleys sank down) "to the place you assigned for them. You set a boundary they cannot cross; never again will they cover the earth" (Psalms 104:8–9).

Different regions of the earth now had different climates. For the first time, distinct seasons responded to the earth's annual journey around the sun (Genesis 8:22). A rainbow, that colorful prism, the Bible asserts, appeared in the skies (Genesis 9:13).

Bible Lesson

When the fountains of the deep exploded, the Bible reports that the ocean above the earth collapsed. The power of this eruption combined with the collapse of the canopy was such a cataclysmic force that the earth's axis was tilted to its current twenty-three-and-a-half degrees. The oceans literally moved across the land mass.

Noah's Drunkenness

The Bible says that Noah left the ark and got drunk (Genesis 9:21). It's hardly a fitting ending to a historical tale of faith and righteousness. It's hard to say what happened here, but there are various theories.

One theory is that Noah was just a victim of science. Assuming that the water canopy measured forty feet or more of potential rainfall, the surface atmospheric pressure before the Flood would be 2.18 pounds per square inch. This increases the partial pressure of carbon dioxide by a multiple of 2.18. As a result, the rate of fermentation of grapes slowed down. Before the Flood, wine took a long time to ferment because of the doubled partial pressure of carbon dioxide. After the canopy condensed, the rate of fermentation significantly increased. This hypothesis supposes Noah was simply caught off guard by the uncharacteristically high alcohol content in his drink.

It's a fact that drunkenness occurs much more rapidly at lower atmospheric pressures. One theory is that Noah was used to an atmospheric pressure of 2.18. So, when he drank wine under the new post-Flood atmosphere, he unintentionally got drunk. God never punished Noah for drunkenness, and the Bible doesn't say anything about him ever getting drunk again.

Look in the Book

In the Bible, God does not often shy away from confronting even his most devoted followers when they sin. Yet the account does not say that Noah sinned when he became drunk. In ancient times, wine consisted of one part grape juice and three parts water. It's possible that Noah's watered-down grape juice was more fermented than he realized because of the change in the atmospheric pressure.

Changing Life Spans

Christians believe the oldest person who ever lived was named Methuselah. When he died, shortly before the global Flood, he was 969 years old. How could anyone live for almost 1,000 years? Well, the Bible says the average life span before the Flood was 912 years. For example, Adam lived to be 930. His son Seth was 912 when he died. Enosh was 905; Jared was 962; and Lamech, the father of Noah, was 950. But after the Flood, life spans dramatically decreased. Here are some examples:

- **Noah:** 950 years old
- **Shem:** 600 years old, only one generation from Noah
- **Eber:** 464 years old, four generations from Noah
- **Peleg:** 239 years old, five generations from Noah
- **Terah:** 205 years old, nine generations from Noah
- **Abraham:** 175 years old, ten generations from Noah
- **Jacob:** 147 years old, twelve generations from Noah
- **Moses:** 120 years old, seventeen generations from Noah

The norm eventually became the famed "three score and ten" (Psalms 90:10), which happens to be the average lifespan of men and women in today's world.

Voyage to the Bottom of the Sea

The earth's surface exhibits a world that recently, albeit slowly, emerged from the depths of a universal ocean. Evidence that water levels were once higher than they are now is seen throughout the earth. All of the internal-drainage lakes and seas (e.g., Caspian Sea and the Great Salt Lake) reveal old beach lines far up their adjacent slopes. Most rivers have old terraces preserved on the sides of their banks. These terraces are underfit streams that course through valleys that are much too large to have been carved by their present streams.

Fantastic Find

Archaeological evidence indicates that, far in the past, streams flowed throughout our great deserts. Large lakes supported thriving communities in what is now the Sahara desert, the Gobi desert, the Arabian desert, and the Great Basin of the western United States. Mountains are much higher today than before the Flood. Mount Everest is not the highest mountain on earth. The island of Hawaii, which descends to the Pacific Ocean floor, is actually the top of the largest mountain.

The extremely desolate Dead Sea region was practically a paradise in the time of Abraham (ca. 2090 B.C.). The "plain of Jordan was well watered, like the garden of the Lord, like the land of Egypt, toward Zoar. (This was before the Lord destroyed Sodom and Gomorrah)" (Genesis 13:10). The sea is "vast and spacious, teeming with creatures beyond number" (Psalms 104:25), has "wonderful deeds in the deep" (Psalms 107:24), and has deep places (Psalms 135:6). These verses describe a fertile land and deep sea filled with wondrous and mysterious life.

If there was some way to remove all the ocean's waters, we could see the rugged, mountainous land and numerous volcanoes hiding beneath. Incredibly, we would also find springs of water flowing from beneath the ocean's depths. When Jonah was swallowed by the great sea creature that

God created, he said, "The engulfing waters threatened me, the deep surrounded me; seaweed was wrapped around my head. To the roots of the mountains I sank down" (Jonah 2:5–6).

Oceanic Canyons

The Grand Canyon, rightfully considered a national wonder, is 277 miles long, up to eighteen miles wide, and more than 5000 feet deep. However, scientists have discovered one submarine canyon that is three times deeper than the Grand Canyon and another one that is ten times longer. Submarine canyons—great oceanic canyons—practically encircle the earth. Some of these huge trenches measure almost eight miles beneath the ocean floor.

Timeless Truth

The Mid-Oceanic Ridge was discovered by map pioneers Bruce Heezen and Marie Tharp in the 1950s. The Bible contends that before the Flood, the earth was one landmass. As the crack encircled the earth, it caused the great continental plates to move away from each other, forming the various continents. Many say the science of plate tectonics reflects this.

At the time of the Flood, it is believed that sixty- to ninety-mile jets of hot water burst through the ocean floor ("the fountains of the deep"). The jets caused a microscopic crack in the ocean floor to split open. Both ends of the split zipped around the earth at the incredible rate of about three miles per second—circling the globe in less than two hours. When one end of the crack slammed into the path left by the other end, beneath the Indian Ocean, a 40,000-mile Y-shaped mountain range was formed.

Ancient Creatures

The Bible mentions at least 160 different species of animals, from the common cattle and sheep to the more elusive leviathan of Job. Believe it or not, dragons are among the mentioned species. The word dragon is from the

Greek *drakon*, which is a translation of the Hebrew *tannim* ("terrible lizard"). In fact, tannim is first found on the very first page of the Bible: "And God created great tannim" or dragon (Genesis 1:21). The Hebrew word is found twenty-four more times throughout the Old Testament. Its last appearance, Malachi 1:3, says that God "laid his [Esau's] mountains and his heritage waste for the dragons of the wilderness" (KJV).

Look in the Book

According to other biblical references, dragons apparently had poisonous fangs (Deuteronomy 32:33), "snuffed up the wind" (Jeremiah 14:6; KJV), and made a wailing sound (Micah 1:8; KJV). Moses' rod miraculously became a snake (*nahash*); however, the rods belonging to Aaron and the Egyptian magicians became dragons (*tannim*; Exodus 4:3; 7:15; KJV).

What exactly did these dragons look like? And what happened to them? Their descendants are seen today. For instance, komodo dragons of Indonesia are terrible lizards, though smaller than the dragons of the Old Testament. Of course, gigantic dinosaur remains have been found. The largest dinosaur found today is the argentinosaurus, who was 120 feet long, 50 feet tall, and weighed 220,000 pounds. The seismosaurus was the longest at 140 feet long. And the ultrasaurus was 60 feet tall.

The Behemoth

Job, who lived after the Flood, endured grief, hardship, and sickness because of his steadfast trust in God. All his many children were killed, his numerous flocks and herds were stolen, and he became covered with painful boils and sores. In all this, though, Job did not curse God (Job 42:1–6). Despite his steadfastness to holiness, however, Job didn't fully understand God's creative greatness. In Job 38 and 39, God quizzes Job on his knowledge of creation. Job fails to answer the questions; however, these two chapters provide an amazingly accurate understanding of scientific principles.

Following his rhetorical questions, God describes the two greatest animals that he created. In Job 40:15–24, God took Job to the Jordan River Valley, which is the deepest river valley of the world today. Once there, God describes the *behemoth*, which means "gigantic and powerful beast," a creature that "ranks first among the works of God" (Job 40:19). In other words, the behemoth is God's greatest land creature (possibly the argentinosaurus). It is described as using the muscles in its stomach to sway its tail "like a cedar" (Job 40:17). Can that possibly mean its tail is over twenty feet long? Absolutely. The behemoth is the dinosaur of dinosaurs.

Bible Lesson

The Bible makes a distinction between beasts of the field, which are domestic animals, and the beasts of the land, which are the predators. No dinosaur footprints have ever been found within a city's limits. Ancient civilizations knew how to protect themselves from the behemoths and the other beasts of the land. They built thick walls that surrounded their cities.

The Leviathan

The second great creature that God describes is his largest sea animal (Job 41). The leviathan has heavy, close-set scales (Job 41:15–17, 23), breathes fire (vss. 18–21), has a chest as "hard as rock" (vs. 24), and makes the sea boil (Job 41:31). It is called "a king over all that are proud" (Job 41:34).

Before scoffing at the notion that the leviathan breathed fire, think back to your childhood. Did you ever catch fireflies on a dark summer night? These little bugs light up. Additionally, eels produce electricity and bombardier beetles produce explosive chemical reactions. There is no scientific evidence ruling out the possibility that the leviathan breathed out certain gaseous fumes that, when combined with oxygen, briefly ignited.

Other Scriptures also refer to this enormous sea creature called leviathan. It is said to be of great size and ferocity in the Psalms (74:13–14; 104:25–26). The prophet Isaiah describes leviathan as "the gliding serpent" and "the coiling serpent" (Isaiah 27:1). Eyewitnesses of these sea beasts supposedly wrote these descriptions.

chapter 9

The Old Testament

"In the beginning. . . ." With this familiar opening, the biblical history of mankind unfolds from creation through the days of the prophets. In the thirty-nine books of the Old Testament, several different authors tell the history of the Hebrews and their interactions with other ancient peoples. The attention to detail that characterizes these books, including the naming of specific people and places, has convinced many people that the accounts therein are historical and true. In this chapter, you'll observe reasons why some believe that the Old Testament writers knew what they were talking about.

The Walls of Jericho

Here's the battle plan that God gave to the Israelites' new leader after Moses' death, Joshua son of Nun: March around the city of Jericho seven times and blow your trumpet seven times. Known for his readiness to heed God's word, Joshua carried out this unusual military tactic. According to his own account, at the sound of the trumpet the walls of the great city came tumbling down (Joshua 6:20). This Old Testament story's common dismissal as folklore isn't a surprise. After all, how many battles are won by a mere trumpet blast? However some archaeologists suggest that is exactly what happened.

Fantastic Find

Prominent archaeologists who have excavated the site of what they believe to be ancient, biblical Jericho include Carl Watzinger (from 1907 to 1909), John Garstang (in the 1930s), Kathleen Kenyon (from 1952 to 1958), and Bryant Wood (from the 1970s to the present).

Jericho, an important city located near the Jordan River, was inhabited by the Canaanites. Like similar strongholds of the time, it was surrounded by great walls to protect the citizens from warring tribes and animal predators. The people felt secure behind their giant barriers. Archaeologists, in excavating the supposed site of ancient Jericho, uncovered a phenomenal fortification system. The mud-brick retaining wall surrounding the city stood fifteen feet high. An eight-foot brick wall, supported by an earthen rampart, topped the retaining wall.

Before marching on Jericho, Joshua sent two spies to the city. A woman named Rahab hid them on the rooftop of her home. The biblical account says that Rahab's home was on the city wall. The spies promised that if Rahab hung a scarlet thread from her window, she and her family would be protected when the Israelites attacked the city (Joshua 2:18). During the excavations, the archaeologists discovered domestic structures between the skyscraping outer wall and a second inner brick wall. Many believe the Bible account of Rahab's home accurately describes what archaeologists found.

Usually the inhabitants of a city such as Jericho were safe from an attacking army until their food ran out. A patient army waited until the desperate and hungry citizens became too weak to defend themselves or surrendered. However, archaeologists found huge stores of grain in Jericho's excavations. When Jericho fell, it was not because of a siege. Of course, this doesn't prove that the walls simply collapsed. But archaeologists also uncovered large piles of bricks along both the outer and inner walls. By observing these bricks, some of the archaeologists determined that the walls fell outward; however, if attackers were destroying the walls to break into the city, it makes sense that the walls would have fallen inward. The outward-falling bricks formed a ramp into the city for the Israelites to enter (Joshua 6:20).

Bible Lesson

Some scholars attribute the collapse of the wall to an earthquake. Such a natural phenomenon would also explain the damming of the Jordan, which allowed the Israelites to cross the river on foot (Joshua 3:9–17). Christians believe that God could have caused an earthquake to accomplish his tasks.

The biblical destruction account describes a great fire (Joshua 6:24). Interestingly, archaeologists found a thick layer of soot throughout the city. The walls and floors were burnt and fallen bricks were found in every room. God forbade the Israelites to plunder the city, but commanded they completely destroy it (Joshua 6:17–21). The archaeological evidence seems to prove that the city believed to be Jericho was totally demolished.

A careful chronology coupled with archaeological evidence dates the exodus of the Hebrews from Egypt under Moses' leadership at 1440 B.C. The biblical account states that the Hebrews wandered in the desert for forty years before entering the Promised Land. This places the crossing of the Jordan and the attack on Jericho at 1400 B.C.

Fantastic Find

Among the debris found in Jericho, researchers found a piece of charcoal that they dated at 1400 B.C. through the testing known as carbon-14 dating. The date matches the time when Joshua destroyed Jericho.

In ancient tombs located northwest of Jericho, Egyptian amulets were found that were inscribed with the names of Pharaohs. These date from 1500 to 1386 B.C. indicating that the cemetery was used during that time period. Could the Hebrews have brought the amulets from Egypt? The Bible says that the Egyptians gave them gold and other treasures as they left (Exodus 12:35–36).

The House of David Inscription

One of the more popular Old Testament personalities is the harp-playing shepherd David who slew Goliath with a sling and five stones, became Israel's second king, committed adultery with the beautiful Bathsheba, arranged the murder of her husband, and wrote many of the Psalms. Such a colorful life is too much for some scholars to believe. But for others, the discovery of an inscribed stone fragment confirms the existence of the Israelites' King David.

Dr. Avraham Biran is an Israeli archaeologist who was in charge of excavations taking place at Tel Dan, located at the foot of Mount Hermon in northern Israel. Work crews found a basalt stone fragment, measuring about 32 centimeters by, at its widest, 22 centimeters, on July 21, 1993. The inscription translated "the House of David." About a year later, in June 1994, two additional fragments of the same stele were found. Many believe this confirms that King David was a real person.

Timeless Truth

A stele is a stone slab, higher than its width, inscribed with names and titles that were either carved in relief or painted onto the slab. It was erected as a ceremonial or funerary monument or as a territorial marker. The "David inscription" is the earliest mention of David, or any other biblical person, outside of Scripture.

Because of pottery fragments found beneath the flagstones, archaeologists believe that the pavement and wall where the fragments were found date to the late ninth or early eighth century B.C. Certainly the fragments date before 732 B.C., the year that Tiglath Pileser III and his Assyrian army conquered Israel. The debris from this destruction covered the entire pavement.

The Amulet Scroll

The rolled-up silver amulet scroll is inscribed with the Tetragrammaton, or the sacred name of God (YHWH), and is the oldest historical artifact, outside of the Bible, that confirms Yahweh as God's name. The Scripture passage inscribed on the amulet, which dates to the end of the seventh or early eighth century B.C., comes from Numbers 6:24–25.

Timeless Truth

Aristotle's famous dictum is highly applicable to the study of the history of the Bible: "He who asserts must also prove." So much of the Bible and its history are up for interpretation. Thus, in a discussion of fallacy versus fact, an honorable scholar must do her best to prove, as Aristotle says, what she asserts to be the truth.

The scroll was found in a trove of approximately 700 burial gifts, including pottery and alabaster vessels, silver jewelry and beads, arrowheads, bone and ivory artifacts, and a rare coin. Students from the Institute of Holy Land Studies, now Jerusalem University College, discovered this exciting find with their professor, Israeli archaeologist Gabriel Barkay, in 1979. The tombs are in Jerusalem near the Scottish Presbyterian Church of St. Andrew, on what is known as the Shoulder of Hinnom, the southwestern slope of the Hinnom Valley.

The Hittite Empire

The Hittites, who lived in Canaan, are mentioned several times in the Old Testament, beginning with Genesis 15:20. This verse says that Abraham and Sarah lived near them. Bathsheba's first husband, the murdered Uriah, was a Hittite. Later we read that the Hittites bought horses and chariots from King Solomon. Despite their prominence in the Old Testament narrative, however, absolutely no evidence of their existence could be found outside of the pages of the Bible for centuries. Critics pointed to this lack of historical testimony to support their assertions that the Bible was untrustworthy as a historical document.

Many believe this changed in 1876 when A. H. Sayce, a British scholar, discovered inscriptions carved on certain rocks found in Turkey referring to the Hittites. Clay tablets found in Turkey a decade later prompted Hugo Winckler, a German cuneiform expert, to launch his own investigation. At a place called Boghaz-koy, Winckler found a clay tablet that was actually a treaty between the Egyptian Pharaoh Ramses II and a Hittite king. From the 10,000 clay tablets found in this excavation, researchers decided that it was originally the capital of the Hittite empire. The Hittite city, called Hattusha, allegedly spread over 300 acres.

Fantastic Find

Winckler and his team reportedly found massive sculptures, five temples, and a fortified citadel during their painstaking excavation of Hattusha. The art and buildings supposedly confirm not only the existence of the Hittites, but also the fact that theirs was a mighty empire. This potential evidence is commonly used as a defense against those who asserted that the Hittites were a biblical myth.

Within the temples, archaeologists found clay tablets describing the priestly rites and ceremonies, including purification rites and the ceremony for purifying a new temple. The lengthy, elaborate instructions are thought to disprove criticism that the laws found in Leviticus and Deuteronomy are too complicated for such an ancient culture. Furthermore, texts found in Egypt and along the Euphrates show that the Hebrew ceremonies were consistent with the ceremonies of other contemporary cultures.

The translations of the Hittite tablets, including about two dozen treaties, potentially enhance the scholarly understanding of the patriarchal period and of the early Hebrews.

The Baruch Bulla

Official documents were rolled up like scrolls and tied with string. The impression from a signet ring was pressed into a lump of clay on the string's knot to authenticate the document. The hardened clay impression is called a bulla (plural *bullae*). Because of the nature of the clay, bullae, with the knotted cord often still attached to its underside, have survived the ravages of history even though the papyrus has not. Archaeologists have found literally hundreds of bullae, many hardened by fires. Clandestine diggers also look for bullae to sell to antiquities dealers and collectors.

Dr. R. Hecht acquired a bulla in 1970 bearing the stamp and name of a scribe called Baruch. This is known as the Baruch Bulla. The impression is divided into thirds by double horizontal lines and bordered by a single line. The writing is the pre-exilic ancient Hebrew linear script as opposed to the post-exilic script that the Jews adopted from the Aramaic. It reads:

brkyhw
bn nryhw
hspr

Though Hebrew is read from right to left, it's written here from left to right. The first two lines translate: "Belonging to Berechiah son of Neriah." The *yhw* is a shortened form of Yahweh, most likely pronounced "yahu." Baruch's name means "blessed of the Lord (Yahweh)." The impression may be that of Baruch ben Neriah (Baruch son of Neriah), the scribe who recorded the dictated prophecies of Jeremiah (Jeremiah 36:4).

Fantastic Find

Now housed in an Israeli museum, the Baruch Bulla measures 17 millimeters by 16 millimeters and the oval seal measures 13 millimeters by 11 millimeters. It was published by Dr. Avigad, and is thought to have come from a burnt house excavated by Yigal Shiloh.

The Israeli archaeologist who published the inscription, Dr. Nahamm Avigad, also published a seal inscribed, "Belonging to Seraiah (ben) Neriah." Seraiah is identified in Jeremiah 51:59 as being the chief chamberlain to King Zedekiah, the last king of Judah who ruled from 597 to 586 B.C. Both he and his brother, Baruch ben Neriah, were close friends of Jeremiah. Seraiah was instructed to read a written oracle from the prophet to the Babylonians that concerned the impending destruction of Babylon. After reading the document, he was told to toss it into the Euphrates River (Jeremiah 51:63).

The Ekron Inscription

The Bible shows that the ancient Hebrews often fought with the Philistines. At the request of the Philistine leaders, who sweetened their plea with money, the beautiful Delilah sweet-talked Samson into revealing the secret of his strength (Judges 16:17). About 300 years later, King Saul offered his daughter Michal in marriage to David in exchange for 100 Philistine foreskins (1 Samuel 18:25). Philistine warriors eventually defeated Saul and killed three of his sons in battle (1 Samuel 31).

Bible Lesson

The Philistines lived in five major cities, known as the pentapolis. One of these, Ekron, is mentioned several times in the Old Testament. Archaeologists Seymour Gitin, of the W. F. Albright Institute of Archaeological Research, and Trude Nothan, of Hebrew University, Jerusalem, reportedly located the ancient city of Ekron while excavating at Tel Miqne in Israel in 1993.

At the supposed site of Ekron, archaeologists uncovered a royal dedicatory inscription carved onto a limestone slab that names the city and five of its rulers. The slab was found in a temple complex that was most likely destroyed during the Babylonian conquest, which dates it to 603 B.C. The inscription, divided into five lines, translates as:

1. The temple which he built, 'kysh (Achish, Ikaus) son of Padi, son of
2. Ysd son of Ada, son of Ya'ir, ruler of Ekron,
3. For Ptgyh his lady. May she bless him, and
4. protect him, and prolong his days and bless
5. his land.

Assyrian records identify Padi and his son Ikausa as kings of Ekron. Padi is also mentioned in the annals of Sennacherib, king of Assyria (reigned from 708–681 B.C.), in connection with Assyria's attack on the city in 701 B.C. During this conquest, Assyria laid siege to King Hezekiah's Jerusalem. A royal clay seal indicates that Padi paid taxes, including a light talent of silver (67.5 pounds) to Assyria in 699 B.C.

Along with eleven other regional kings, Ikausa transported building materials to Nineveh to build the palace of Esarhaddon (680–669 B.C.). He is also listed as fighting beside Ashurbanipal, the king of Assyria from 668 to 626 B.C., against the Egyptians in 667 B.C. The three other kings named in the above inscription haven't been identified through other archaeological evidence.

The third letter in the name *Ptgyh* is damaged and may be an "n," changing the name to *Ptnyh*. Read as *Pontia*, this name means "mistress" or "lady," a formal title in ancient Greek for various goddesses. It may refer to Asherah, a Semitic deity idolized by many disobedient Hebrews.

Mount Ebal Altar

The Bible says that Joshua built an altar of uncut stones on Mount Ebal and then read "all the words of the law—the blessings and the curses" to the Hebrews (Joshua 8:30–35). The passage says that half the people stood in front of Mount Ebal and the other half in front of Mount Gerizim, known as the mountain of blessings. The ruins of ancient Shechem, near modern Nablus, are thought to be in the valley that separates the two mountains.

Fantastic Find

Adam Zertal, an Israeli archaeologist, excavated a site on Mount Ebal after finding pottery shards among a large pile of stones. The pottery dates to the Iron Age I, ca. 1220–1000 B.C., which is when the Israelites inhabited Canaan. The excavations, beginning in the fall of 1982, uncovered the outer walls of a large compound.

A rectangular stone structure interested the archaeologists because it had distinct layers of earth, stone, ashes, animal bones, and potsherds. Within the ash layers, the researchers found 962 burnt bones belonging to sheep, goats, domesticated cattle, and fallow deer. Such Iron Age sites usually include donkey and dog bones, too, but none were found at the Mount Ebal site. The site was abandoned by 1130 B.C.

Timeless Truth

The Israelites were not allowed to eat pork because pigs were considered scavengers. Pigs frequently carry parasites, such as *Trichinella spiralis*, which causes the disease trichinosis in humans, and *Echinococcus granulosis*, which causes cancer of the liver and lungs. Also, pigs often carry the tapeworm *Taenia solium*. The Jews were forbidden to eat pork (and other animals considered unclean) so that they wouldn't get these diseases.

Pigs and fallow deer are usually found in the same natural environment, so the lack of pig bones was also unusual. Dr. Zertal suggests that Joshua built this altar and that animals were sacrificed and eaten here (Joshua 8:31). Given the prohibitions against eating pork, this hypothesis explains the absence of pig bones. Neither would they have sacrificed donkeys or dogs.

The Cylinder of Cyrus

The prophet Ezra writes, "In the first year of Cyrus king of Persia, in order to fulfill the word of the Lord spoken by Jeremiah, the Lord moved the heart of Cyrus king of Persia to make a proclamation throughout his realm and put it in writing: 'This is what Cyrus king of Persia says: "The Lord, the God of heaven, has given me all the kingdoms of the earth and he has appointed me to build a temple for him at Jerusalem in Judah. Anyone of his people among you—may his God be with him, and let him go up to Jerusalem in Judah and build the temple of the Lord, the God of Israel; the God who is in Jerusalem"'" (Ezra 1:1–2).

At this time, known as the exilic period, the majority of the Israelites were living in Persia and only a remnant remained in Jerusalem. A clay tablet inscribed with cuneiform writing, found in the nineteenth century, says that Cyrus permitted the Jews to return to Jerusalem so that the temple could be rebuilt. The tablet dates to 538 B.C.

Look in the Book

The passage 2 Kings 3:4–5 says, "Now Mesha king of Moab raised sheep, and he had to supply the king of Israel with 100,000 lambs and with the wool of 100,000 rams. But after Ahab died, the king of Moab rebelled against the king of Israel." The Moabite stone, found in 1868, details King Mesha's plan to rebel against Omri the new king of Israel—even calling him by name. Many believe this confirms the biblical account.

Hezekiah's Tunnel

In 2 Kings 20:20, it says: "As for the other events of Hezekiah's reign, all his achievements and how he made the pool and the tunnel by which he brought water into the city, are they not written in the book of the annals of the kings of Judah."

The Siloam inscription, found in 1880 beneath the old city of Jerusalem in an underground water conduit, was written in Old Hebrew and dates to 702 B.C. It shows that Hezekiah ordered the construction of the tunnel and provides details of its engineering. Beginning at opposite ends, the workers chiseled the tunnel out of solid limestone until they met in the middle.

Fantastic Find

Hezekiah's tunnel is about a third of a mile long and less than three feet wide. In some places it is less than five feet high. Beginning at the Gihon Spring, outside Jerusalem, the tunnel ran beneath a hill and under the city wall to the Siloam Pool.

Hezekiah built the tunnel as a defense against the imminent siege of Sennacherib, ruler of the Assyrians, which happened in 701 B.C. (2 Chronicles 32:2–4, 30). The Prism of Sennacherib, housed in the University of Chicago Oriental Institute, provides an account of Sennacherib's siege of Jerusalem.

The Bible says that the Assyrian king Sennacherib captured Judah's fortified cities, including Lachish, during the reign of King Hezekiah. The Assyrian king demanded a tribute from King Hezekiah that included "all the silver that was found in the temple of the Lord and in the treasuries of the royal palace" (2 Kings 18:13–17). Sennacherib's campaign against Judah is recorded on the Prism of Sennacherib and on the Lachish reliefs. Second Kings 19:37 says that Sennacherib was assassinated by two of his sons, Adrammlech and Sharezer. This is shown in the annals of a third son, Esarhaddon, who succeeded his murdered father as king.

Other Old Testament Discoveries

Many other events that are mentioned in the Old Testament books are believed to have been confirmed by various historical and archaeological sources. For example, archaeologists have found and identified three separate pools that supposedly related to biblical accounts:

- After King Saul's death, his only surviving son Ishbosheth battled David for the throne of Israel at the pool of Gibeon (2 Samuel 2:12–32).
- The eyes of the lovely Shulammite woman were compared to the pools of Heshbon (Song of Songs 7:4).
- After Ahab, King of Israel, was killed in a battle against the king of Aram, his bloody chariot was washed clean at the pool of Samaria (1 Kings 22:29–38).

But the pools are not the only discoveries that have inspired many to believe that the biblical stories are historical and true. The following list contains some more accounts, all reportedly confirmed by various discoveries:

- The attack on Jerusalem by the Egyptian Pharaoh Shishak is recorded in 1 Kings 14:25–26 and supposedly on the walls of the Temple of Amun in Thebes, Egypt.
- The rebellion of Moab against Israel is recorded in 2 Kings 1:1; 3:4–27 and apparently on the Mesha inscription.
- The fall of Nineveh is predicted by the prophets Nahum (1:14) and Zephaniah (2:13–15), and is also believed to be recorded on the Tablet of Nabopolasar.

- The fall of Jerusalem to Nebuchadnezzar, king of Babylon, is recorded in 2 Kings 24:10–14 and also, many believe, in the Babylonian Chronicles.
- The captivity of Jehoiachin, king of Judah, in Babylon is recorded in 2 Kings 24:15–16 and, reportedly, in the Babylonian Chronicles.

There is reason to believe that archaeologists have also discovered the royal palace in Susa of Xerxes, King of Persia. According to the Bible, this is where Esther lived after becoming the king's wife (Esther 1:2; 2:3, 5, 9, 12). King Belshazzar's Babylonian palace has also reportedly been discovered. The Bible says it was here that handwriting mysteriously appeared on a wall during the king's great feast. Daniel interpreted the handwriting for the king (Daniel 5).

chapter 10

The New Testament

The birth, death, and resurrection of Jesus are the central events of the New Testament. Many Christians hold that if Jesus wasn't born of a virgin, if he wasn't crucified, and, most importantly, if he didn't rise from the dead, then nothing else in the Bible really matters. The Gospel writers provide detailed accounts of what Jesus said and what he did. But can their accounts be trusted? After all, they were his friends and followers. What are the earliest manuscripts? This chapter looks at what some people had to say about the details of the New Testament.

Early Manuscripts

Critics of the Bible claim that the New Testament books, especially the Gospels, were written centuries after the first century. They believe that legend dictated what the New Testament says. However, archaeologists may have discovered New Testament manuscripts dating back to the first century. These manuscripts are believed to be closer to their original autographs than any other literature in the ancient world.

The John Rylands Papyrus (P52)

A papyrus fragment was discovered in Egypt in 1920 that has the Scripture passages of John 18:31–33 and 37–38. This phenomenal find is called the John Rylands Papyrus and is designated as P52. It is currently located at the John Rylands Library in Manchester, England, and is dated at A.D. 100.

Scholars hold that the Gospel of John is one of the last of the New Testament books to be written. This Gospel dates somewhere in the early 90s of the first century. The dating of the John Rylands Papyrus at A.D. 100 opposes critical argument.

The Magdalen Papyrus (P64)

In 1901, three small fragments of a papyrus of the Gospel of Matthew were discovered in Luxor, Egypt, and sent to the Magdalen College Library in Oxford, England. Classified as Papyrus 64, these three fragments were examined by the famed German scholar Carsten Thiede in 1995, who dated the fragments between A.D. 30 and 70. He demonstrated that the Magdalen Papyrus was actually a part of two other fragments, Papyrus 67, a fragment of Matthew housed in Barcelona, and Papyrus 4, a nearly complete page from the Gospel of Luke, which is housed in Paris. In three places in the Magdalen fragments, the name Jesus is written as "KS," an abbreviation of the Greek word *Kyrios*, or Lord.

Chester Beatty (P46)

A huge papyrus manuscript containing almost all of Paul's letters was reportedly discovered in 1930 near Fayrum, Egypt, together with two earlier manuscripts of the Gospels, Acts, and Revelation. Classifed as Papyrus 46, fifty-six leaves are housed in Dublin, Ireland, in the Chester Beatty Collection. Thirty leaves are housed in Ann Arbor, Michigan.

In 1988, scholar Young Kyu Kim studied P46 and determined that it was written before Domitian became Emperor in A.D. 81. Kim believed that the handwriting styles and linguistic changes from papyri of various known dates in the first century match those of P46.

The Oxyrhynchus Papyri and Papyri from Qumran Cave 7

These documents contain sayings of Jesus that have parallels in the Bible's four Gospels. They were discovered in Oxyrhynchus in Egypt and are dated at A.D. 150. Fragments of 1 Timothy 3:16–4:3 (7q4 1,2), James 1:23–24 (7q8), Mark 4:8 and Acts 27:38 (7q6 1,2), and Mark 6:52–53 (7q5) were discovered among the Dead Sea Scrolls. The Dead Sea Scrolls were written before A.D. 70 when the Romans destroyed Jerusalem. That suggests that these passages from 1 Timothy, James, Mark, and Acts were all written before A.D. 70.

The Bodmer Papyrus (P66, P72–75)

This collection comprises fifty Greek and Coptic manuscripts from codices and scrolls that were discovered in Egypt. Most are papyri, but three are written on parchment. They include the Old and New Testament texts and writings of the early Church Fathers. They date at A.D. 200.

Historical Accuracy of Luke

Luke's New Testament writings, his Gospel and the book of Acts, were once considered unreliable because they named places and people for which there was no other historical evidence. However, some archaeologists believe that Luke was an unerringly accurate historian and his two books are reliable historical documents.

Bible Lesson

According to the Bible, the Tower of Antonia was located on part of the Temple Mount. It was covered with a tessellated pavement. A bema was placed on this pavement outside the hall of the Praetorium called "Gabbatha" (John 19:13). This is the place where Jesus was sentenced to death by Pontius Pilate (John 18:28; 19:13). Some have called "Gabbatha" a myth, while others say that the court "Gabbatha" has been discovered by archaeologists and is frequently visited by tourists to Jerusalem.

For example, it is believed that Luke gives the correct titles to a variety of government officials, from politarchs in Thessalonica, temple wardens in Ephesus, proconsuls in Cyprus, and even "the chief official of the island" in Malta (Acts 28:7). In Luke's Gospel announcement of Jesus' public ministry, the Gospel refers to Lysanius, tetrarch of Abilene (Luke 3:1). However, for centuries the only known Lysanius ruled Chalcis from 40–36 B.C. Eventually, though, archaeologists found an inscription of a temple dedication that seemingly referred to someone named Lysanius as the tetrarch of Abila near Damascus. This inscription dated to the time of Tiberius, who ruled from A.D. 14–37.

Fantastic Find

The Bible says that the apostle Paul stood trial before the proconsul Gallio at the bema, or tribunal, in the city of Corinth (Acts 18:12–17). A bema was a platform or "judgment seat" for public addresses where trials were held. Critics claimed that there was no such bema in Corinth, but archaeologists say that it stood in the forum (agora, marketplace). They hold that Corinth's bema was built in 44 B.C. of blue and white marble.

An inscription of a letter from Emperor Claudius was discovered near Delphi that refers to "Lucius Junios Gallio, my friend, and the proconsul of Achaia." The inscription is dated at A.D. 52, which is about the time Paul was there.

One of Paul's fellow Christians, Erastus, is named as the city treasurer of Corinth in both Acts 19:22 and Romans 16:23. When archaeologists excavated a Corinthian theater in 1928, they discovered an inscription that said, "Erastus in return for his aedileship laid the pavement at his own expense."

It is called the "Erastus inscription." The pavement that the inscription refers to was laid in A.D. 50. An aedileship designates the office of treasurer.

When Luke called Publius "the chief official of the island" of Malta (Acts 28:7), scholars questioned the strange title. However, recently discovered inscriptions suggest that this was Publius' title. Altogether, many believe Luke accurately names an amazing thirty-two countries, fifty-four cities, and nine islands.

The Pool of Bethesda and the Pool of Siloam

The Gospel of John describes how Jesus healed a man who had been lame for thirty-eight years at the Pool of Bethesda (John 5:1–15). This pool, which was fed by a spring, was known for its healing properties. Countless invalids waited their turn on its five porticoes.

Just like Luke, the Gospel of John has also been criticized for its supposed inaccuracies. For example, some believed that John only invented the porticoes, meaning them to symbolize the five books of the Torah. But in 1956, archaeologists excavating at Bethesda uncovered a rectangular pool forty feet underground. A portico was found on each of three sides and two separate porticoes were found on the fourth side. Some believe this discovery substantiates the biblical account.

Fantastic Find

The site of the Pool of Siloam, which is mentioned in the Gospel of John (John 9:7), was supposedly discovered by archaeologists in 1897. If the discovered site is, in fact, the location of the Pool of Siloam, then the critics who asserted that the pool never existed have been proven wrong.

Capernaum and Peter's House

The Gospel of Mark says that Jesus and his disciples "went to Capernaum, and when the Sabbath came, Jesus went into the synagogue and began to teach" (Mark 1:21). Archaeologists found small houses, built in the first century, beneath a sixth-century Byzantine basilica. The roofs were made from clay, branches, and straw. Remember the story told in Mark 2 of the paralyzed man's friends lowering him through the ceiling? It wouldn't have been difficult for men who were so determined to get their friend to Jesus to make a hole in the straw and clay roof.

A synagogue visible today is dated to the fourth or fifth century. However, after long years of research, the synagogue of the time of Jesus has been uncovered at a lower level on the same spot. According to Luke 7:4–5, the first-century synagogue was built by a Roman centurion.

The Bible says that Jesus went into "the house of Peter" (Matthew 8:14), also called "the house of Simon and Andrew" (Mark 1:29) and "the house of Simon" (Luke 4:38). The Bible also says that Jesus healed Peter's wife's mother in Peter's home (Matthew 8:14–15).

Graffiti and inscriptions were uncovered in one of the larger houses. The vast majority, 101, were in Greek, but there were also eighteen Syriac and fifteen Hebrew inscriptions. But what astonished the researchers was that so many were prayers thanking God for "our brother Peter" who opened his home to his brothers and sisters in Christ. Some believe this is the house of the apostle Peter.

Fantastic Find

On the remains of the wall plaster, 131 graffiti inscriptions were recovered, written in Greek, Aramaic, Syriac, and Latin. Among the inscriptions are invocations to the "Lord Jesus Christ." Peter is also mentioned. Several symbols and patterns, such as flower crosses, pomegranates, figs, trefoils, stylized flowers, and geometric drawings, decorate the walls.

Capernaum's main north-south road was located between the synagogue, which Jesus would have attended, and Peter's house to the east. Ten living quarters were discovered alongside the road. Inside the home, doors didn't separate rooms. The residents lived together as one large family. The women performed their domestic chores inside the courtyard and the children played in the road.

In front of Peter's home, archaeologists reportedly found a large space free of buildings just as Mark 1:33 and 2:2 state. The roof was made of a mixture of mud and straw sustained by wooden bars. Outside of the home is a staircase that would lead to the roof. One could repair the layer of mud every year before the beginning of the rainy season.

Timeless Truth

While excavating the south wall of the temple mountain in 1968, it is believed that Professor Benjamin Mazar uncovered the broad steps that Jesus would have climbed to enter the temple.

The Galilee or Jesus Boat

The Sea of Galilee's water level was dramatically lowered in 1985–86 due to a severe drought. During this time, when large areas of the shoreline were no longer covered with water, the brothers Moshe and Yuval Lufan found the remains of a 2,000-year-old boat along the northwest shore near the city of Tiberias.

An expert in marine archaeology, Shelley Wachsman, examined the boat where it lay. Noting that the planks of the hull were edge-joined with mortise and that wooden pegs held together the tendon joints, the antiquity of the boat was confirmed. It was moved to a specially constructed conservation pool in February 1986 so that it could be properly studied and preserved. Seventeen pieces of pottery, including a complete lamp and cooking pot, were found in the boat.

Fantastic Find

Based on similar pottery found in other Galilean excavation sites, researchers dated the boat from the late first century B.C. to the mid-first century A.D. Carbon-14 dating of the pottery resulted in dates of 120 B.C. to A.D. 40. This boat was most definitely a first-century A.D. sailing vessel discovered at the very same place, the Sea of Galilee, where Jesus and his disciples sailed.

The boat, which could be used with sails or oars, had room for four oarsmen, a helmsman, and about ten passengers. Some believe such a boat could easily have transported Jesus and his twelve disciples across the Sea of Galilee. The boat is currently exhibited at Kibbutz Ginnosar in Israel. Many think this first-century boat just might have been one that Jesus sailed in.

Ossuary of Caiaphas

Joseph, of the family of Caiaphas, served as the Jewish high priest from A.D. 18 to 37 and, as leader of the Sanhedrin, the Jewish high court. A member of a wealthy family and son-in-law of Annas, who served as high priest from A.D. 6 to 15, Caiaphas belonged to the Sadducee sect. He viewed Jesus' popularity as a threat to his own religious authority and accused Jesus of blasphemy during one of six middle-of-the-night illegal trials held before Jesus' crucifixion.

Caiaphas' family tomb was reportedly discovered in November 1990 when a dump truck accidentally smashed through the roof of the burial chamber. Common to that place and time, the chamber was cut into rock in an old cemetery dating to the late Second Temple era (first century B.C. to first century A.D.). The cemetery was on the southwest side of old Jerusalem in what is now known as the Jerusalem Peace Forest.

Timeless Truth

Family members shared the same tomb. The enshrouded body was laid on one of the burial platforms cut from the rock of the hollowed-out chamber. From the first century B.C. to about A.D. 70, the burial custom was to place the remains in a limestone box, the ossuary, about a year after the initial burial. This freed the platform for other burials. The ossuaries were stored side by side, each marked with the person's name. Family members visiting the chamber said prayers for their dead relatives.

About a dozen ossuaries were found in the Caiaphas' family tomb. Two of these are inscribed with a form of the name Qafa, or Caiaphas. Rosettes, zig-zag patterns, and other designs were carved into the boxes with a nail or a shard of glass. The inscriptions vary greatly depending on the literacy of the individual doing the inscribing. Several hundred ossuaries have been discovered dating to the first century A.D.

The name Yehosef bar Qafa, or Joseph son of Caiaphas, appears twice on the underside of the most intricately carved ossuary. Two circles of five rosettes each decorate the box. Inside, researchers found the bones of two infants, a young child, a teenage boy, and an adult man and woman. The bones of the man, believed to be about sixty years old when he died, is believed to be Joseph the high priest.

Ossuary of James

Some archaeologists believe they have located the ossuary containing the bones of James, the half-brother of Jesus and New Testament writer. The announcement was made on October 21, 2002, by the *Biblical Archaeological Review*. The limestone box dates to A.D. 63 and bears the following inscription in Aramaic: "James, son of Joseph, brother of Jesus." Scientists at the Geological Institute of Israel examined the ossuary.

Unlike standard ossuaries, this one seems designed to hold the remains of only one person. It is twenty inches long, but its width measures ten inches at one end and twelve inches at the other. The inscription appears to have been carefully placed in proportion to the box's dimensions. Because the rosettes carved into the box are faint and weathered, it is believed that the less faded inscription was added much later.

Fantastic Find

A private collector obtained the James ossuary on the antiquities market in 1986. A paleographer at John Hopkins University, P. Kyle McCarter, believes that the style of the Aramaic script (which changes with time) confirms a date of mid-first century A.D. for the ossuary. The inscription is unusual—only one other ossuary is known to mention a brother. For one inscription to name Joseph, James, and Jesus is astounding.

James is named as Jesus' brother both in biblical and historical accounts. The Bible says that Jesus had four brothers and two sisters (Matthew 13:55–56; Mark 6:3). The Gospel of Paul says that Paul met with "James, the Lord's brother" (Galatians 2:1–10). James is also mentioned in Acts 15:13–21 and Galatians 2:1–10 as presiding over a discussion about circumcision. He was a leader in the Christian church at Jerusalem until dying as a martyr in A.D. 62. The Jewish historian Josephus writes about "the brother of Jesus—who was called Christ—whose name was James" (*Antiquities* 20:9:1). After an exhaustive investigation, it appears that the James ossuary is authentic.

Herodian Building Project-Sites

During Herod the Great's reign over Judah, he completed several major building projects, which included expansive fortified palaces and the rebuilding of the Temple in Jerusalem. Excavations have uncovered the architectural grandeur of the Herodium, Masada, and Machaerus. These ruins tell their own stories about life in Judah during the years before and after the transition from B.C. to A.D.

Bible Lesson

Herod the Great was king of Judah during the year of Jesus' birth. After the Magi returned to the East without telling Herod where Jesus could be found, the king ordered the death of all male infants under the age of two. After his death in 4 B.C., his son, Herod Antipas, succeeded him to the throne. Jesus' fifth trial was before Herod Antipas, but it seems Jesus never spoke a word to him (Luke 23:6–12).

For years critics have dismissed Herod and his many building projects as a literary invention. But now, archaeologists have potentially uncovered the spectacular building projects of Herod the Great.

The Herodium

Herod the Great built the Herodium, which he named after himself, as a memorial to his victory over his enemies. This particular palace-fortress, according to the Jewish historian Josephus, was built where Herod defeated the Hasmoneans and Parthians in 40 B.C. (*Antiquities* XIV, 352–360).

Josephus writes that the Herodium was located on a hill about sixty stadia from Jerusalem (one stadium equals approximately two hundred meters). What the historian calls "pleasure grounds" were at the base of the hill and were notable for "the way in which water, which is lacking in that place, is brought in from a distance and at great expense." He mentions the fortress's round towers, steep stone steps, and the expensive royal apartments, which were designed both for ornamentation and security. "The surrounding plain was built up as a city second to none," writes Josephus, "with the hill serving as an acropolis for the other dwellings" (*War* 1, 31, 10; *Antiquities* XIV, 323–325).

Look in the Book

The Jewish historian Josephus says that Herod died from some disease, perhaps a sexually transmitted one. He was extremely hungry, suffered from a high fever and convulsions and had foul discharges. It was said an aqueous liquid settled about his feet and that his putrefied "privy member" produced worms. He found it difficult to breathe when he sat upright (*Antiquities* 17.6.5).

The Herodium was identified as Herod's fortress in the nineteenth century, but most excavations of the hilltop palace, standing 758 meters above sea level, occurred in the early 1960s. Off and on since 1972, archaeologists have excavated the buildings at the foot of the hill. The excavations confirm Josephus' account that the Herodium was actually two separate areas.

When Herod the Great died, his body was carried on a jewel-studded golden bier from Jericho to the Herodium. His family members and hundreds of slaves swung censers as they followed the bier. Herod's body was clothed in purple. He wore a gold crown and held a golden scepter. Five hundred servants carried the spices used to bury Herod's body.

A circular wall punctuated by towers surrounded the grand palace, on top of the hill. Other buildings were grouped around a large pool on the northern plain. Josephus also provides a historical account of the king's funeral procession and burial at the Herodium in a tomb he had built (*War* 1, 33, 8; *Antiquities* XVII, 196–199).

Masada

Towering 1,400 feet above the western shore of the Dead Sea stands the rock fortress of Masada. Built as a place of refuge between 37 and 31 B.C., Masada was a rather sophisticated fortress. Thirty towers and four gates were set in the wall enclosing the rock plateau. Archaeologists have uncovered two aqueducts and numerous deep cisterns that provided water for daily use and the gardens, decorative fountains, and assorted bathhouses.

Bible Lesson

After David killed Goliath, King Saul tried to kill David. First Samuel 23:14 states that David hid in the desert strongholds of the northwestern part of the Dead Sea territory. Most scholars believe that David hid on top of Masada. "The Lord is my rock," writes David in Psalm 18:2, "my fortress and my deliverer; my God is my rock in whom I take refuge." The Hebrew word for "fortress" is the same word as for "Masada."

On the northern edge of the cliff, Herod's palace was built in three tiers connected by a staircase. Its roofs were supported by rows of columns. Within these frescoed walls and on these mosaic floors, Herod the Great entertained his guests. Other buildings were used for various purposes including residences, offices, storehouses and workshops, and military barracks.

Machaerus

The Hasmonean ruler Alexander Jannaeus (103–76 B.C.) built Machaerus nine miles east of the Dead Sea in the gorge of Callirhoe as a frontier fortress against his Arab enemies. Also known as the Black Fortress, it towers 3,860 feet above the Dead Sea and 2,546 feet above the Mediterranean. During Herod the Great's restoration of the fortress, Josephus writes that the king built a wall round the very summit and erected towers at the corners, each 27.4 meters. In the middle of this enclosure he built a palace, breathtaking in size and beauty.

Though not mentioned by name in the Bible, Machaerus has an important biblical connection. Three of the Gospels provide varying accounts of how John the Baptist angered Herod Antipas by openly condemning his divorce and subsequent marriage to Herodias, his brother's wife (Matthew 14:1–12; Mark 6:21–29; and Luke 9:7–9). Herod imprisoned John at Machaerus. The infamous dance of his stepdaughter Salome, which ended with John's head on a platter, also took place here at Machaerus. Josephus confirms John's death in his writings (*Antiquities* 18: 116–119). The ruins of Machaerus, now known as M'khaur, are thought to still be visible on the northern end of Jebel Attarus.

chapter 11

The Dead Sea Scrolls

In March 1947, a young Bedouin goat herder followed two of his wandering goats into the cliffs along the northwestern shore of the Dead Sea. After one of the goats entered an opening in the rocks, Muhammad picked up a rock and tossed it through a second opening. Hearing the sound of breaking pottery, he entered the cave and found scrolls wrapped in linen cloth inside clay jars. This chapter explores the significance of this great archaeological discovery.

Eleven Treasure Caves

From 1947 through 1956, some of the most important ancient documents have been discovered. Hundreds of Hebrew and Aramaic scrolls were found in the caves only a mile west of the Dead Sea. This area, known as Qumran, is approximately ten miles south of the city of Jericho. Other scrolls were found in sites further inland.

Overlooking the Wadi Qumran are eleven caves where most of the scrolls were discovered. The caves are located near the ruins of a long-ago settlement known as Khirbet Qumran. In excavating these ruins, archaeologists discovered a walled site made up of various buildings, including a bakery, a potter's workshop, and a dining hall. Artifacts found at this site are similar to artifacts found with the scrolls in the caves.

Fantastic Find

Some of the scrolls that were discovered described what it was like to live in a community like Khirbet Qumran. However, these types of scrolls have been found throughout Israel and there is no evidence that these scrolls belong to this specific settlement.

The discovery of the Dead Sea Scrolls wasn't important because of community scrolls. The more valuable and famous scrolls are the biblical manuscripts. Many of these scrolls were preserved in jars and are almost complete manuscripts, such as the large Isaiah scroll found in Cave 1. Other scrolls were lying unprotected on the cave floors. These fragments are more difficult to decipher. Using carbon-14 dating and standard archaeological and paleographical principles, scientists dated these scrolls from between 250 B.C. and A.D. 70. The majority of these scrolls are kept in the Rockefeller and Israel Museums in Jerusalem. However, the most mysterious scroll, known as the Copper Scroll, is in Amman, Jordan.

The Qumran Quandary

Many scholars believe that a Jewish sect called the Essenes copied the manuscripts and hid the scrolls in the Dead Sea caves. So far, there is no scientific evidence to support this theory. Josephus, the first-century Jewish historian, described the Essenes as a Jewish sect.

Pliny the Elder, who lived in the first century A.D., wrote about the Essenes. He said that they lived near the Judaean town of En Gedi on the western shore of the Dead Sea. But Pliny did not say that the Essenes lived at Qumran. In fact, it seems that there is no first-century testimony that the Essenes ever resided at Qumran, though many assume it's true.

Look in the Book

According to Pliny the Elder, the Essenes avoided commerce, abhorred weapons, did not marry (scorning sexual desire), and lived in isolation. Another first-century writer, Philo Judaeus, said that the Essenes were a peaceful community without arrows, shields, swords, or helmets.

Less than fifty meters east of the building at Qumran, archaeologists found a large cemetery. The remains of forty men, seven women, and four children were found in forty-three tombs. Some of the bones were broken and others had been burnt. From the evidence, archaeologists believe that these people were massacred and quickly buried. They were Jewish freedom fighters who lost a fight with the conquering Romans. Keeping in mind Pliny's assertion that women did not live with the Essenes, this cemetery bears witness that a celibate order did not live in the Qumran community.

Qumran's Walls Destroyed in Battle

An ancient military technique for conquering an enemy fortification was to dig tunnels beneath a city's walls. After the wooden beams used to construct the tunnels were set on fire, the walls collapsed and the conquering soldiers swarmed over the fallen debris. In excavating Qumran, archaeologists discovered these kinds of destroyed tunnels beneath the walls. They also found that the building ruins were sealed in layers of ash as from a great fire. Such evidence strongly demonstrates that Qumran was a military fortress that was captured by the Romans. Abhorring war and weapons as much as they did, it is unlikely that the Essenes defended the Qumran settlement.

Buildings at Qumran

The excavation uncovered 140 locations within an area of 4,800 square meters. Food storage, a mill, an oven, a kitchen, and a stable were identified. But archaeologists also uncovered a forge and a massive defensive tower. Once again, these findings were not consistent with what is known of the Essenes. One of the many excavated rooms was thought to be a council hall and scriptorium.

Timeless Truth

A scriptorium is a place where manuscripts were copied. Piles of debris found near this hall resulted from the collapse of the building's second story when the Romans breached the walls. Though archaeologists found a table, its height and pitch were not suitable for copying scrolls. Besides, it is believed that scribes did not sit at this type of table. Instead of a scriptorium, this room was a military office or headquarters where Roman military leaders took their meals.

If the Essenes resided here, many believe archaeologists would have found the tools used to copy manuscripts. However, no parchments, needles, thread, line markers, pens, or styluses were found among the rubble. This absence of tools does not definitively prove that the community did not exist, but it also doesn't provide proof that it did.

Reservoirs

Scholars who believed the Essenes resided at Qumran point to the water reservoirs as evidence. Because of the stair steps leading into these reservoirs, these scholars claim they were ritual baths. However, those in opposition to this theory believe that all Jewish groups, not just the Essenes, participated in ceremonial bathing because of biblical laws for cleanliness. For those people, the reservoirs neither prove nor disprove anything.

Fantastic Find

The claim by some scholars that only the Essenes could have secretly stored these manuscripts in pottery and hidden them in caves is not verified. It was a common practice in the ancient Near East to store manuscripts of all types in jars. The pottery found in Qumran has wide necks, but similar jars have been found at Quailba and Jericho. This being the case, it's hard to say that there's anything unique about the Qumran pottery.

Material Possessions

Many believe the Essene sect was not interested in material possessions and they lived in poverty. These theorists hold that there isn't any archaeological evidence that suggests Qumran was inhabited by the Essenes or any other celibate and impoverished community. Though the Essenes had a settlement somewhere in the desert, they say it was not at Qumran.

The Copper Scroll, found in Cave 3, is considered a treasure map that lists sixty-four locations where forty-eight metric tons of silver and eight metric tons of gold were buried in Israel. Those who agree that the Essenes had no interest in material possessions tend to think that they could not be responsible for the Dead Sea Scrolls.

Timeless Truth

Those who believe that the Essenes lived at Qumran and wrote the Dead Sea Scrolls can provide no explanation for the fortune in gold and silver as described in the Copper Scroll. The Copper Scroll is a list of the greatest treasure in the history of the world.

Documents from the Jerusalem Temple Library

If the Essenes didn't write the Dead Sea Scrolls and hide them, who did? And why? It is suggested that these scrolls were part of the library of the Temple in Jerusalem. Some say that since they were aware of the impending danger from Rome, the Jewish religious leaders took measures to safeguard many of their sacred writings and other important Temple possessions. The Dead Sea caves were ideal hiding places for the library's scrolls. Under this theory, the caves kept their secrets for over 1,900 years.

Sectarian Beliefs?

The sectarian works found in Qumran include the so-called *Manual of Discipline*, which details the daily life, activities, and hierarchy of a secret community. Another manuscript appears to be a letter to the priests of Jerusalem. Supposedly written by the sect's leader, the Teacher of Righteousness, it outlines the differences between the sect and the Jewish priests. Their largest preserved manuscript, known as the *Temple Scroll*, is a rewrite of the Torah.

Fantastic Find

Several Hebrew and Aramaic apocryphal and pseudepigraphal works were among the scrolls found both at Qumran and at Masada, a rock fortress on a plateau 1,800 feet above the western shore of the Dead Sea. Masada was a refuge for many Jews during the Roman conquest, but the Romans finally conquered it in A.D. 74. Thanks to these discoveries, we now have the books of Jubilee, Enoch, Sirach, and the Testament of Levi in their original languages.

Additional details about how the sect began are found in the *Damascus Covenant*. This manuscript, along with other legal documents, provides information regarding the community's special laws. Referring to themselves as the "sons of Light," the sect tells of a future war against the "sons of Darkness" in what is known as the *War Scroll*. Expressions of hope and grief are found in their *Thanksgiving Hymn*. Exegetical writings, known as the *pesarim*, center on the relevance of the biblical books.

Biblical Works

About 190 biblical scrolls were found in the eleven Qumran caves. Except for the book of Esther, portions of all the other books of the Hebrew Bible were reportedly discovered. Some scrolls were almost complete and others were only fragments. Similarly, researchers found multiple scrolls for some books and only single copies for others. The scripts vary, but the vast majority of the scrolls were written in Aramaic. Only sixteen were written in Old Hebrew (paleo-Hebrew). Similar scrolls dating from the beginning of the second century A.D. have been found in other Judean desert locations.

Translation

Until the Qumran discovery, the Masoretic Text (MT) was the oldest copy of the Old Testament canon known to be in existence. It was written in approximately A.D. 916. Remember that the Dead Sea Scrolls date from 250 B.C. to A.D. 70. The spelling style of most of the Dead Sea Scrolls is the same as in the MT. This is considered by some to be incredible evidence of the painstaking care taken in copying biblical manuscripts.

Fantastic Find

The Masoretic Text (MT) includes the Old Testament and was completed by the school of scholars called the Masoretes in A.D. 916. These same scholars added vowels to the Hebrew consonants and provided accent marks to the words. The Greek Septuagint, known as LXX, is the first translation in history of one language to another. It is the Old Testament translated from Hebrew to Greek by seventy Jewish scholars in A.D. 250. The Samaritan Pentateuch is a Hebrew scroll of the Torah.

Other Caves and Discoveries

Traveling about eleven miles south of Qumran, you come to the caves of the Wadi Murabba'at. At one time, Murabba'at was occupied by a garrison commanded by Simeon Ben Losebah, the leader of the second Jewish revolt against Rome (A.D. 132–135). Manuscripts from this time period, including two letters from the commander himself, were found here in 1952.

Many fragments of biblical texts dating to this same time period were also found at Wadi Murabba'at. A fragment from the Minor Prophets written in Greek, along with other scrolls, was found in the caves of nearby wadis.

The rock fortress of Masada was conquered by the Romans in A.D. 74. During the 1963–1965 excavations, several manuscript fragments were found in these ruins, including portions of what appear to be Psalms, Leviticus, Ecclesiasticus (the Wisdom of Ben Sira), and Jubilee.

Bible Lesson

Remember the discussion from Chapter 6 about apocryphal and pseudepigraphal texts? Some believe Ecclesiasticus and Jubilee, respectively, fit into those categories. According to some scholars, neither the pseudepigraphal nor the apocryphal works have any authority or credibility. Their texts claimed that their authors were biblical writers. However, some believe that the texts date to centuries later than when Jesus and the apostles lived.

Midway between Qumran and Murabba'at, manuscripts were found at Khirbet Mird. These collections, dating between the fifth and eighth centuries A.D., reportedly contained several biblical texts written in Greek and in Palestinian Syriac. It is believed that the Greek texts included New Testament fragments of the uncial codices (books) of Mark, John, and Acts. The Syriac texts are thought to be fragments of Joshua, Luke, Acts, and Colossians.

What Do the Scrolls Contain?

The 850 Dead Sea manuscripts are classified as follows: biblical texts, biblical commentaries, sectarian texts, pseudepigraphal texts, apocalyptic texts, and mystical or ritualistic texts.

Timeless Truth

The Old Testament book of Isaiah was written in 800 B.C. The copy of the Biblical Isaiah in the Masoretic Text dated to A.D. 916—a gap of 1,716 years. How accurate can the MT be? Well, one of the Dead Sea Scrolls is supposedly a complete manuscript of the book of Isaiah that dates to 125 B.C. But the MT Hebrew manuscript matches more than 95 percent of the Dead Sea scroll word for word. The slight variations can be attributed to slips of the pen and spelling variations. So, it seems the Dead Sea scroll of Isaiah was copied 1,041 years before the Hebrew manuscript of the Masoretic Text.

Cave 1, discovered by the young goatherder, contained seven scrolls and fragments. The complete Isaiah scroll, designated Isaiah A, was apparently found here. It is the earliest known copy of any complete biblical book. A scroll designated Isaiah B was also found, but it is an incomplete text. Fragments from Genesis, Leviticus, Deuteronomy, Judges, Samuel, Isaiah, Ezekiel, and Psalms were reportedly found here, along with some nonbiblical works including Enoch, the Sayings of Jubilee, the Book of Noah, the Testament of Levi, Tobit, and the Wisdom of Solomon. Finally, fragments of commentaries on Psalms, Micah, and Zephaniah were also discovered.

About 100 manuscripts were found in Cave 2. These included two of Exodus, one of Leviticus, four of Numbers, three of Deuteronomy, one each of Jeremiah, Job, and the Psalms, and two of Ruth. The intriguing treasure map, the Copper Scroll, was hidden in Cave 3.

Literally thousands of fragments from hundreds of manuscripts were discovered in Cave 4. Copies of all the Old Testament books except Esther were found here. In addition, a fragment of Daniel 7:28–8:1 consisted of a change from the original Hebrew to Aramaic. Lastly, fragments of commentaries of the Psalms, Isaiah, and Nahum were also located in Cave 4.

Fantastic Find

A fragment of what is to be Samuel, which dated to the third century B.C., was found in Cave 4. If this is, in fact, a fragment of Samuel, then it is the oldest known biblical text written on papyrus.

Though no Old Testament manuscripts were found in Caves 7 through 10, fragments from the New Testament were apparently found in Cave 7. These are possibly the earliest New Testament copies in existence. In Cave 11, researchers claim to have found thirty-six Psalms, the apocryphal Psalm 151, part of Leviticus, and an Aramaic Targum (paraphrase) of Job.

The Copper Scroll

The mysterious Copper Scroll is a list of hidden treasures. Unlike most scrolls, this one was not made from parchment nor papyrus, but of thin copper sheets. The Hebrew text consisted of sixty-four sections, which were arranged in twelve columns. Each one described a hiding place and its secret treasure. The scroll implicates that forty-eight metric tons of silver and eight metric tons of gold were buried throughout the land of Israel, equivalent in wealth to the gold in Fort Knox. This would be like burying all the gold in Fort Knox throughout the state of Vermont!

Many of the descriptions in the Copper Scroll identified specific items belonging to the Temple or to the priests. According to the story, the Romans were marching toward Jerusalem to crush the Jewish Revolt and the Jewish priests feared that the soldiers would loot their holy relics. According to the Copper Scroll, they buried their sacred treasures and hid their buried-treasure map in the Dead Sea caves.

Fantastic Find

The Copper Scroll dates to sometime in the four years between the First Jewish Revolt in A.D. 66 and the destruction of Jerusalem in A.D. 70. The archaeologists who discovered the Copper Scroll were under the joint auspices of the American School of Oriental Research, the Ecole Archeologique Francaise de Jerusalem, and the Palestine Archaeological Museum.

Archaeologists discovered the Copper Scroll on March 20, 1952. Four years later, it was archived in the Archaeological Museum of Amman, Jordan, where it remains to this day. Scholars were allowed access only to early handwritten copies of the scroll and to photographs of the scroll taken in 1994.

Hammered on Copper

The Copper Scroll, which is actually a replica of a standard parchment scroll, consisted of three copper sheets that were riveted together. However, it was found in two rolled-up pieces. The sheets were 99 percent copper and only about one millimeter thick. Such exceptionally pure and thin metal was a treasure in itself.

The Copper Scroll was written in an early form of Mishnaic Hebrew. The style of the letters was different on each of the copper sheets. From this, it can be deduced that the text was hammered into the metal with a punch by three different metalworkers. As they were probably illiterate, they would have merely copied what earlier scribes had written. Unfortunately, the copper is now completely oxidized.

Timeless Truth

It is believed that illiterate metalworkers were given the task of hammering the text onto the Copper Scroll because they could not decipher the locations of the hidden treasures. The script seems to exhibit the work of three different "hands" or inscribers.

The Contents

The Copper Scroll was one of the few autographs (original copies) among the Dead Sea Scrolls. Most of the other manuscripts were copies of works that belonged in the Temple library. Though the prospect of deciphering a treasure map is a thrilling one, the Copper Scroll is a rather dry administrative document, something like a grocery list. Except, of course, that it supposedly contains the locations of the greatest buried treasure in the history of mankind. The sixty-four sections include the following information:

- An assigned concealed site
- An additional stipulation of the concealed site
- A command to dig or measure
- A distance stated in cubits
- A treasure description
- Further comments
- Greek letters

Opening the Scroll

Though the two pieces of the scroll were discovered in 1952, they couldn't be opened because the oxidized copper crumbled when it was touched. A few years later, H. Wright Baker and John Allegro, both professors at the University of Manchester, England, devised a method to open the scrolls. Professors Baker and Allegro first coated the rolled-up pieces with an adhesive. Then, using a small circular saw, they cut the scrolls into twenty-three narrow strips and cleaned them. The concave sides of the strips revealed the inscribed text.

Fantastic Find

Unfortunately, as H. Wright Baker and John Allegro slid the saw through the scrolls, the cuts destroyed some letters. This is one of the reasons why some of the words remain a mystery. A French team of scientists used modern technology to make a facsimile of the Copper Scroll. The technology enabled them to make out the engraving of damaged letters.

The Rosetta Scroll

The very last strip of the Copper Scroll mentions a second scroll that deciphers some of the phrasing that will unlock the code and reveal the locations of the treasure. According to the Copper Scroll, this second scroll is buried in the lost city of Janoah.

The Copper Scroll was featured in an exhibition called "Treasures from the Dead Sea: The Copper Scroll after 2000 Years." The exhibition was part of the Dead Sea Scroll Jubilee held at the University of Manchester, England, from October 21, 1997, through January 10, 1998. This exhibition was the second largest attended in history. The first was arranged for viewing the moon rocks brought back by the Apollo astronauts.

chapter 12

Unwrapping the Nativity

Now it's time to take a look at one of the most well-known and beloved biblical events for Christians: the momentous occasion of God the Son coming to earth as an infant. In this chapter, you'll investigate ancient documents, languages, and archaeological discoveries to view the birth of Jesus against its historical and cultural background. How did it really happen? Who was actually there? Your nativity scene may never look the same again.

The Virgin Mary

Luke 1:26–38 introduces you to a young Jewish girl who was a descendant of King David and of the tribe of Judah. Her name was Mary and she lived in the Galilean city of Nazareth. From other biblical passages, it's clear that the Galileans, and particularly the citizens of Nazareth, were despised by their fellow Jews (John 1:45–46). It's also clear that Mary was a *parthenos*, or virgin maiden (Isaiah 7:14; Luke 1:27). The angel Gabriel told her that she was "highly favored" (Luke 1:28).

Look in the Book

In Mary's culture, an engagement was as binding as a marriage, even when the union had not been consummated. Breaking the engagement was equivalent to a divorce (Matthew 1:19). Mary was betrothed to a young man named Joseph. During the betrothal, Mary and Joseph would each have had a chaperone who accompanied them wherever they went.

Mary was engaged to Joseph, a carpenter (Matthew 13:55). Though Hollywood characterizes the pregnant Mary as a young woman in her late teens or early twenties, historical evidence of the first-century Jewish culture indicates that girls were commonly married between the ages of ten and thirteen. Roman law decreed that the minimum age for a betrothal was ten years for girls and boys. Thus, Mary was no more than thirteen years old when she gave birth to Jesus.

Bible Lesson

Our English word *carpenter* comes from the Greek word *tekton*, which means "stonemason." Jesus worked with wood, but he primarily worked with stone. Even today in Nazareth stone can be seen everywhere. A carpenter in the ancient world was powerfully built and strong due to the physical labor. For this reason, paintings of a skinny, feminine-looking Jesus are likely inaccurate.

When Was Jesus Born?

Christians celebrate Jesus' birth on December 25, but is this really his birthday? Our calendar year supposedly reflects how many years have passed since Jesus was born. But was Jesus born in A.D. 0? Well, no. There is no such year as either A.D. 0 or 0 B.C. The year A.D. 1 immediately followed 1 B.C.

The Scythian monk Dionysius Exiguus, in the year A.D. 534, calculated the birth of Jesus by reading Luke 3:1 and 3:23, but he ignored the date of Herod's death and Matthew 2:19. He designated A.D. 1 as the year Jesus was born. Thus, he made a five-year mistake. Take the current year and add five. That's what year it should really be. So, in what year was Jesus born?

During the Roman Emperor's Decree

The Gospel of Luke says that Jesus' birth occurred when the Roman emperor Caesar Augustus ordered that "a census should be taken of the entire Roman world" (Luke 2:1). This indicates that Caesar ordered censuses to be regularly taken throughout the whole provincial empire. Top-notch scholars have learned that a census was taken every fourteen years. This census had two purposes, enrollment and taxation, and required Jewish males to return to the hometown of their ancestors.

Timeless Truth

Octavian, also known as Augustus, was the first Roman Emperor and reigned from 31 B.C. to August 19, A.D. 14. The name *Augustus* was a title given to Octavian that means "revered one." As the adopted son of Julius Caesar, Octavian defeated Marc Antony and Cleopatra to gain world dominance at the naval Battle of Actium in A.D. 31. This ended the Roman Republic and was the beginning of the Roman Empire with Octavian as its first emperor.

Before Herod's Death

The Gospels of both Matthew and Luke specified Jesus' birth as being in the days of King Herod. Therefore, Jesus was born before Herod died in

4 B.C. (Matthew 2:1; Luke 1:5). The Jewish historian, Josephus, says that an eclipse of the moon happened shortly before Herod died. History reveals that this eclipse occurred on March 12–13, 4 B.C. History also shows that a Passover took place after Herod died. Since the Passover for that year was April 11, Herod must have died between March 12 and April 11. This dates Jesus' birth before March or April of 4 B.C.

After Herod Murdered His Sons

In 7 B.C., Herod executed two of his sons, Alexander and Aristobulus. His other sons openly maneuvered to succeed their father to the throne. In the next three years, Herod changed his will three times. Angered at the tumultuous situation, Caesar Augustus began treating Herod as a subject rather than a friend. Recognizing the king's weakness and the instability of the province, Caesar ordered the census of Israel. The census, therefore, is dated after 7 B.C. and before 4 B.C.

Bible Lesson

In the ancient world, the concept of friendship was much different than it is today. It meant that you were obedient and loyal to another person, not that you were buddies. The context of a given situation tells who was obedient to whom. In John 15:14, Jesus said, "You are my friends if you do what I command." At Jesus' arrest, the Jews shouted at Pilate, "'If you let this man go, you are no friend of Caesar'" (John 19:12). Pilate understood their blunt threat; his loyalty and obedience to Caesar was being denied.

According to Luke, Caesar Augustus' census took place before Quirinius was governor of Syria (Luke 2:2). Here is where a quandary arises: Two different governors of Syria were called Quirinius. The first was governor in 11 B.C. A coin honoring this Quirinius named him as proconsul of Syria and Cilicia from 11 B.C. until Herod's death in A.D. 4. The second Quirinius became governor in 3 or 2 B.C. Either could have been governor before the census was taken. Based on the dates of the eclipse and the Passover, however, it makes sense to assume that Luke referred to the first Quirinius.

While Shepherds Tended Their Flocks

The night Jesus was born, shepherds tended their flocks in the hills outside Bethlehem. A Jewish document called the Mishnah says that sheep around Bethlehem remained outside all year except for the ones selected for the Passover offerings. Thirty days before the feast, these Passover sheep were brought closer to the town.

Look in the Book

Throughout Israel, sheep were brought out of the wilderness and tended closer to the towns and villages during the winter months. This is exactly what the Gospel writer Luke maintains. He writes, "And there were shepherds living out in the fields nearby, keeping watch over their flocks at night" (Luke 2:8). Jesus was therefore born during the winter months.

Examining all this historical evidence, it can be confidently stated that Jesus was born sometime between December 5 B.C. and January 4 B.C. The exact date is harder to determine. The Church Father Hippolytus (A.D. 165–235) was the first to claim December 25th as Jesus' birthday. In A.D. 386, Chrysostom, the Patriarch of Constantinople (A.D. 345–407) officially declared December 25th as the date of Jesus' birth.

Where Was Jesus Born?

The land of Israel was under Roman occupation during Octavian's reign as emperor. To be counted in the census, Joseph and Mary had to travel the eighty miles from their home in Nazareth to Joseph's ancestral home of Bethlehem. When they arrived, Joseph's name, occupation, property, and family were recorded by the imperial census-takers.

When the young couple arrived in Bethlehem, they found it bustling with other travelers who were also forced to obey the emperor's decree. The story is familiar: There was no room in the inn (or guest-room), so they found shelter in a stable.

No Room in the Inn

The typical Jewish peasant home had two stories. The family lived in the upper quarters and the animals were stabled on the ground floor. Luke 2:6 states that "while" Mary and Joseph were in Bethlehem, meaning they were in the town for some time, Mary gave birth to Jesus. The word commonly translated "inn" in Luke 2:7 is the same word translated "guest room" in Luke 22:11 (referring to the upper room where the Last Supper took place). There was no room in the inn, or the guest room of any house in Bethlehem, because other travelers were staying there. The only place left was the bottom floor of someone's home where the animals were kept. This is where Joseph and Mary stayed while they were in Bethlehem.

Forcing Mary to give birth with the animals was an unthinkable insult, particularly for a culture known for its hospitality. Apparently, no one was willing to give up his place in any of the guest rooms for Mary. It seems that the Jewish people in Bethlehem and Herod, the Jewish king, were not aware that their Messiah was soon to be born. Only the lowly shepherds and the Magi, who were non-Jews, were looking for Jesus' coming.

Bible Lesson

The Church of the Nativity in Bethlehem, which can be visited today, was built over the site that Christians have claimed as the place of Jesus' birth since the second century A.D. This place appears to be the first floor of a peasant's two-story house. Animals drank from a trough kept here. Supposedly, Mary laid Jesus in the trough (manger).

Settling amidst the animals stabled there, Mary gave birth to her firstborn, Jesus (Luke 2:7), in this dank and smelly place. Like any other Jewish woman, Mary wore a colorful girdle around her waist during her pregnancy. After Jesus was born, this girdle became his swaddling cloth. Though this was the usual custom, the swaddling of her infant had special significance for Mary.

Mary Swaddled Jesus

The angel Gabriel had told Mary that her son was the king, the long-awaited Messiah whose reign would be forever and "will never end" (Luke

1:31–35). She knew what to do for her noble newborn (Ezekiel 16:4). Mary gently washed Jesus with salted water and then wrapped ("swaddled") him in her girdle to protect his tiny limbs. The salt cleaned the skin and symbolized truth and honesty. Swaddling helped the baby's nervous system to develop. It was also thought that a swaddled baby would grow up to be tall and righteous.

It's interesting to see how Luke parallels Jesus' birth and his death:

- Luke 2:7: "wrapped him in cloths and placed him in a manger"
- Luke 23:53: "wrapped it [Jesus' body] in linen cloth and placed it in a tomb"

Wise Men Myths

Who were these travelers from the East bearing gifts for the baby Jesus? Known as the Magi, they are often depicted in nativity scenes as three kings who join the shepherds in worshiping the newly born Christ-child. *Ben Hur* (1959), the Academy Award–winning movie, opens with the three wise men visiting the newborn Jesus. Is this what really happened? Are our Christmas traditions and Hollywood movies historically accurate?

Timeless Truth

> The popular carol "We Three Kings," written by John Henry Hopkins Jr., in 1857, perpetuated the three-wise-men myth. The familiar names of Caspar, Melchior, and Balthazar came from clergyman Henry Van Dyke's story, "The Other Wise Man," written in 1896.

Two common myths are easily dispelled. First of all, even though Jesus was born in a stable, the Gospel of Matthew says that the Magi found him in a house (Matthew 2:1–12). The wise men weren't present at Jesus' birth, but arrived months, perhaps even a year or so, later. When the Magi returned home without telling King Herod that they had found the child, the Gospel writer says that the angry king ordered the death of all the boys under the age of two who lived in and around Bethlehem (Matthew 2:16–18). By

Herod's calculations, the baby he considered his rival would be killed in this horrendous slaughter.

Second, just because the Gospel writer named only three gifts doesn't mean there were only three wise men (Matthew 2:11). The number of Magi is never given in the biblical accounts, nor are their names.

In all ancient cultures, gifts of gold, frankincense, and myrrh were presented to a newborn king as a matter of regal protocol. Those offering their gifts bowed first to the reigning king and queen and then bowed to the newborn king. But the Magi didn't bow to Joseph and Mary. They bowed only to Jesus (Matthew 2:11).

Bible Lesson

The Magi's expensive gifts provided the means for Joseph to flee with his family to Egypt to escape Herod's evil and murderous plan. The text doesn't tell us where in Egypt they went, but history tells us that the city of Alexandria was divided into five sections, known as quarters. One of these five sections was a Jewish quarter where they would have been taken in as family. This was most likely where they went to live until they returned to Nazareth.

Who Were the Wise Men?

Who were these unnamed, unnumbered Middle Eastern travelers known as the wise men? To answer that question, you have to journey back into the centuries before Jesus' birth. History tells us that four great world empires successively ruled the ancient world. These were, in order: the Babylonian Empire; the Medo-Persian Empire; the Greek Empire ruled by Alexander the Great; and, at the time of Jesus' birth, the Roman Empire under the emperor Octavian (Caesar Augustus).

Though the Medes became part of the second great world empire, they lived at the time of the Babylonian Empire. They can be traced to the city of Ur of the Chaldeans, the city where Abraham lived (Genesis 11:27–12:5). The term *Chaldeans* is synonymous with *Magi*, the name for an ancestral priesthood clan who were natural philosophers and expert astronomers. This clan was part of the Medean society.

Politicians of Enormous Power

The Magi, priests who were chosen to conduct the Medes' religious observances, obtained enormous political power. Gaining a reputation for their wisdom, they became consultants to the kings and rulers of the East. In Jeremiah 39:3, you can read of a wise man named Nergal-Sharezer who was the head of the Magi in the court of the Babylonian king Nebuchadnezzar. This king elevated the Magi to exalted positions within his court. The biblical prophet Daniel was given the designation of a principal Magi for his ability to interpret dreams. Belteshazzar was named as the lord of the magicians in Nebuchadnezzar's court (Daniel 4:9; Daniel 5:11). Notice the similarity between the words *Magi* and *magicians*.

The King Makers

In time, the Magi became the kingmakers. Their authority was so entrenched in the Medo-Persian culture that no one became king without being personally instructed in the academic disciplines by the Magi. These wise men both sanctioned and crowned the new king. With this kind of power, the Magi controlled the known Middle Eastern world.

Darius was crowned king of the Medo-Persian Empire in the sixth century B.C. At this time, there were three orders of Magi. One was dedicated to the belief of Zoroastrianism, another to the belief system of the Medo-Persian Empire. The third gave allegiance to Judaism and to the God of Daniel. The descendants of this third order are the ones that traveled to Bethlehem.

The Megistanes

The Medo-Persian Empire eventually fell to the military might of Alexander the Great. In time, this legendary conqueror's empire was systematically crushed by the juggernaut of the ancient world, the Roman war machine. The old Medo-Persian Empire evolved into the Parthian Empire. The Magi, now known as the Megistanes, still wielded immense power.

Fantastic Find

In modern nativity scenes, it's common to see the wise men ambling along on their camels. But from Parthian history it's clear that whenever the Megistanes made a journey, they were accompanied by 1,000 mounted cavalry. These Megistanes galloped thunderously into Jerusalem, and the entire city, along with their king, quaked in fear.

At the beginning of the first century A.D., the Parthians forced their king from his throne. In their search for a different kind of king, the Megistanes and their thousand-man mounted cavalry galloped into Jerusalem. When Herod learned that the Megistanes had arrived, he was "disturbed, and all Jerusalem with him" (Matthew 2:3). The Greek word translated "disturbed" is *etarachtha* and means "to shake violently." The kingmakers were on his doorstep and they were not looking for him.

Look in the Book

It seems that the Star of Bethlehem that guided the Megistanes (Matthew 2:2) was a supernatural phenomenon, and not a star like the sun, because it appears and disappears. Only the Megistanes see it. Neither Herod nor his court had seen the star; he had to ask the Megistanes when it appeared. After the Megistanes left Herod, "the star they had seen in the east went ahead of them until it stopped over the place where the child was" (Matthew 2:9). The star *moved* and then it *stopped*.

When the Megistanes found Jesus in a house in Bethlehem, they worshiped him (Matthew 2:11). They were guided by their knowledge of Scriptures, which came from Daniel's long-ago influence. The Megistanes knew the words of Micah, which predicted that the Messiah would be born in Bethlehem (Micah 5:2). They were looking for a powerful political king, but found a humble servant-king instead.

chapter 13

Jesus' Death

For Christians, the cross symbolizes the sacrifice of Jesus for mankind and the hope of eternal life. It is a reminder of the humiliation and torture Jesus endured because of his great love. After his arrest, he was beaten and scourged almost to the point of death. Then he spent six long hours on the cross, struggling for each breath. While hanging there, he reportedly made seven statements that were recorded by the Gospel writers. This chapter explores execution by Roman crucifixion and explains the significance of the final words Jesus spoke before he died.

Scourging

Under Roman rule, anyone found guilty of a capital offense was scourged (*verberatio*) with a flagrum before being crucified. The flagrum was made up of several leather thongs with pieces of bone and metal dispersed throughout the strips. Small lead dumbbells were tied to the leather ends. As the victim was whipped by the Roman lictors, the bone and metal tore into his body, ripping and shredding his flesh.

Look in the Book

Eusebius, bishop of Caesarea (A.D. 263–339) writes that a scourged victim's "veins were laid bare . . . The very muscles, sinews, and bowels of the victim were open to exposure" (Epistle of the Church in Smyrna). The highly respected Roman leader Cicero (106–43 B.C.) said the threat of crucifixion oppressed the people. "Even the mere word, cross, must remain far not only from the lips of the citizens of Rome, but also from their thoughts, their eyes, their ears" (Marcus Tullius Cicero, *Pro Rabirio*, V.16).

After the Jewish religious leaders found Jesus guilty of blasphemy, they insisted that Pilate order his crucifixion. According to the Bible, Jesus was stripped of his clothing, and then tied to an upright post. He was beaten by one Roman lictor from his neck to the waist and by another, striking backhanded, from his waist to his ankles. Lictors were expert torturers who beat their victims to near death. They didn't want the victim to die, though, since the terror of crucifixion awaited. Jewish law demanded that no one was to be beaten more than forty times. The Jewish leaders took this very seriously and allowed thirty-nine strikes just in case they miscounted. But the Romans didn't follow any such constraint.

Jesus' Torture

The Bible says that after the scourging, Jesus was taken to the quarters of the Roman soldiers in the Praetorium (Matthew 27:27–30; Mark 15:16–19). With mocking and jeering, the soldiers put a scarlet robe on Jesus' shoulders, placed a crown of thorns on his head, and forced him to hold a staff as his scepter. The soldiers knelt in feigned homage as they shouted, "Hail, king of the Jews!" (Matthew 27:29). They hit him on the head with the staff. After having their fun, the soldiers "led him away to crucify him" (Matthew 27:31).

Bible Lesson

Many believe the crown of thorns Jesus wore wasn't a circlet that surrounded his head, but a cap of the three-inch long thorns that grow around Jerusalem. The puncture wounds covered Jesus' entire head and he probably wore this "crown-cap" throughout the crucifixion.

Jesus' Crucifixion

The Bible says that Roman soldiers tied the horizontal bar of the cross, called the patibulum, to Jesus' shoulders, then led him from the Praetorium. After enduring the scourging and torture, the weight of the cross was practically impossible to bear. When Jesus fell under the weight of the crossbeam, the soldiers pulled a man named Simon of Cyrene (a city in north Africa) from the crowd and forced him to carry the bar the rest of the way to Golgotha, the place of the Skull (Matthew 27:33; Mark 15:22; Luke 23:33; John 19:17). The Gospel of Luke says, "A large number of people followed him, including women who mourned and wailed for him" (Luke 23:27).

Before Jesus was nailed to the cross, the soldiers offered him wine mixed with myrrh and gall, a narcotic prepared by the women of Jerusalem to lessen the pain (Matthew 27:34; Mark 15:23). He tasted it, but refused to drink it. His sacrifice demanded that he endure the complete and overwhelming pain of crucifixion.

Once again, Jesus was stripped of all his clothing. His head was placed in the middle of the horizontal crossbar, which was now on the ground, and his arms were outstretched to both ends. Pinning Jesus' arm with his knee, a soldier hammered a spike into first one wrist and then the other. Nailed to the crossbeam, Jesus was now forced to stand. Ropes were threaded through the rings located at each end of the beam.

Timeless Truth

Crosses were tall enough to be easily seen as people passed through the city gates. The Roman authorities wanted people to see what happened to those who disobeyed their laws. The cross was high enough that a soldier placed a vinegar-soaked sponge on a hyssop stalk, as a kind of extension pole, so that the sponge could touch Jesus' lips (Matthew 27:48; Mark 15:36; John 19:29–30). The cross was in two pieces, the long (*stipes*) piece was about fifteen feet in height and the small crossbeam (*pantibulum*) was around six feet in length.

The vertical part of the cross (*stipes*), which was about fifteen feet tall, was already fastened into a hole in the ground. Wooden scaffolding stood behind the cross and soldiers stood on ladders behind this scaffolding. They caught the ropes as they were thrown up over the wooden scaffolding, and then threw the ends of these ropes to other soldiers standing on the ground. By pulling on the ropes, the soldiers hoisted the crossbeam, and Jesus, to the top of the vertical post. After fastening the horizontal bar to the vertical one, a soldier positioned Jesus' right foot on top of his left and then hammered one large spike through both feet and into the cross.

Look in the Book

The Jewish leaders wanted the sign to read that Jesus claimed to be the King of the Jews. By leaving the inscription as he originally ordered, Pilate was getting revenge for being politically maneuvered by the Jewish authorities into ordering the crucifixion. As vicious and corrupt as Pilate was, he could find no fault in Jesus and tried to free him, but the Jewish leaders threatened him by going to the Roman emperor telling him of his disloyalty and disobedience as "a friend of Caesar."

The Roman custom was to write a victim's crime on a tablet (*titulus*), which was carried by a Roman soldier before the victim as he was led to his execution. Once he was on the cross, the tablet was fastened to its top. Jesus' tablet read, "This is Jesus of Nazareth, the King of the Jews" in the main three languages of the day: Hebrew, Latin, and Greek (Matthew 27:37;

Mark 15:26; Luke 23:38; John 19:19). Though the Jewish chief priests protested, Pilate refused to change the inscription (John 19:21–22).

The First Three Hours

According to the Bible, Jesus was crucified between two guerilla fighters (John 19:18; Isaiah 53:12) at 9:00 A.M. on a Friday morning. To exhale, he slumped into a Y position, then pushed up with his legs and arms to a T to inhale. His first words after being nailed to the cross were "Father, forgive them, for they do not know what they are doing" (Luke 23:34).

Bible Lesson

A centurion and four soldiers were assigned to each crucified victim. They divided the victim's property among themselves (John 19:23–24). One soldier took Jesus' headgear, another his outer garment, the third his belt, and the fourth his sandals. Jesus also owned an inner garment, described as "seamless, woven in one piece from top to bottom" (John 19:23). The soldiers gambled for the seamless garment by casting lots, thus fulfilling the prophecy of Psalm 22:18.

During Jesus' first three hours on the cross, he was mocked by those traveling to and from Jerusalem and by the chief priests, teachers of the law, and synagogue leaders. They taunted him to save himself if he were indeed the Son of God. The two crucified criminals and the Roman soldiers also mocked and insulted him (Matthew 27:44; Luke 23:36). But when one of the criminals challenged Jesus to save all of them, the other one came to Jesus' defense. "We are punished justly, for we are getting what our deeds deserve," he said. "But this man has done nothing wrong" (Luke 23:41). The repentant criminal asked Jesus to remember him. For the second time, Jesus spoke from the cross. "I tell you the truth, today you will be with me in paradise," he told the criminal (Luke 23:42–43).

The apostle John and four women stood near the cross. The women were Jesus' mother Mary; her sister Salome, the wife of Zebedee and the mother of the two apostles James and John; Mary the wife of Clopas and the mother of James and Joses; and Mary of Magdala (Matthew 27:56; Mark

15:40; John 19:25). The Romans did not know the identity of Jesus' mother and his followers. If they had, no doubt they would have taunted and persecuted them for being associated with a condemned criminal.

Though the other apostles apparently weren't at the cross, John and Jesus' mother were close enough to hear him speak. Looking at his mother and his beloved apostle, Jesus spoke for the third time. To Mary, he said, "'Dear woman, here is your son,' and to the disciple, 'Here is your mother'" (John 19:26–27). These words are significant because they are similar to the language for a legal adoption. By calling his mother, "woman," Jesus was gently reminding Mary that she must view him as her savior. John was now her son and she was John's new mother.

Look in the Book

Jesus called Mary "woman" on only one other occasion: at the wedding of Cana (John 2:1–11), where he turned water into wine. A new relationship was about to begin—i.e., Jesus' public ministry was about to commence. Here, too, Jesus called Mary "woman," which was telling Mary that a new relationship was beginning. No longer would he be at home—he was about to begin his ministry.

When Jesus said, "behold your son," Christians believe he wasn't telling Mary to look at him on the cross. He was entrusting his mother to John's care. At this time, Jesus' half-brothers and sisters were unbelievers (John 7:1–5). Jesus wished his mother to be cared for and protected by someone who did believe in him.

Fantastic Find

Hollywood movies such as *Ben Hur* (1959), *The Robe* (1953), *The Greatest Story Ever Told* (1965), and *The Passion of the Christ* (2004) all show Mary at the cross when Jesus died. They also show Mary holding Jesus after he is taken off the cross. However, the Bible says that though Mary was at the cross for a while, the apostle John took her away before noon. According to the Bible, Mary wasn't at the cross when Jesus died.

"From that time on," John took Mary from Golgotha "into his home" (John 19:27). Mary was not at the cross when Jesus died. The other women did not leave, but they moved some distance from the cross.

The Last Three Hours

The time is now twelve noon, but the bright sun cannot be seen (Luke 23:44–45). For the next three hours, no one mocks or insults Jesus. The darkness keeps anyone from witnessing Jesus' dying moments. Around 3 P.M., Jesus speaks for the fourth time: "'Eloi, Eloi, lama sabachthani?'" which is Aramaic for "My God, my God, why have you forsaken me?" (Matthew 27:46).

Christians believe that Jesus paid the penalty of sin for all mankind, from the first man Adam to the last individual to be born before the second coming. Jesus suffered all aspects of death—physical, spiritual, and eternal—for all men and women. Since spiritual and eternal death signify a broken communion with God the Father and God the Holy Spirit, this means that during Jesus' final three hours on the cross, he was separated from his Father and the Holy Spirit. He endured mankind's loneliness and despair at being separated from God. During his physical death, which was imminent, Jesus fully experienced death for each person (Hebrews 2:9). Some who heard Jesus' outburst thought he was crying out to the prophet Elijah for help.

Jesus' fifth statement, "I am thirsty" (John 19:28), fulfilled the prophecy of Psalm 22:15, which gives a horrifically accurate description of the thirst and fever experienced in crucifixion. Hearing Jesus' words, a Roman soldier soaked a sponge in a jar of vinegar and raised it on a hyssop stalk to Jesus' lips (John 19:30). This act fulfilled the prophecy of Psalm 69:21.

Bible Lesson

Why did Jesus accept the vinegar after earlier refusing the wine mixed with myrrh? Well, the earlier drink was a narcotic sedative which would have lessened the pain Jesus felt on the cross. Christians believe he was not willing to do anything less than offer his full self as a complete sacrifice. But the vinegar (*posca*) was the equivalent of a first-century Gatorade, a sour wine that the soldiers drank to prevent dehydration in hot and humid climates.

After tasting the vinegar, Jesus cried out in a loud voice (Mark 15:37) for the sixth time. "It is finished," he said (John 19:30). The phrase is only one word in the Greek and means that a commercial transaction has been completed. The connotation is that payment has been made in full or that a debt has been completely discharged. The phrase was also used in a military sense. The winning Roman general stood on the losing general's neck, raised his sword to the sky, and shouted, "It is finished." In this one word, Jesus was declaring that he had fully paid the debt for mankind's sin by suffering mankind's eternal punishment, Hell, while on the cross (Romans 3:25).

Jesus' seventh and final statement before dying was a child's prayer. "Father, into your hands I commit my spirit" (Luke 23:46; John 10:17–18). "With that," writes the apostle John, "he bowed his head and gave up his spirit" (John 19:30). The Greek word "bowed" means to lay one's head down. It is the same word found in Matthew 8:20 and Luke 9:58, which say, "Foxes have holes and birds of the air have nests, but the Son of Man has no place to lay his head."

The Bible says that Jesus did not gasp for a last breath, but purposely and at the moment of his own choosing, shut his eyes, laid his head on the crossbeam as if on a pillow, and died. A Roman centurion who was at the cross during the entire six hours proclaimed, "Surely he was the Son of God" (Matthew 27:54).

Miracles Accompanying Jesus' Death

At the exact moment of Jesus' death that Friday afternoon, the Bible says that the Temple veil separating the Holy Place from the Holy of Holies split in two from its top to its bottom. This veil was a large piece of material measuring sixty feet long, twenty feet wide, and four inches thick. As large as it was, no one could have torn it and certainly no one could have torn it from its top. Christians believe that God ripped the veil to end the separation of the people from the Holy of Holies, a place that could be entered only by specifically chosen priests. Now every single person could approach God through Jesus.

Bible Lesson

Why did Jesus die at approximately 3:00 P.M. on that Passover Friday after-noon? Well, the Jewish priests began to slit the throats of the sacrifi-cial lambs, which were to be eaten as part of the Passover meal, at precisely 3:00 P.M. (Matthew 27:45–46). Jesus, the lamb of God, is the Christian's Passover (John 1:29; 1 Corinthians 5:7). This is why Jesus chose to die at 3:00 P.M. The New Testament writers are adamant that Jesus "gave" his life and no one took it from him (Galatians 1:4: 2:20; Titus 2:14).

The Bible says that an earthquake also occurred at the same moment, splitting rocks and opening many tombs (Matthew 27:52). Dead saints arose from these tombs, though they didn't appear in Jerusalem until after Jesus' resurrection. After that, they appeared to many people.

chapter 14

Jesus' Burial

There is more information about the death and burial of Jesus than of any other historical figure from ancient history. The Gospel writers devote much of their attention to providing specific details of what happened that fateful day. Christians believe their description of how Jesus died is verified by what is known of both Roman and Jewish customs. The Jewish historian Josephus (A.D. 37–100) also comments on Jesus' death. This chapter takes an in-depth look at Jesus' final moments on the cross through his burial in a borrowed tomb.

After He Died

To make sure that Jesus was dead, a Roman soldier thrust his lance into Jesus' side. The Gospel of John says that "blood and water" came out of the wound (John 19:34). If Jesus was still alive when pierced with the lance, many believe blood would have spurted out with every heartbeat. However, modern medicine shows that when a knife pierces the side of someone who has recently died, a dark blood clot seeps from the wound followed by a watery serum. The Roman soldiers were death professionals who were very good at their job—making sure their crucified victim was actually dead.

Jesus' body was wrapped in seventy pounds of spices after being placed in Joseph of Arimathea's tomb. Some still question ancient people's ability to tell if a person were completely dead at that time in history, while others argue that those who loved him would not have enshrouded him until they knew for sure that he had died.

Preparing for the Sabbath

Jesus was crucified on a Friday. For the Jews, this was the day of preparation before the Sabbath began at sundown—i.e., 6:00 P.M. (John 19:31). This particular Friday was part of the Passover Feast and also the second paschal day dedicated to the ceremonial wave sheaf offering (Leviticus 23:10-14). During the spring, before any grain could be harvested, stalks of barley were brought to the priest who waved the stalk before God. Then the harvesting could begin.

Timeless Truth

The Sabbath Day is the seventh day of the week, Saturday, the day God rested after spending six days creating the universe. However, as the Hebrews calculated time, the Sabbath began at sundown on Friday and continued until sundown on Saturday. After the sun set on Friday, the rules prohibiting working on the Sabbath were enforced.

Because of their sacred regard for the Passover, the Bible says the Jewish religious leaders asked Pilate's permission to break the legs of the three crucifixion victims to ensure their death before the Sabbath began (John

19:31). This practice was called *crucifragium*. With their legs broken, the victims couldn't raise themselves up to a T position to breathe. In the Y position, the victim couldn't breathe and suffocated. Using an iron mallet, the Roman soldiers crushed the legs, from the kneecaps down, of the two guerilla fighters. But they didn't break Jesus' legs because he was already dead (John 19:32–33). The prophets had said that none of Jesus' bones would be broken (Exodus 12:46; Number 9:12; Psalm 24:20; John 19:36; cf. 1 Corinthians 5:7; 1 Peter 1:19).

Bible Lesson

According to Deuteronomy 21:22–23, anyone hanged on a tree was not to remain there overnight. Because the crucified person was under God's curse (Galatians 3:13), leaving him there overnight desecrated the land. Before crucifixion became an accepted method of execution, victims were impaled upon poles and left in prominent places where everyone could see them. The long sharp pole was thrust under the person's sternum. Sometimes only the victims' heads were placed on top of the poles.

Joseph of Arimathea was a wealthy and prominent member of the Sanhedrin, the Jewish Supreme Court. He was also a secret disciple of Jesus. Joseph owned the tomb where Jesus was buried. He and another Sanhedrin member, Nicodemus, provided the linen cloth and spices needed for burial. But before they could proceed, Joseph went to Pilate to request Jesus' body (Matthew 27:57; Mark 15:43, 46; John 19:38–39). Under Roman law, someone crucified for sedition was left for the vultures. For Joseph to go to Pilate showed great courage and devotion.

Look in the Book

The Jewish historian Josephus, in *The Jewish War*, writes that the Jews "proceeded to that degree of impiety as to cast away their dead bodies without burial, although the Jews used to take so much care of the burial of men, that they took down those that were condemned and crucified, and buried them before the going down of the sun." When three of Josephus' acquaintances were crucified, he courageously asked the Roman Emperor Titus to take them from the cross. Joseph of Arimathea made a similar request to the Roman Governor Pilate.

After listening to Joseph's request, Pilate sent for the centurion in charge of the crucifixion and questioned him about the victims (Mark 15:44). The centurion said that he saw how Jesus died (Mark 15:39). In addition, four soldiers were required by Roman law to sign a document certifying that Jesus was dead. The soldiers, death specialists, were punished for falsifying information so they didn't make mistakes. After all this, Pilate released Jesus' body to Joseph's care.

Pilate expressed surprise that Jesus was dead after only six hours on the cross (Mark 15:44). Yet it's clear he believed that Jesus was dead or he wouldn't have released Jesus' body to Joseph of Arimathea. Since the Jewish religious leaders requested guards for the tomb, they, too, must have believed Jesus was dead. Pilate's approval of their request may reflect his belief in Jesus' innocence.

The Burial

The Bible says Joseph and Nicodemus, most likely with the help of their servants, lowered the cross to the ground. They removed the nails from Jesus' body and wrapped it in a linen shroud (Mark 15:46). Jesus was buried in a tomb called a *meartha*. This word, which occurs thirty-two times in the Gospels, refers to a cave hewn from the rock, not a natural cave. A nine-foot-square area within the entrance, known as a court, was used for performing the burial rites. Then the dead were laid on a niche, or *kukhin*, in the meartha. The tomb belonged to Joseph of Arimathea and was "new" (Matthew 27:60; John 19:41). No one else had been buried in it.

Fantastic Find

According to the legend of Herai, or Shingo, when Jesus was twenty-one years old he went to Japan and stayed there eleven years. His brother Isukiri was crucified in his place. Jesus settled in the village of Herai, married a woman named Miyuko who bore him three children, and died when he was 106 years old. The legend says that Jesus and his brother, along with locks of Mary's hair, were buried in the same tomb.

Joseph and Nicodemus, most likely with the help of servants, placed Jesus' body on a stone ledge in the tomb's court area. They wrapped it with seventy pounds of spices and linen (John 19:40; Luke 23:53). The spices were a fragrant mixture of powdered myrrh and aloe, and aromatic sandalwood, often used by the Jews for anointing and burial. They also placed flowers from the vicinity with the body. The spices both preserved the body and acted as an adhesive for the linen shroud. Additional spices were placed under and around the body to alleviate the body's decaying odor. Once Jesus' body was completely and tightly wrapped, a piece of cloth similar to the shroud, but much smaller, was placed over his head (John 11:44).

Look in the Book

The Jews always buried their dead and they also buried their enemies (2 Samuel 2:32; Tobit 1:17–19; 2:3–7; 12:12–13; Sirach 7:33; 38:16; Joshua 8:29; 10:27; Josephus's *Jewish War* 3.377). The Temple Scroll, one of the Dead Sea Scrolls, records a command to bury a crucified body on the same day. Josephus also mentions such a command—to bury on the same day one who has been hung on a tree after being stoned to death (*Antiquities* 4:202 and *Jewish War* 4.317).

After Joseph and Nicodemus completed the rites, an "exceedingly great stone" called a *golel* was rolled in front of the tomb's entrance (Matthew 27:60; Mark 15:46). Men pushed the large disk from its initial resting place and then it rolled along a groove designed for this purpose. Weighing at least 2,000 pounds, the stone was a barrier against wild animals.

Some biblical critics claim that the reason the tomb was empty was because Jesus' followers went to the wrong tomb. Christians refute this assertion, saying that Joseph of Arimathea was a wealthy and prominent man and this was a new tomb. Joseph's family and colleagues knew where his tomb was located and so did the workers who cut it from the rock. The Jewish religious leaders obviously knew where the tomb was located since they wanted it guarded. Pilate knew where it was and so did the Roman soldiers who guarded the tomb.

Bible Lesson

In the fourth-century manuscript *Codex Bezae*, there is a gloss, which is a phrase written in a parenthesis, at Mark 16:4 that says, "And when he [Jesus] was laid there, he [Joseph] put against the tomb a stone which twenty men could not roll away." Many of these stones are seen in Israel. Based on the size of these stones and the entrances of the tombs, engineers have estimated that they average at least a ton.

Additionally, the Gospel writers record that a group of women, including "Mary Magdalene and Mary the mother of Joses" followed Joseph and Nicodemus and "observed where he [Jesus] was laid" (Matthew 25:47; 27:61; Mark 15:47; Luke 23:55). Before the stone was rolled in front of the tomb, the women left to prepare more spices so that they could continue the burial process after the Sabbath had ended. These women saw Jesus being buried and knew where the tomb was located.

These women returned to the tomb on Sunday morning with their additional spices (Matthew 28:1; Mark 16:2; Luke 24:1). It's absurd to claim that they didn't know where Jesus was buried. When Peter and John were told that the tomb was empty, the two apostles ran to the tomb to see for themselves. They knew exactly where to look (Luke 24:12; John 20:3–8).

Timeless Truth

In one view of Hinduism, Jesus was in India/Kashmir from A.D. 30 to 50. While there, Jesus told King Shalivahan that he was *Isa Masih* (Jesus the Messiah). Buddhism teaches that Jesus (Avalokitesvara) wasn't crucified, but traveled to Tibet and was buried in India.

Guarded by Roman Soldiers

Aware that Jesus had predicted his resurrection and fearing that his followers would steal the body to make it appear as if he had risen, the Jewish leaders asked Pilate to secure the tomb (Matthew 27:62–66). Pilate gave them a Roman guard, known as a *kustodian*, to secure the tomb.

Look in the Book

Some wonder if the Roman guard selected to secure the tomb could have been the Jewish Temple guard. However, the temple guards are never referred to as a kustodian, which refers to an elite Roman military unit. Besides, after the soldiers deserted their post, they asked the Jewish religious leaders to intervene with Pilate on their behalf (Matthew 28:11–14). It seems Pilate had nothing to do with the Jewish Temple guard.

Kustodians were highly-trained special military units of sixteen men each who protected the Emperor's treasure and whatever else belonged to him. One kustodian could hold off a small army of three to 400 soldiers for about a half hour, which gave time for reinforcements to show up. As a convicted criminal, Jesus' body belonged to Rome and the emperor, so Pilate's sending of the guard, particularly in view of the concerns raised by the Jewish leaders, was a sensible decision.

Timeless Truth

According to the ancient Roman law, a soldier who left his post faced the death penalty. To avoid such a severe punishment, the soldiers were particularly attentive to their duties, especially during the night watches (Dion. Halm *Antiq. Rom.* VIII.79; Polybius VI.37,38; *Justinian Digest* 49.16). The kustodian was the most disciplined military unit of the ancient world, making it unlikely that a soldier would have fallen asleep while on duty.

Each kustodian soldier carried a pike, which was a six-foot wooden spear with an iron head. He held a large shield on his left arm. In his belt, he had a three-foot short-sword designed for thrusting and close fighting. He also carried a dagger in his belt. These soldiers were the deadliest ever known.

After Jesus' tomb was secured and sealed, four of the soldiers stood battle-ready at the tomb's entrance in four-hour shifts. The remaining twelve formed a semicircular perimeter in front of the tomb where they were relaxed, but wary. If anyone approached the tomb, the kustodian immediately got into a formation of four rows of four men. They killed anyone entering their perimeter.

The Sealing of the Tomb

The Gospel of Matthew says that the Jewish religious leaders "made the tomb secure, sealing the stone and setting the guard" (Matthew 27:66). The Roman seal was a cord that stretched across the stone. It was fastened at each end with sealing clay (Daniel 6:17). Before the tomb could be opened, the fastenings would have to be broken. The seal indicated Roman power and the Emperor's ownership.

Breaking the Roman seal was a capital offense that carried the death penalty. The Roman guards witnessed the sealing after confirming that what they were to guard—Jesus' dead body—was indeed in the tomb. The seal was sacred to the Roman guard.

Timeless Truth

J. D. Crossan of the Jesus Seminar believes that Jesus' burial is "wishful thinking" and nothing more than a tradition. He claims Jesus was either eaten by birds while still on the cross or that he was buried in a shallow common grave where his body was eaten by wild dogs. In this view, Joseph of Arimathea was invented by the writer of the Gospel of Mark to shift responsibility for Jesus' burial to his friends.

While some critics deny the story as it appears in the Bible, others believe that passages stating that Joseph of Arimathea took Jesus' dead body from the cross and laid him in his own new tomb verify the truth of the event. The Jewish burial process and customs are well documented in the Bible. Some also believe that both Jesus' followers and his enemies knew exactly which tomb held his body. The tomb was supposedly located in a garden outside the walls of Jerusalem near the crucifixion site.

The Swoon Theory

Another theory about Jesus' burial is that his followers conspired to fake Jesus' death. According to this theory, Jesus was drugged in such a way that even the Roman executioners believed he was dead. Then later he was revived and it appeared he had risen from the dead. Some criticize this theory, saying that it doesn't quite explain how the Sanhedrin was manip-ulated into convicting him of blasphemy in the first place, nor why Jesus endured the crucifixion for the sake of such a hoax.

For this hoax to succeed, Jesus faced six illegal trials, endured beat-ings, a scourging, the crown of thorns, crucifixion, and a spear thrust into his side. Then he revived in the tomb and unwrapped his burial garments. Though he had gone three days without medical treatment, he managed to move the one-ton stone blocking the tomb's entrance and singlehand-edly defeated an elite Roman guard. After all that, he walked seven miles to Emmaus (on nail-punctured feet) and proclaimed himself the risen Mes-siah. Of course, this would be difficult for a normal man, but plausible for a person like Jesus, who had performed many miracles in the past.

Timeless Truth

Schonfield calls the biblical account of Jesus' burial and resurrec-tion the "fairy dust of faith." However, many Christians believe that Schonfield's own work lacks credibility, integrity, and scholarship. Like many biblical accounts and their accompanying theories, this one has raised a significant amount of controversy.

According to Hugh Schonfield's book *The Passover Plot*, Jesus was to take a narcotic so he could sleep on the cross. But those involved in the plot didn't expect the Roman soldier to thrust his spear into Jesus' side. Joseph took Jesus from the cross and placed him in his tomb as planned. However, according to Schonfield, Jesus died from the side wound while in the tomb. The book depicts another young man disposing of Jesus' body, and then being mistaken for the risen Jesus.

chapter 15

The Empty Tomb: Miracle or Hoax?

Was Jesus' tomb really empty on that early Sunday morning? What happened to Jesus' body? The answers to these pivotal questions determine whether or not the Bible can be believed. Many believe that if Jesus' body was still in the tomb, or if it was stolen, then Christianity is a false religion. However, if he truly rose from the dead, then the Bible can be considered trustworthy. This chapter provides the historical background for Jesus' death and resurrection while addressing these questions.

An Angel or Jupiter?

The Bible says that at the request of the Jewish religious leaders, Pilate ordered a Roman kustodian to guard Jesus' tomb. The soldiers took up their post late Friday afternoon around 6:00 P.M. Sometime during the fourth watch on Sunday morning, between 3:00 A.M. and 6:00 A.M., while it was still dark, an angel dressed in dazzling white came down from the sky "like lightning" (Matthew 28:3).

Like most Romans, the soldiers were extremely superstitious. For example, they believed that Jupiter, the king of the Roman deities, hurled lightning bolts. In fact, it's possible they mistook the angel's presence for that of Jupiter. The soldiers of a kustodian were the military elite and feared no one, but they had never fought against a Roman god before. Or an angel. The angel walked through the kustodian's formation, dislodged the great stone from the tomb's entrance, picked up the enormous rock, carried it away from the tomb, and sat on top of it. The greatest fighting men on the face of the earth "became like dead men" (Matthew 28:2–4).

Bible Lesson

The stone was not rolled away from Jesus' tomb. The trench that was used to roll the stone in place begins on a hill and descends downward. The stone could not be rolled backwards up the hill. The Greek word *airo* doesn't mean "to roll," but to pick up an object and carry it a distance from its original location. According to the Bible, the angel had incredible strength.

Since the stone probably weighed at least a ton, the kustodian's fear is understandable. They believed in a false god, Jupiter, who had the strength to move the stone. It's hard to imagine the disciplined kustodian leaving their post for any reason. But they wouldn't have dared stand up to their king of the gods. Some of them ran to the Jewish religious leaders instead of Pilate because the penalty for leaving their post was death.

Moving the Stone

The showdown between the angel and the Roman kustodian, such as it was, occurred before the women arrived early that Sunday morning. Carrying the additional spices they needed to complete the anointing of his body, they talked about the huge stone that blocked the entrance to the cave. They knew it was too large for them to move on their own and wondered how they could get someone to help them (Mark 16:1–3).

Bible Lesson

The women didn't know that the Roman kustodian were guarding the tomb. If they had arrived any earlier, no doubt the soldiers would have killed them. The only ones who knew about the kustodian guarding the tomb was Pilate, the Jewish religious leaders who requested the guard, and the kustodian itself. The apostles and the women followers had no knowledge of a guard being posted at Jesus' tomb.

When the women got to the tomb, they were amazed to see that the stone was no longer in front of the tomb. And they were frightened when they saw the angel, who told them not to be afraid and encouraged them to look into the tomb (Matthew 28:5–6). The angel didn't move the stone to let Jesus out of the tomb, but to let people in so they could see that Jesus wasn't inside. However, it's not accurate to say that the tomb was empty. Read on to discover what occurred on that Sunday morning.

Sunday Morning

The Bible says that it was still dark when Mary Magdalene and the other women arrived at the tomb. Seeing that the stone had been moved, they ran to tell the apostles Peter and John (John 20:2). Just after sunrise, another group of women arrived at the tomb and they also saw that the stone had been moved (Mark 16:4). Entering the tomb, they "saw a young man dressed in a white robe sitting on the right side" (Mark 16:5). This angel and another one with him approached the women and "stood beside them" (Luke 24:4). The terrified women fell before the angels, who said, "Don't be alarmed . . .

You are looking for Jesus the Nazarene, who was crucified" (Mark 16:6). The Gospel of Luke phrases it a little differently: "Why do you look for the living among the dead? He is not here; he has risen" (Luke 24:5–6).

Timeless Truth

In the first century A.D., women had a very low social status. "Sooner let the words of the Law be burnt than delivered to women" and "Happy is he whose children are male, and alas for him whose children are female" (B Kiddushin 82b) were common Jewish beliefs. But the risen Jesus appeared to Mary Magdalene before anyone else, even Peter and John.

The Gospel of Mark states that the angels reminded the women that Jesus had told them of both his crucifixion and his resurrection. After one of the angels instructed the women to tell the disciples that Jesus would meet them in Galilee, they left the tomb "trembling and bewildered" (Mark 16:7–8).

Mary Magdalene and the women with her "came running to Simon, Peter, and the other disciple, the one Jesus loved, and said, 'They have taken the Lord out of the tomb, and we don't know where they have put him'" (John 20:2). Hearing this, Peter and John immediately ran to the tomb. The younger man, John, got there first. He stopped at the entrance and peered inside. Jesus wasn't there, but he saw the linen cloths that had been left behind.

When Peter got to the tomb, he went inside without stopping. He "saw the strips of linen lying there, as well as the burial cloth that had been around Jesus' head. The cloth was folded up by itself, separate from the linen" (John 20:6–7). John followed Peter inside and he now "saw and believed" (John 20:8). John is the first person to have a full understanding of Jesus' resurrection. The Bible says that both he and Peter returned home, still wondering about these amazing events.

Many think that the presence of the linen burial cloths proved that Jesus' body had not been stolen. The argument is that it would have been extremely difficult to unwrap the shroud after it was adhered to his body. Furthermore, many wonder how a group of fishermen and a tax collector could have defeated the battle-hardened kustodian. Christians believe there is another story behind Jesus' disappearance from the tomb.

Jesus' Post-Resurrection Appearances

The Bible says that Jesus appeared to many different individuals and groups of individuals after his resurrection. For Christians, these appearances prove that Jesus is God the Son. He defeated death, crushing Satan's head, as God promised Adam and Eve before banishing them from the Garden of Eden (Genesis 3:15). However, some critics attribute the testimony of those who saw the resurrected Jesus as the result of wishful thinking or mass hysteria. In response to this theory, Christians argue that Jesus' followers, with the exception of John, weren't even brave enough to go to the cross. To them, it seems unlikely that these frightened men made up the resurrection appearances, and later died for that lie. (All of the apostles, except the traitor Judas and the beloved apostle John, died martyr's deaths.)

The Bible states that several people actually saw the risen Jesus. These include Mary Magdalene, a group of women, two disciples on the road to Emmaus, and several of the apostles.

To Mary Magdalene

After Mary Magdalene told Peter and John her news, she returned to the tomb. By the time she got there, the two apostles had already come and gone again. Standing at the tomb by herself, Mary wept (John 20:11). Peering inside, she "saw two angels in white, seated where Jesus' body had been, one at the head and the other at the foot. They asked her, 'Woman, why are you crying?' 'They have taken my Lord away,' she said, 'and I don't know where they have put him'" (John 20:12–13).

Timeless Truth

Dr. Simon Greenleaf, renowned nineteenth-century Harvard law professor, believed that if the evidence regarding Jesus' resurrection was examined by an unbiased jury, their verdict would be that Jesus did, indeed, rise from the grave. He thought the eyewitness testimony of Mary Magdalene, the other women, and the disciples could withstand any cross-examination.

Turning from the tomb, Mary noticed someone standing in front of her. Still crying, she mistakenly thought Jesus was the gardener. When Jesus asked her who she was looking for, she begged him to tell her where Jesus' body had been taken. At this point, Jesus called her by name and Mary recognized him, calling him *Rabboni*, the word for "exalted teacher" (John 20:14–16). She also grabbed Jesus' feet and he told her not to hold onto him because he had "not yet returned to the Father" (John 20:17). He sent her to the disciples to share with them the good news that she had seen the risen Lord (John 20:18).

Bible Lesson

The other women who had gone to the tomb with Mary Magdalene early that Sunday morning also went back to the tomb. Once there, they saw Jesus, "clasped his feet," and worshiped him. Jesus instructed them to tell his disciples to meet him in Galilee (Matthew 28:9–10).

To Two Disciples on the Road to Emmaus

Two men set out from Jerusalem on the seven-mile journey to Emmaus that Sunday afternoon. While walking, they discussed all the strange things that had happened that morning—Peter and John's race to the tomb, the folded head cloth but no body on the burial platform, and how Peter, John, and Mary Magdalene believed that their crucified Savior had risen from the dead. A stranger approached and wanted to know what the two travelers were talking about. They told him all about what had happened during the Passover season, how a prophet of God and the redeemer of Israel was crucified, and the reports of the open tomb (Luke 24:13–28).

Timeless Truth

Carsten Thiede, professor of papyrology at the Academy of Theology in Basel, Switzerland, discovered the city of Emmaus. By retracing the steps of Jesus and the two disciples (Mark 16:12–13; Luke 24:13–32), he and his students identified Motza-Kolonia as the ancient Emmaus. It's located about seven miles west of Jerusalem.

As they continued to Emmaus, the stranger taught them what Moses and the Old Testament prophets said about the Messiah. When the travelers asked the stranger to eat with them, he acted as the host instead of the guest. Giving thanks for the unleavened bread, he passed it to them. When they took it, a miracle happened—their eyes were opened. They realized the stranger was Jesus and why their hearts burned within them when he talked about the Scriptures (Luke 24:31–32). Though it was dark (and traveling was dangerous), the travelers immediately returned to Jerusalem and told the eleven apostles, "It is true! The Lord has risen" (Luke 24:29–33).

Jesus' Appearances to the Apostles

According to the Bible, Mary Magdalene, the women, and the two disciples on the road to Emmaus were not the only people to whom the risen Jesus appeared after the resurrection. He also appeared to several of the apostles at various different times.

To Ten of the Apostles

On Sunday evening, all of the apostles except for Judas (who had killed himself) and Thomas were hiding because they were afraid of the Jewish leaders. Jesus suddenly appeared among them, saying, "Peace be with you" (Luke 24:36; John 20:19). Naturally, this scared them, too, but Jesus reassured them and showed them the wounds and scars in his wrists, feet, and side. He invited them to touch him and he ate fish with them. The apostles were overjoyed (John 20:20).

Bible Lesson

The sudden appearance didn't mean that Jesus had his resurrection body like Christians believe they will receive at the second coming, only that Jesus miraculously appeared behind closed doors. He received his physical resurrection body at his ascension. Appearing behind locked doors is in the category of the miraculous, like feeding the 5,000, walking on water, etc. Jesus appeared in the very same physical body in order to give proof that he had indeed physically risen from the dead.

Jesus repeated his greeting, "Peace be with you" to his apostles (John 20:21). This peace strengthened the disciples when they, who no longer belonged to this world, would willingly go out into the world to share the good news of Jesus' resurrection.

When the ten apostles later told Thomas, also called Didymus, or Twin, that Jesus had appeared to them, he refused to believe them. "Unless I see the nail marks in his hands," he said, "and put my finger where the nails were, and put my hand into his side, I will not believe it" (John 20:25).

To Eleven of the Apostles

A week later, the Bible says, Jesus appeared in the same locked room and greeted the apostles once more with "Peace be with you" (John 20:26). This time, Thomas was with the others and Jesus invited him to touch his wounds, to "stop doubting and believe" (John 20:27). Thomas didn't need to take Jesus up on his offer, though. Seeing Jesus alive was enough for him to believe (John 20:28). Jesus pronounced a blessing on Thomas for believing and also on those who believe in Jesus without seeing him (John 20:29; 1 Peter 1:8–9).

Look in the Book

Some critics state that no one ever called Jesus "God." But the Gospel of John says that the apostle "Thomas said to him [Jesus], 'My Lord and my God'" (John 20:38). Others beside Thomas also referred to Jesus as God. Even Jesus called himself God and the titles that were only reserved for God.

Jesus summarized his instructions to the eleven apostles, saying, "This is what I told you while I was still with you; Everything must be fulfilled that is written about me in the Law of Moses, the Prophets and the Psalms" (Luke 24:44). Jesus "opened their minds so they could understand the Scriptures" (Luke 24:45). The eleven apostles were told to stay in Jerusalem until the Holy Spirit came (Luke 24:49).

To Seven of the Apostles

The third time Jesus appeared to the disciples, they were by the Sea of Tiberius (John 21:1–25). The Bible says the apostle John was there, along with his brother James, Peter, Thomas, Nathanael, and two of the other apostles. They fished all night but didn't catch anything. When they were still about 100 yards out to sea the next morning, a stranger on the shore called to them and asked them if they had caught anything (John 21:1–5). In the Greek, the question's structure expects the answer to be no. He told them to lower their net on the right side of the boat and when they did, they caught so many fish that they were unable to get the net back into the boat (John 21:6).

John realized the stranger was Jesus and hearing this, Peter jumped into the sea and swam to shore (John 21:7–8). By the time the boat landed, Jesus had a fire going and was cooking fish. Peter helped the men with their catch—153 fish (John 21:11). The disciples and Jesus ate a breakfast of fish and bread together (John 21:12).

Bible Lesson

When Peter came up out of the water to meet Jesus on the shore, the first thing he saw was the fire that Jesus had built. It's probable that Peter remembered how he denied knowing Jesus the night he was arrested (Mark 14:54; Luke 22:55–56; John 18:18, 25). Jesus asked Peter three times if he loved him (John 21:15–17). Most likely Jesus deliberately made that fire because he knew the impetuous Peter would swim to shore. This gave him the opportunity to speak to Peter alone before the other apostles brought the boat to shore.

After the meal, Jesus asked Peter, "Do you truly love me more than these?" (John 21:15). Peter had boasted at the Last Supper that he would stand by Jesus no matter what happened, but then he denied knowing who Jesus was after his arrest (Mark 14:29; John 13:37). Peter quickly answered, "You know that I love you" (John 21:15). When Jesus asked his question, he used the Greek word for selfless love, but when Peter replied, he used the word for friendship. Jesus told Peter, "Feed my lambs" (John 21:15).

Jesus again asked Peter the same question, using the same word for self-less love. Peter replied, once again using his word for friendship. Jesus told him, "Take care of my sheep" (John 21:16). Jesus addressed the question a third time, but this time he used the word for love that Peter had used (John 21:17). Though Peter was hurt because Jesus asked him the same question again, he answered, "Lord, you know all things; you know that I love you" (John 21:17). Peter denied knowing Jesus three times during the night of the trials and beatings. Jesus now asked him to confess his love three times. Once again, Jesus responded, "Feed my sheep" (John 21:17).

Look in the Book

Jesus talked to Peter about the sufferings his commitment would bring to him (John 21:18–19). Peter's ministry would last a long time, until his old age, but then he would be crucified. Peter wanted to know what would happen to John, but Jesus wouldn't tell him (John 21:20–21).

To the Eleven Apostles in Galilee

The seven apostles who saw Jesus on the shore and the four other apostles met with Jesus in the mountains and "worshiped him" (Matthew 28:17). He commissioned them to be his witnesses on earth and to "go, make disciples, baptize believers, and teach all nations" and promised them that he would be with them always, "to the very end of the age" (Matthew 28:19–20).

These disciples were to make other disciples by preaching the word that Jesus had delivered to them, persuading people to accept Jesus as God. The disciples were then to baptize those who put their faith in Jesus "in the name of the Father and of the Son and of the Holy Spirit" (Matthew 28:19). The believer's baptism would identify them with the Trinity (or Godhead) God. Those baptized were taught to obey everything Jesus commanded them (Matthew 28:20).

To the Eleven Apostles in Jerusalem

The Gospel of Mark records this appearance where Jesus told the eleven, "Whoever believes and is baptized will be saved" (Mark 16:16). The person who refuses to believe in Jesus cannot be saved. Now that Jesus was authorizing the eleven to go as his witnesses, he conferred the same power on them (2 Corinthians 12:12).

The Report of the Roman Guard

In the Bible, some of the Roman soldiers guarding the tomb reported to the Jewish religious leaders that a man dressed in dazzling white opened the tomb and that the body was gone. Instead of doubting this report, the leaders bribed the kustodian guard to spread the falsehood that the disciples stole Jesus' body as they slept. The leaders even offered to protect the soldiers from the governor's anger should he hear the report. The soldiers feared the governor would sentence them to death (Matthew 28:11–15).

Bible Lesson

The New Testament Greek word baptism (*baptidzo*) means "to immerse." In fact, it still means "to immerse" in modern Greek. In A.D. 1311, at the Council of Ravenna, Italy, the Roman Catholic Church decreed that sprinkling and pouring water were proper ways to baptize. The priests felt it was undignified for them to get wet while immersing people in water. So they added the two additional ways. However, for the first 1300 years of the Christian Church, baptism was always done by immersion.

Christians make the point that if the soldiers were so irresponsible as to fall asleep when they were on duty, they would have been executed. This punishment is not something many of them would deliberately face. Furthermore, Christians wonder how the kustodian knew who stole the body if they were asleep.

Jesus' Ascension

On the day of his ascension, Jesus and his apostles walked from Jerusalem to the Mount of Olives (Luke 24:50). On the slopes, Jesus lifted his hands and, while blessing the apostles, "he left them and was taken up into heaven" (Mark 16:19–20; Luke 24:50–53; Acts 1:9–12). The angel told the disciples that as Jesus was taken up into heaven, so would he come back—i.e., visibly. This is one of the reasons why Christians believe in the second coming of Jesus.

The Gospel of John is a very detailed account, but it doesn't come close to divulging all the many things that Jesus did. The Gospel of John says that if everything Jesus did during his earthly ministry was written down, there wouldn't be room enough in the whole world for all the books that could be written. For most Christians, what is written in John's Gospel is sufficient to persuade men that "Jesus is the Christ, the Son of God" so that "by believing you may have life in his name" (John 20:31).

chapter 16
The Shroud of Turin

A mysterious and ancient linen cloth is kept under lock and key in the Italian town of Turin. Could it possibly be the burial cloth of Jesus? If so, by what means did it get there from Jerusalem? Is there really an image of a crucified man imprinted onto the cloth? Known as the Shroud of Turin, the cloth has a long history of being treasured by church officials. In this chapter, you'll learn eye-opening details about the famous shroud.

The Mysterious Linen Cloth

Though many have doubts that the shroud was actually Jesus' burial cloth, it is difficult to dispute the antiquity of the material. The linen cloth measures 14' 3" in length and 3' 7" in width. The weaving, known as herringbone twill, is a common weave of the first century A.D. Since the cloth has been hidden in Turin for centuries, one might logically conclude that it is a European artifact. But researchers say that the woven material comes from a plant called *Gossypium herbaceum*. This cotton plant is not found in Europe; however, it is common in the Middle East.

Fantastic Find

Hidden within the threads, researcher Avinoam Danin, a botany professor at the Hebrew University of Jerusalem and a leading authority of the flora in Israel, found microscopic pollen grains from fifty-eight different plants. He said, "This combination of flowers can be found in only one region of the world. The evidence clearly points to a floral grouping from the area surrounding Jerusalem."

Dating the Shroud

If the cloth was woven somewhere in the Middle East in the earliest years of the first millennium A.D., how did it end up in Turin? Many believe ancient evidence proves that a man named Jude Thaddeus brought the shroud to Edessa, Turkey, which is modern-day Urfa. It may have been taken to the Brito Edessenorum, the Castle of Edessa, the home of King Abgar. Statues identified as Jude Thaddeus do, in fact, show him with a shroud. At some point, it was hidden in the city's walls. After it was found in A.D. 544, reproductions were made of the shroud's image. The artists of the Renaissance seemed to find inspiration from the shroud. Amazingly, portrayals of Jesus from this time on resemble the shroud's haunting image.

Timeless Truth

Historical documents refer to an artifact called the Mandylian, a cloth that shows a man's facial image. Researchers believe that the Mandylian and the Shroud of Turin are the same cloth, but only the facial image was seen because of the way it was folded. The Mandylian was given to Constantine VII in A.D. 944. The folding method is known as tetradiplon or "doubled in four."

Knights of the French Crusade took the shroud to Lirey, France, during the sack of Constantinople (modern Istanbul) in A.D. 1204. On April 10, 1349, the Christian emperor Constantinople gave the cloth to a French knight named Geoffrey de Charny. In 1355, it was displayed in the town of Lirey, France. A year later, the shroud was in the possession of de Charney's son, Geoffrey II.

Bible Lesson

Legends abound of the search for the Holy Grail, the so-called cup that collected the blood of Jesus. There is no scientific or archaeological evidence of a cup that Jesus used when he instituted the Lord's Supper. Perhaps the Holy Grail doesn't refer to a cup at all, but to the burial cloth that absorbed the blood of Jesus. The Knights could have been looking for the Shroud.

In November 1389, the Bishop Pierre d'Arcis of Troyes claimed the cloth was Jesus' burial shroud. He described it as bearing the double imprint of a crucified man. For unknown reasons, Pope Clement VII ordered the bishop not to speak any more of the shroud. This happened on January 6, 1390. By A.D. 1457, the shroud was with the ruling House of Savoy, in Turin.

A 3-D Negative Photographic Image

Though the antiquity and origin of the material are fascinating, this information is not what attracts researchers to the shroud. Unlike any other cloth, ancient or modern, this large rectangular shroud holds a secret. Imprinted upon the material is the detailed image of a crucified man, both a front view and a back view. These are opposite one another with the head in the middle as if the cloth was draped over the top of the head. No side images are seen, though, not even near the two images of the head. Some go so far as to say that the shroud is the first example of photographic film.

Look in the Book

The prophet Isaiah predicted that the Messiah's beard would be pulled out (Isaiah 50:6). Although the Gospel writers don't say that Jesus' beard was plucked out, Jewish law says this is the punishment for blasphemy—i.e., claiming to be God. Anyone accused of this crime had clumps of his beard pulled out with pliers. The Jewish religious leaders claimed Jesus was guilty of blasphemy. Furthermore, the man whose shape is evident in the shroud seems to have had portions of his beard pulled out.

How did this photographic negative imprint itself upon this ancient cloth? This is one of the questions baffling researchers. A theory posed by one scientist is that the image is an iron oxide–based pigment painted onto the cloth. However, if the image were a painting, one would expect to find brush strokes. Not only are there no brush strokes, but the image doesn't penetrate into the cloth as pigment would. Instead, the image rests on the cloth's surface. And unlike a painting, the outlines of the images are blurred. It's true that particles of relatively pure iron oxide were found in the cloth, but this is not unusual. The preparation and fermentation of flax result in iron oxide traces.

Further research shows that the image's high resolution is due to its pixels—tiny individual dots so close together that they form a picture. Though our computers have pixel points, the sophistication of these pixels, the result of particle radiation, cannot be reproduced with our current technology.

The shroud was first photographed in 1898 by the Turin Councilor Secondo Pia. These negative plates revealed a clearer photograph of the images. Looking at the negative plates was like looking at the negative of a negative of the photographed subject—in other words, the photograph itself. This photograph allowed researchers to analyze the image.

The photograph is of an incredibly tall and severely abused man. Measuring six feet, nine inches tall, the images show signs of beating, scourging, and bleeding. In fact, bloodstains soil the cloth near the wrists, feet, head, and side. Two strands of hair curl at the forehead and his closed eyes are swollen. His left eyebrow is higher than the right one and the nasal cartilage looks like it might have separated from the bone. The man's right wrist is covered by his left hand, but the left wrist is wounded in a lesion typical of a puncture. The thumbs are drawn inward. This happens when a nerve in the wrist is pierced. Many researchers deem this evidence of crucifixion.

Timeless Truth

Though it's true that Hollywood movie directors often show the Roman soldier hammering the long pointed spikes into the palms of Jesus' hands, this is more legend than fact. A person's hands are too fragile to hold up the weight of his hanging body, especially for one so tall. The Romans actually hammered each spike into the hollow of the wrist, which would pierce the largest nerve in the hand, the median nerve. Once that nerve was transected, it would draw the thumbs inwardly and could produce constant electrical shocks throughout the hands.

The shroud's image shows other signs that this photographed man was crucified. Not only that, but additional evidence on the shroud strongly indicates other abuses that correspond to the biblical accounts of the torture Jesus endured before his death. For example, lesions appear on both the front and back. These wounds were possibly caused by a horrific scourging.

About thirty puncture wounds are seen on the man's head. One knee is severely scraped, but neither leg was broken. Blood from the wounds soaked the cloth. The Gospels say that a crown of thorns was placed on Jesus' head. His tormentors crushed the thorns on his head so that they pierced his skin. They also say that Jesus fell while carrying the cross to Golgotha. Despite all the torture the Romans inflicted, the ancient prophecy was fulfilled: "Not one of his bones will be broken" (John 19:36).

Bible Lesson

The whip the Roman soldiers used when scourging someone, called a flagrum, had two or three leather thongs with chunks of metal or bone attached along the leather strips. Small iron dumbbells were tied to the ends. These ripped and gouged the victim's flesh. From the angles of the lesions on the man in the shroud, researchers have deduced that two men of different heights scourged the victim. This was common Roman practice.

Without a doubt, the shroud's image is that of a man who had been scourged, wounded, and crucified. Of course, many criminals and enemies of Rome were crucified, and many of them surely suffered other wounds. But there is additional evidence that this shroud may have once held Jesus' dead body. The apostle John records how Jesus was stabbed in the side by a Roman spear. The sun was setting, signaling the beginning of the Passover. The Romans broke the legs of the two others being crucified with Jesus to hasten their death. Jesus' legs weren't broken because he was already dead. Still, just to be sure, a Roman soldier thrust his lance upward into Jesus' side. The Gospel of John says that blood and water poured out (John 19:31–34).

This is significant because if Jesus were still alive at the time of the stab, only blood would have poured from the wound. However, the sac that surrounds the heart holds a watery fluid. Under extreme stress, the sac expands. If the Roman's spear punctured the sac, the water would mix with the blood and flow from the wound. A different explanation is that Jesus' chest cavity filled with blood as a result of the internal hemorrhaging from the scourging. This watery blood flowed from the spear wound. Actually, the spear most likely entered both the chest and the pericardium sac.

Many believe the shroud's image shows a long upward wound that pierces the diaphragm, the thoracic cavity, the lung, and the heart. It seems that blood cells and clear serum drained onto the shroud from this wound, indicating that it occurred after death. Once the body was laid on the burial cloth, the drainage leaked and gathered in a small pool beneath the man's back.

Timeless Truth

Many scholars and physicians who have studied the issue agree that Jesus was already dead when the spear wound was inflicted. Crucified individuals usually died of asphyxiation because it was difficult to repeatedly raise up their bodies so that they could breathe. The strain on the lungs and chest muscles was horrific, causing blood and fluid to compress the lungs. The diaphragm would drop into the abdomen. The man in the shroud has a "bloated" abdomen, likely demonstrating the dropping of his diaphragm.

Skeptics question whether someone deliberately bloodied the shroud to fit the biblical accounts of Jesus' wounds. Keep in mind that the shroud's image was documented in the 500s. A person concocting such a hoax would have to have medical knowledge of blood flow, physiology, and pathology, which is possible but not likely. Researchers can't help but be impressed at the medical accuracy of the shroud's image.

Burial Practices

Three Greek terms are important to understanding the Jewish burial customs of the first century. The first, *sindon*, refers to a large burial shroud that wraps around the body. The second, *soudarion*, refers to a small cloth, about the size of a dinner napkin, that is placed over the head. The Gospels of Matthew, Mark, and Luke mention that Joseph of Arimathea, the wealthy owner of the tomb where Jesus was laid, used a sindon to bury Jesus. The Gospel of John includes the third term, *othonia*, to refer to all of the burial cloths.

Those wrapping the body in the shroud must have been in a hurry because the images show no evidence of bandages on the hands, feet, or head. Those who believe the Shroud of Turin actually held Jesus' body claim this matches the biblical account: Due to the imminent Passover, Jesus' friends hastily prepared his body for burial. The Bible says that they planned to finish the interrupted burial process the following Sunday morning—the first Easter Sunday.

Burning the Shroud

In past centuries, the shroud was "boiled in oil, tried [boute] by fire and steamed many times, without either effacing or altering the said imprint and figure," said Antoine de Lalaing on Good Friday of 1503. The shroud was placed in a protective silver casket, which melted in a fire on December 4, 1532. However, the cloth's image wasn't altered by the high temperatures or by the water thrown on the casket to dowse the flames. This possibly provides further evidence that the image wasn't painted onto the cloth. Many believe that heat and water damage to paint would be easily seen.

Though the image was unaffected, the cloth was burnt. When it is folded, four burn holes are arranged in an L-shape, as if a hot poker penetrated the layers. Interestingly, a Budapest prayer book known as the "Prayer Manuscript" includes an illustration of a shroud of the same weave and with the unique L-shape burn pattern. The image of the man is on the shroud. This Prayer Manuscript dates to A.D. 1192.

In addition, the unique features of the man are found in iconography dating back to the sixth century A.D. When researchers superimposed the face of the shroud on a sixth-century icon from St. Catherine's monastery in Sinai, they found 170 points of congruity. The same facial features are found in the gold solidus of Justinian II (A.D. 692).

Testing the Shroud

Reputable scholars and researchers were given access to the shroud in recent years to determine its authenticity. They have performed a variety of tests to establish the antiquity and nature of the cloth, the origin of the image, and probability of its being Jesus' own burial shroud.

A. D. Adler and J. H. Heller analyzed a blood particle from one of the cloth fibrils. Their microspectrophotometric analysis identified hemoglobin. Subsequently, Pier Baima Bollone, a pathologist, typed it in the AB blood group. At least twelve independent scientific methods verified that blood is on the shroud. High levels of bilirubin in the blood prove the person endured severe trauma.

In 1988, scientists performed radiocarbon testing on small samples of the shroud. These tests are used to date ancient artifacts by measuring the amount of their C14, a radioactive isotope of carbon. The margin of error was 100 years either way. These tests concluded, with ninety-five percent accuracy, that the shroud dated from A.D. 1260–1390. The shroud was determined a hoax!

However, Dr. Leoncia Garza-Valdes, from the University of Texas in San Antonio, had the privilege of examining a sample of the shroud in 1993. As soon as he looked at the sample in a microscope, he realized it was heavily contaminated. The 1988 tests weren't performed on the shroud at all, but on the mixture of microscopic linen, bacteria, fungi, and bioplastic coating (the symbiosis between the bacteria and the fungi) growing on the fibers.

Fantastic Find

Once Dr. Garza-Valdes's suspicion was independently confirmed, he examined shroud fibers obtained from Dr. Harry Gove, inventor of the 1988 dating method tests. He concluded that the fibers have a fifty-seven percent coating. Skeptics had claimed that a sixty percent coating was needed to cause a 1300-year error. The effects of the 1532 fire could also have caused an error of several hundred years. The bottom line: The 1988 tests were not necessarily reliable.

So, after all the studies and research and examinations, what is known for sure? The shroud is a burial cloth depicting the image of a severely wounded man who had been crucified. How the image imprinted itself onto the burial cloth remains a mystery. Another mystery is the lack of damage to the cloth fibrils. Many believe they would have been torn if anyone had removed the body from the shroud. Christians believe the body disappeared while still wrapped within the shroud, and the image imprinted itself on the cloth as it collapsed when the body vanished.

Scientists can't prove that this is what happened; nor can they prove that the crucified man is Jesus. After all, science can't repeat the one-time events of Jesus' crucifixion and resurrection and thus prove any of its hypotheses. But it's extremely interesting to find parallels between the biblical accounts of what happened to Jesus and what seemingly happened to the man once wrapped in the Shroud of Turin.

What Did Jesus Look Like?

Only one Scripture passage, a prophecy of Isaiah, describes Jesus' appearance. "He had no beauty or majesty to attract us to him, nothing in his appearance that we should desire him" (Isaiah 53:2). This seems to state that Jesus was not a handsome man. People were attracted to Jesus because of his goodness, compassion, and intellect.

Timeless Truth

Artists have attempted to draw portraits of the man from the Shroud of Turin's image. Their task isn't easy, though, because the image's face is severely swollen from brutal beatings and a possible fall on his face from a weight on his shoulders. The nose cartilage and right eyelid appear torn.

Artists often portray Jesus with long flowing hair. But Paul asks, "Does not the very nature of things teach you that if a man has long hair, it is a disgrace to him?" (1 Corinthians 11:14). In ancient times, Jewish men did not have long hair. In fact, many Jewish texts ridiculed men who had long hair. It is clear just by looking at ancient statues and coins that Jews, Greeks, and Romans had short hair during this time. A frieze on Rome's Arch of Titus, built after the Romans destroyed Jerusalem in A.D. 70 depicts captive Jewish men. All had short hair.

Throughout history and with only a few exceptions, men have worn their hair short. The Spartan Warriors had long hair and so did a very few Hebrews under a Nazirite vow, such as Samson and John the Baptist (Numbers 6:1–21; Judges 13:2–7; Matthew 3:14). Russian university students grew their hair to protest Vladimir Lenin's communism after the Bolshevik Revolution overthrew the Russian provisional government on November 25, 1917. American university students in the 1960s (hippies) did the same thing to protest the Vietnam War.

The image on the shroud depicts a muscular man standing six feet nine inches tall. People tend to think that people in the ancient world were short, but excavations of countless cemeteries from all cultures indicate an average height of about five feet nine inches tall. This is the average for most cultures in the ancient world and it is the same average for the twenty-first-century world. Still, the man of the shroud is a foot taller.

The shroud's image is of a man with long hair. In fact, the image shows one long braid down the man's back. But that doesn't mean the image isn't of Jesus. Jewish law allowed an exalted teacher to wear such a braid so that others recognized the teacher as a special rabbi. It's difficult to know the true length of Jesus' hair.

Also, don't forget that Jesus descended from kings. According to the Bible, the first king of Israel, Saul, was "a head taller than any of the others" (1 Samuel 9:2; 10:23). King David and his heirs were also tall men. Therefore, it's easy to believe that Jesus was also a tall man. Because he worked as a carpenter, with heavy wood and stone, he would have been a powerful and muscular man. The Bible's testimony that he was able to endure such severe scourging and torture, surviving six hours on the cross, and crying in loud voices as he spoke from the cross suggests even more evidence of his physical strength and stamina. Though it's almost impossible to prove for sure that the Shroud of Turin once covered the body of Jesus, many cherish this piece of ancient history as the closest link to Jesus' life. Even if it didn't cover Jesus, but another sufferer of crucifixion, it makes the story of Jesus' experience more accessible to the modern world.

chapter 17

Archaeology and the Crucifixion

Crucifixion is an unusually cruel and humiliating punishment that, according to the Dead Sea Scrolls, was abhorred by both the Jews and the Romans. The texts say that only slaves and enemies of the Roman Empire were sentenced to this horrid death. The Jewish religious leaders convinced Pilate that Jesus was a political threat to Rome, so Pilate ordered his crucifixion. In this chapter, you'll read about archaeological discoveries that some say confirm the biblical accounts of Jesus' existence, Pilate's existence, and execution by crucifixion.

Jesus: A Real Historical Person?

For many, the primary evidence that Jesus was a real person comes from the New Testament, and particularly the four Gospels. If Jesus was not a real person, then it is pointless to examine the archaeology of crucifixion. Many believe that these texts are historically accurate and trustworthy. However, other historical documents also attest to Jesus having been a real person.

Josephus's Testimony

The Jewish historian Josephus (A.D. 37–100) recorded the history of the Jewish people in Israel. In his work *Antiquities*, Josephus states:

> *Now there was about this time, Jesus, a wise man, if it be lawful to call him a man, for he was a doer of wonderful works, a teacher of such men as receive the truth with pleasure. He drew over to him both many of the Jews and many of the gentiles. He was the Christ and when Pilate, at the suggestion of the principal men amongst us, had condemned him to the cross, those that loved him at the first did not forsake him. For he appeared alive again the third day, as the divine prophets had foretold these and ten thousand other wonderful things concerning him; and the tribe of Christians, so named from him, are not extinct to this day.*

Josephus confirms the principles held by Christians: Jesus performed miracles, had many followers, was crucified, and rose again. Despite his attesting to Jesus' deeds, Josephus was a Jew and no friend of Christianity.

Jewish Rabbinical Tradition

The Tannatic period, between A.D. 70 and 200, is so called because the rabbis of those years were known as the *Tanna'im*, or the "repeaters" of the traditions confirmed in the Mishnah or Tosefta toward the end of the period. From this period came the traditions called the *baraithoth*, which was material external to the Mishnah but preserved in the Gemara.

The Sanhedrin (43a) states, "Jesus was hanged on Passover Eve. Forty days previously the herald had cried, 'He is being led out for stoning, because he has practiced sorcery and led Israel astray and enticed them to apostasy. Whosoever has anything to say in his defense, let him come and declare it.' As nothing was brought forward in his defense, he was hanged on Passover Eve."

Look in the Book

The Mishnah is the entire body of religious oral law that was written down into six orders with sixty-three separate tractates. The Gemara are Rabbinic discussions on a host of items. The Mishnah plus the Gemara equals the Talmud.

To this *baraitha* (tradition) was attached a statement by Ulla, a rabbi who lived in the third century. "Ulla said: 'Would you believe that any defense would have been so zealously sought for him? He was a deceiver, and the All-merciful says: "You shall not spare him, neither shall you conceal him." It was different with Jesus, for he was near to the kingship.'" Here Ulla said Jesus was a special case being "near to the kingship." With the reference to his descent from King David, this means that Ulla believed that Jesus was related to royalty.

Pliny the Younger

Pliny the Younger, imperial Roman Legate of Bythynia in northwestern Turkey, in a letter to Emperor Trajan in A.D. 112, writes, "They were in the habit of meeting on a certain fixed day before it was light, when they sang an anthem to Christ as God, and bound themselves by a solemn oath not to commit any wicked deed, but to abstain from all fraud, theft and adultery, never to break their word, or deny a trust when called upon to honor it; after which it was their custom to separate, and then meet again to partake of food, but of the ordinary and innocent kind."

Justin Martyr

Justin Martyr addressed his *Defense of Christianity* (A.D. 150) to the Roman Emperor Antoninus Pius. In this text, he cites Psalm 22:16 to the emperor: "But the words, 'They pierced my hands and feet,' refer to the nails which were fixed in Jesus' hands and feet on the cross; and after he was crucified, his executioners cast lots for his garments, and divided them among themselves. That these things happened you may learn from the 'Acts,' which were recorded under Pontius Pilate." Justin Martyr also stated, "That he performed these miracles you may easily satisfy yourself from the 'Acts' of Pontius Pilate."

Tacitus

In A.D. 115, Tacitus, the important Roman historian, recorded Nero's persecution of the Christians. He writes "Christus, from whom the name had its origin, suffered the extreme penalty during the reign of Tiberius at the hands of one of our procurators, Pontius Pilate, and a most mischievous superstition, thus checked for the moment, again broke out not only in Judea, . . . but even in Rome."

Timeless Truth

The Roman Emperor Nero burned the city of Rome in July of A.D. 64 because he wanted to build a new city named Neropolis, or city of Nero. By October of A.D. 64, he and his henchmen had the Roman citizens convinced that the Christians were responsible for burning the city. As evidence, Nero cited a passage from 2 Peter 3:10–13 that speaks of the world being destroyed with fire.

The historian Tacitus also said, "They got their name from Christ, who was executed by sentence of the procurator Pontius Pilate in the reign of Tiberius."

Suetonius

Suetonius, a Roman historian, compiled a biography of the first twelve Roman emperors in his *Life of Claudius*. He states that Claudius "expelled the Jews from Rome, on account of the riots in which they were constantly indulging, at the instigation of Chrestus." Chrestus, a common slave name, was a frequent misspelling of the name of Christ.

Thallus and Julius Africanus

In A.D. 52, Thallus wrote a history of the Eastern Mediterranean world from the Trojan War until his own day. Julius Africanus quotes this work as describing the strange darkness that occurred during Jesus' crucifixion as an eclipse of the sun. However, he says that Thallus's explanation isn't possible because Jesus was crucified during the time of a full moon. Eclipses of the sun don't occur during a full moon.

Mara bar Serpion

Sometime after A.D. 73, Mara bar Serpion, a non-Christian, wrote a letter to his son that suggests he believed Jesus was a historical person. He asks, "What advantage did the Athenians gain from putting Socrates to death? Famine and plague came upon them as a judgment for their crime. What advantage did the men of Samos gain from burning Pythagoras? In a moment their land was covered with sand. What advantage did the Jews gain from executing their wise King? It was just after that that their kingdom was abolished."

Pontius Pilate Inscription

Before his crucifixion, Jesus was tried before Pontius Pilate, the fifth Roman governor of occupied Judea. If Pilate was not a real person of history, then there was no crucifixion of Jesus. The emperor Tiberius appointed Pilate to this post in A.D. 26. However, in A.D. 37, the Roman governor of Syria, L. Vitellius, removed Pilate from the post because he slaughtered many Samaritans at Mount Gerizim.

Bible Lesson

The Bible says that during "the affair of the Roman standards," Pilate ordered his soldiers to march into Jerusalem carrying medallions bearing the Emperor's image among their military standards. This caused a five-day demonstration by the Jews at Pilate's provincial capital of Caesarea. Pilate finally relented and had the images of Caesar removed.

Pilate is mentioned in several passages of the Gospels. He is also mentioned in the writings of the historians Josephus, Philo, and Tacitus.

Pilate built an aqueduct from cisterns near Bethlehem to improve the water supply of Jerusalem. But he paid for this aqueduct with the funds from the Temple treasury. Pilate brutally crushed the ensuing riot. At another time, Pilate set up several golden shields bearing an inscription to the Emperor Tiberius in his Jerusalem headquarters. The Jewish people protested in vain. Finally, the emperor warned Pilate to respect the Jewish religious and political customs.

Additional evidence for Pilate is found in the coins issued while he was governor. Antonio Frovo, director of the Italian excavations at Caesarea Maritima, discovered a dedicatory stone in 1961. The inscription on the ancient stone, which had been reshaped for use in the building of a Caesarean theater, was damaged. However, it can still be read. Inscribed in three lines, it says: 'Tiberieum/[Pon] tius Pilatus/[the roman emperor of the period]/Pontius Pilate/Prefect of Judea." The inscription confirms that Pilate existed and his title was governor. The stone is displayed in the Israel Museum in Jerusalem.

The Crucified Man of Giv'at ha-Mivtar

Ossuaries dating to the first century A.D. were found by Dr. Vassilios Tzaferis during excavations on Mount Scopus near Jerusalem. The name on one of the bone boxes was Yehohanan, or Yohan ben Ha'galgol, which translates as John. Researchers examining the remains at Jerusalem's Hadassah Medical School concluded that the man was in his mid- to late twenties. He was five feet six inches tall, had a cleft palate, and one long nail stuck through both ankle bones. He had been crucified.

Apparently when the seven-inch spike was being driven through the Achilles' tendons of the man's feet, it hit a hard knot in the wooden cross. The end of the nail bent and couldn't be pulled out of the bones. This type of archaeological evidence is unique.

Additionally, the man's lower forearms had been punctured with nails. The bones of the upper arms were smoothly worn just as one would expect of a crucified victim. Remember how difficult it is to breathe when hanging on a cross—the victim pulled his body up by his arms and pushed up with his feet. The apostle John told how the Roman soldiers broke the legs of the two men who were crucified with Jesus to hasten their death (John 19:31–35). Someone crushed Yohan's leg bones right beneath the knee.

Fantastic Find

Some believe archaeology confirms the details of Jesus' crucifixion as recorded in the four Gospels. Yehohanan was discovered with thirty-five other bodies in a Jerusalem gravesite at Giv'at ha-Mivtar in 1968. Their remains showed they died a violent death, perhaps during the Jewish revolt against Rome in A.D. 70. The remains of Yehohanan the crucified man are first-century evidence of a Roman execution by crucifixion.

The Historian Thallus

The works of Thallus, written in the middle of the first century A.D., no longer exist. However, he is quoted in a text called *Chronography* written by Julius Africanus. Regarding Jesus' crucifixion, Africanus quotes Thallus: "On the whole world, there pressed a most fearful darkness, and the rocks were rent without reason, an eclipse of the sun." This is extrabiblical evidence that confirms the Gospel accounts of the midday darkness and the violent earthquake that occurred while Jesus was on the cross (Matthew 27:45, 51; Mark 15:33; Luke 23:44).

Timeless Truth

The Roman emperor Claudius decreed that anyone found guilty of disturbing a grave would be put to death. Claudius reigned from A.D. 41–54 so the decree was made sometime during those years. Had Claudius heard the stories of Jesus' resurrection and the false claims that his body was stolen? Claudius's decree was found on a stone slab in Nazareth in 1878.

The Titulus of St. Croix

The wooden placard nailed at the top of the crucified victim's cross was called a titulus. The victim's name and his crime were written on the placard so that the public knew who was being executed and why. All four Gospels assert that Jesus' titulus said, in three languages, "The King of the Jews" (Matthew 27:37; Mark 15:26; Luke 23:38; John 19:19).

After Jesus' death and resurrection, it is believed that many Christians journeyed to Jerusalem to search for his tomb. The Roman emperor Hadrian, in A.D. 135, constructed a temple in the area for the false Roman deities Venus and Jupiter. Hadrian didn't want the Christians going on their pilgrimages and hoped to tempt them to the temple.

A couple of centuries later, the Roman Empress Helena was told by a man named Judas that hundreds of years of debris covered the area. During the excavation that she ordered, the diggers found three crosses and nails in a cave close to where it was believed Jesus' tomb was located. They also found a wooden placard that said, "King of the Jews." This titulus was taken to Rome in A.D. 326. The placard, known as the *titulus Christi*, is kept in the Basilica di Santa Croce (St. Croix) in Gerusalemme, Rome.

Fantastic Find

Weighing 687 grams, the titulus measures 25 × 14 centimeters and is 2.6 centimeters thick. The inscription, written in three languages, is on one side of the placard. The first line, practically destroyed, was written in Hebrew, the second in Greek reversed script, and the third in Latin reversed script. All three languages translate the same phrase: King of the Jews.

The titulus was examined by the renowned scholar Carsten Thiede. He concluded that it was made of walnut wood, a common tree in the first-century Middle East. Stone inscriptions known to date from the first century have similar textual characteristics as the writing on the placard—evidence that it also dates to the first century A.D.

For example, the line written in Latin includes the word *Nazarinus* (Nazarene), a common first-century spelling. Fourth-century Latin texts read *Nazarenus*. Also, the letter "I" is used for Jesous (Jesus), a common abbreviation that is not used in later years.

Timeless Truth

Is it possible for wood to survive for 2,000 years? Well, wood similar to that of the titulus, also analyzed to be 2,000 years old, has been found in excellent condition near Hadrian's Wall on the England-Scotland border. Wood objects from other cultures, even before the first century A.D., have been discovered and are now in museums. For example, wooden board games and boats have been discovered in ancient Egypt.

The Hebrew language, unlike Greek, Latin, and English, is written and read from the right to the left. On the titulus, the Hebrew line is written this way. Strangely though, the Greek and Latin lines are also written from right to left. Scholars speculate a Jewish or Roman scribe wrote the text on the placard (on Pilate's order). He inscribed all three of the languages for a Jewish audience accustomed to reading from right to left. Some believe that this linguistic error proves the authenticity of the titulus. They think it's doubtful that a forger would have made such a mistake.

Golgotha and the Tomb of Jesus

According to the Gospel writers, Jesus was crucified at Golgotha (Matthew 27:33; Mark 15:22; John 19:17). The Latin translation of this Aramaic word is "Calvary"; in English it's translated "skull." Golgotha was a hill located outside Jerusalem's wall near a heavily traveled road (John 19:20; Hebrews 13:12). The Gospels of Matthew and Mark both say that those traveling to and from Jerusalem mocked Jesus as he hung on the cross (Matthew 27:39; Mark 15:29–30).

Exactly where is Golgotha? It might be a place north of Jerusalem's Old City called Gordon's Calvary. It was named to honor General Charles Gordon, a nineteenth-century British military hero who thought the site resembled a human skull.

Timeless Truth

A tomb cut out of rock is located in a quiet garden near Gordon's Calvary. Those who believe it was Jesus' burial place call it the Garden Tomb. Most likely, the General made a mistake. His hill is part of a larger ridge that archaeologists believe was a mine. Only in the past two or three centuries did this site become skull-like. It didn't look that way in the first century.

More likely, Jesus was crucified on an outcropping of rock inside where the Church of the Holy Sepulcher now stands. Located in the Christian Quarter of Jerusalem's Old City, the enormous building actually encloses a hill. Known as the Latin Calvary, the tomb traditionally thought of as Jesus' burial place is nearby. Ancient walls, uncovered by archaeologists, ran south of the current Holy Sepulcher site. The Turkish Sultan, Suleiman the Magnificent, built the present wall in the sixteenth century. Archaeologist and supervisor Lirgilio Cordo claims that this was the site of Golgotha.

History of Golgotha

Excavations of the Latin Calvary site indicate that it was originally a quarry dating back to the seventh century B.C. After being abandoned in the first century B.C., it was made into a garden. When the Roman emperor Hadrian crushed the second Jewish revolt in A.D. 135, much of Jerusalem was demolished. Hadrian built a new city called Aelia Capitolina, which enclosed Golgotha. The garden was destroyed and a sacred building called the Capitolium was built on top of it. Golgotha was now under a basement.

Fantastic Find

Two different kinds of tombs were carved into the rock of the Golgotha garden. The first type was for single burials and the entrance had what is known as an arcosolium arch. Only the wealthy, such as Joseph of Arimathea, could afford this type of tomb. The second type of tomb, called kochim, had shelves cut in the rocks for multiple bodies.

The historian Eusebius writes that Hadrian's destruction of Jesus' tomb was deliberate. From Jerome, it is evident that statues of the false Roman deities Jupiter and Venus were erected at the site. Ironically, Hadrian's efforts helped preserve evidence of the location of Jesus' burial place.

Eusebius accompanied the Empress Helena on a pilgrimage to Jerusalem in A.D. 326. While looking for Jesus' burial place, they were told that it was beneath the Temple of Venus. Helena had the Temple demolished and the excavation of the site began. Several ancient tombs were uncovered but most importantly, the archaeologists found the rocky outcrop of Golgotha. A few years later, in A.D. 335, a church was built next to the hill. That church was eventually replaced by the Church of the Holy Sepulcher.

The Tomb of Jesus

Which of the tombs in the garden belonged to Joseph of Arimathea? Some believe it's the tomb that's known as the Garden Tomb, but it was carved from the rock in the eighth or seventh century B.C. This dates back to the years when the kings of Judah reigned. There are several clues that help archaeologists date the tomb. For example, the type of chisel used to cut into the rock can be determined by marks on the walls. In addition, they can tell from the layout of the tomb's rooms and the artifacts found inside.

The Garden Tomb can't be Jesus' tomb because the Gospel writers stated that the tomb he was laid in was brand new. One can surmise that Joseph of Arimathea commissioned the construction of the tomb. No one had yet been buried in it.

Timeless Truth

The Greek Orthodox, the Armenian Orthodox, and the (Latin) Roman Catholic churches control the Church of the Holy Sepulcher. The Syrian Orthodox, the Egyptian Coptic Orthodox, and the Ethiopian Orthodox communities also possess certain rights and properties around the building. Visitors are welcome to visit the tomb and the rock (Golgotha) in the Church of the Holy Sepulcher.

The tomb or sepulcher inside the Church of the Holy Sepulcher is most likely the tomb where Jesus was buried. The tomb itself stands in an elaborate structure within the rotunda, surrounded by columns supporting an ornamented domed roof.

As you go into the tomb itself, you enter into a small outer chamber before you would go into the inner chamber where the body would have been placed. This tomb of the Holy Sepulcher perfectly matches a rich man's tomb (such as Joseph's new tomb) and, many believe, has a long historical tradition as confirmation of being the tomb where Jesus was buried.

Chapter 18
The Mystery of Miracles

The miracles recorded in the Bible were abundant and instantaneous. According to the Bible, miracles were witnessed by huge numbers of people, both those who supported Jesus and those who didn't. In fact, Jesus' critics never denied the authenticity of the miracles—only the power behind them. Did these unexplained happenings come from God or Satan? This chapter delves into that question and defines miracles and their supposed origin. You'll also read about important relics treasured by Christians throughout the centuries. Some believe these relics possess miraculous powers.

What Is a Miracle?

Christians believe that a miracle is the direct, extraordinary, and creative work of God. During certain times in history, it is believed that God intervened in a special way. The miracles recorded in the Bible were powerful signs that the miracle-worker was his spokesperson (Mark 2:10–11). The ones witnessing the miracles understood that they were witnessing a singular event. Christians believe that even though God created a universe that is providentially ordered, he can bypass his own natural law for his own purposes.

Look in the Book

For his first miracle, Jesus turned water into wine at a wedding feast at Cana (John 2:1–11). The Bible says that Jesus told some servants to fill six stone water jars, used for ceremonial washing, with water—about 180 gallons of water (John 2:6). Of course, they would have drawn the water from a well. Then Jesus said to draw water again, and they drew out wine instead of water. Jesus turned the entire well of water into wine.

It didn't take faith to see the miracles that Jesus performed. Even his enemies didn't deny that he restored a man's withered arm, but they were furious that he performed this miracle on the Sabbath (Matthew 12:9–14; Mark 3:1–6; Luke 6:6–11). There's a good reason Jesus performed so many miracles in Galilee. The Israelites brought their sick relatives and friends to the city of Tiberius, located on the Sea of Galilee, so they could be placed in the waters for healing. No wonder the Bible said that multitudes went out to Jesus with their sick; they came from the hospital town of Tiberius.

Who Performed Miracles?

Only a select few performed the miracles recorded in the Old Testament. Moses was given the power to perform miracles when he was demanding that the Egyptian Pharaoh free the Hebrew slaves. The prophets Elijah and Elisha also performed miracles during their ministries. However, Jesus said that John the Baptist was the greatest man who ever lived (Matthew 11:11), yet he never performed a miracle (John 10:41). In the earliest days of the

Christian church, only the apostles performed miracles (Acts 2:43; 4:33; 5:12). But they were able to pass on miraculous gifts to others; for example, when they laid hands on the evangelists Stephen and Philip (Acts 6:6–8; 8:6).

Because miracles were temporary, they didn't meet or satisfy mankind's eternal needs. For instance, except for Jesus, none of those who were raised from the dead are still alive. Each one eventually died again. Those who experienced this miracle include:

- The widow's son (1 Kings 17:22)
- The Shunammite's son (2 Kings 4:32–36)
- The man thrown in Elisha's tomb (2 Kings 13:20–21)
- Jairus' daughter (Matthew 9:25)
- The widow's son (Luke 7:15)
- Jesus' friend Lazarus (John 11:43–44)
- The Old Testament saints (Matthew 27:52)
- The disciple Tabitha (Acts 9:40–41)
- The apostle Paul (Acts 14:19–20)
- Eutychus, who fell from a window (Acts 20:9–12)

When Jesus fed the 5,000 (Matthew 14:21), and later the 4,000 (Mark 8:4–9), they became hungry again. From the moment God rested on the seventh day to when he closed the door of Noah's ark, only one miracle is recorded. Genesis 5:24 reports that Enoch, who "walked with God," was taken to heaven without experiencing death (Hebrews 11:5–6).

An Inseparable Trio

Miracles were unique occurrences that appeared in distinct periods of crisis situations involving revelation and redemption. The four periods are as follows:

- Israel in bondage in Egypt
- Israel in bondage to Baal
- The nation in bondage in the Babylonian exile
- The world in bondage to sin

It is believed that each of these periods had at least one spokesman or deliverer who accurately spoke or wrote God's revelation and interpretation of the redemption. Moses led Israel from bondage and Joshua succeeded him as the one to lead the Hebrews into the Promised Land. Elijah and Elisha were prophets who spoke against the worship of the false god Baal. Many of the Old Testament prophets, such as Ezra, Nehemiah, and Daniel, gave hope to the Israelites during their years of exile in Babylon from their homeland. Finally, Jesus came as redeemer and deliverer to the whole world.

During each of these four periods, miracles confirmed that the spoken message, the revelation, came from God. Whether examining Israel's repetitive need for rescue, or mankind's eternal need, it is evident that God's redemption comes first. This is followed by God's revelation and then by his confirming miracles. In other words, the miracles confirmed the revelation, which correctly interpreted the redemptive events. These three—the redemptive events, revelation, and miracles—are an inseparable trio.

Miracles as Proof

Christians believe that God gave the ability to perform miracles to those who spoke for him as proof that their message came from him. They also believe that the miracles of Jesus prove he was who he said he was: the promised Messiah (Luke 7:20–22; John 10:25; Acts 2:22; Romans 1:4). When Jesus told a paralytic that his sins were forgiven, the teachers of the law accused Jesus of blasphemy. "Which is easier to say," asked Jesus, "'Your sins are forgiven,' or to say, 'Get up and walk'?" (Matthew 9:5). The teachers understood that it was easier to tell a cripple that his sins were forgiven. But so they would know that he had the power to forgive sins, Jesus told the paralytic to get up and walk. Amazingly, he did! For Christians, this proved that Jesus had the authority to forgive sins (Matthew 9:2–8).

Though the evangelist Philip performed miracles himself, he didn't have the power to give this gift to others. The apostles Peter and John traveled from Jerusalem to Samaria, where Philip was evangelizing, to give this gift to the Samaritans who were becoming Christians (Acts 8:14–17). The apostles didn't give miraculous gifts to all the new Christians, though. Luke writes that Simon the sorcerer, who had amazed his neighbors with his magic, was "astonished by the great signs and miracles he saw" Philip perform. Simon wanted to buy this power. But he wasn't given (and absolutely wasn't sold) the power of miraculous gifts (Acts 8:9–25).

Bible Lesson

Luke writes that the apostle Paul laid his hands on twelve Ephesian disciples to impart miraculous gifts (Acts 19:6–7). Moses and Paul teach that signs and wonders identified true prophets and apostles from false ones (Deuteronomy 18:20–22; 2 Corinthians 12:12).

Many Christians believe that the miraculous powers of the apostles decreased as God's objective word was being written down and collected in the first century A.D. The last recorded miracle in the Bible was performed on the island of Malta (A.D. 60) by the apostle Paul (Acts 28:8–9). Three years later (A.D. 63), Paul writes that Epaphroditus almost died from some sickness (Philippians 2:25–27). Why didn't Paul heal him? About four years after the Epaphroditus incident (A.D. 67), Paul didn't heal Timothy's stomach problem, but told him to use a little wine for medicinal purposes (1 Timothy 5:23). Then in A.D. 68, Paul left Trophimus sick in Miletus (2 Timothy 4:20). It seems the apostles' miraculous powers were waning as the New Testament was being written.

Look in the Book

Many Christians today believe that there are only two modern miracles: when God creates a new human soul at the time of conception and when God the Holy Spirit creates a "new creation" in a believing sinner through regeneration (2 Corinthians 5:17; Galatians 6:15; Ephesians 2:10; 4:24). This event is being "born again" (John 3:3–8).

Miracles not only provided credentials for the miracle-worker as God's spokesperson, they also confirmed the message of the miracle-worker as God's messenger (Hebrews 2:3–4). For example, Philip's preaching of Jesus was confirmed by miracles, which in turn authenticated his message to the Samaritans (Acts 8:6). Through the power of Jesus' first miracle, the turning of water into wine, his disciples believed in him (John 2:11). An official from Capernaum believed Jesus' word that a miracle had taken place without seeing it himself (John 4:46–54). "Jesus did many other things as well," said the apostle John. "If every one of them were written down, I suppose that even the whole world would not have room for the books that would be written" (John 21:25).

What Is a Relic?

A relic is an ancient artifact that's considered holy because of its connection with Jesus or another revered person. Such an object is believed to provide a spiritual link to God. The most common relics are called *brandea*. They are everyday objects, such as a piece of cloth that may have been worn by a saint or even dirt from the garden of Gethsemane. It's difficult to verify the authenticity of many of the supposed relics in existence today, but the discussion of relics is quite relevant to any study of the history of the Bible.

The early Christians often created their own brandea. For example, they might rub a handkerchief on the tomb where they believe Jesus was buried. Or they would treasure a small vial of water from the Jordan River where Jesus was baptized. The brandea were often kept in reliquaries, which are boxes specially made to hold the chosen relic. These could even be worn as good luck charms if they were small enough.

Fantastic Find

St. Anthony's coffin is at the Basilica of St. Anthony in Padua, Italy. When it was opened about thirty years ago, his body had decomposed. All, that is, except his tongue. Apparently, it looked normal. St. Anthony's gift was preaching, so this was seen as a tribute to him. His tongue reportedly remains at the Basilica.

After about the seventh century, another type of relic became popular. Churches began collecting a saint's body parts, such as the bones or locks of hair. At first, bodies weren't to be moved from their burial places. But after A.D. 787, new churches needed a relic before they could be consecrated. Eventually, the Church leaders allowed a saint's body to be moved (called *translation*) and even divided (called *partition*). The status and power of an individual church was dependent on its relics. Emperor Charlemagne

(A.D. 742–814), a ruler known for slaughtering pagans who refused to become Christians, accumulated an impressive relics collection for the church he established at Aachen. Other European monarchs followed the Emperor's lead for their own churches.

Timeless Truth

During the Middle Ages, the selling of relics was forbidden. This practice was known as *simony*, after Simon the sorcerer who was rebuked by the apostle Peter for trying to buy the ability to perform miraculous gifts (Acts 8: 9–25). The only exception was when buying the relic would prevent it from being desecrated. Relics couldn't be auctioned because the bidding would drive up the price.

The saint's spirit was believed to be a part of the saint's body. That made these body-relics more valuable than the common brandea. An early church slogan might be: Where the body goes, the spirit will follow. Miracles were said to occur wherever these saint's body-relics were preserved and worshiped. The early worshipers considered such miracles to be a sign of God's approval.

Specific Relics

Problems arose when more than one church claimed to have the same relic. Three different shrines in the eleventh century claimed to have the head of John the Baptist. Even though Jesus' body ascended to heaven, this didn't keep churches from claiming to have his umbilical cord, his baby teeth, Mary's breast milk, or other intensely personal items.

Bible Lesson

When St. Bernadette Soubirous died in A.D. 1879, her body was placed in a glass coffin at her convent in Nevers, France. When the body didn't decompose, it was designated as "incorrupt." Often the phenomenon of incorruptibility is thought to be accompanied by a sweet fragrance called the "odor of sanctity." Sometimes a liquid, the "oil of saints," exudes from the body.

The popes' private chapels in eleventh-century Rome supposedly kept Jesus' umbilical cord and his foreskin preserved in oil in a gold and jeweled crucifix. Other relics kept here include a piece of Jesus' cross, the heads of the saints Peter and Paul, the Ark of the Covenant, the tablets of Moses, the rod of Aaron, a golden urn of manna, the tunic of the Virgin Mary, various pieces of clothing worn by John the Baptist including his hair shirt, the five loaves and two fishes that fed the 5,000, and the table used at the Last Supper.

Fantastic Find

Before Jesus' body was removed from the cross, a Roman soldier pierced his side with his spear. The Hofburg Treasure House, in Vienna, Austria, claims to have this weapon. It's called the St. Longinus Lance after the soldier, whose name supposedly was Longinus. St. Peter's Basilica in Rome claims to have the shaft of the spear.

To end the theft of relics from one church to another, the Roman Church decided in A.D. 1215 that relics were to be stored and displayed in reliquaries. Later, in 1255, removing a relic from its storage for any reason was forbidden. The most important, and impressive, relics were kept in valuable reliquaries adorned with jewels and precious metals. A saint's power depended on how many Christians made the pilgrimage to worship the saint's relics.

Some reliquaries were actually caskets fashioned into full-body statues that were placed on altars and carried in ceremonial processions. The tomb of St. Thomas of Canterbury, completed in 1220, was quite magnificent. During the English Reformation, when Henry VIII closed the monasteries, the jewels and precious metals from St. Thomas' tomb filled twenty-six carts.

Fantastic Find

The officials of the Cathedral of Naples claim that they have a vial of St. Genarro's dried blood. When they place the vial close to his head, they say, it liquefies and boils. Supposedly, this occurs eighteen times a year.

Often pilgrims made a wax model of whatever part of their own body had been miraculously healed. These wax relics were exhibited in the churches as proof of a saint's power to heal. For instance, Henry of Maldon's tapeworm hung on the altar of Canterbury cathedral. Beside it was a shepherd's dismembered finger. Apparently, the shepherd hoped St. Thomas would help him grow another one.

Even a relic that was known to be false became authentic if it performed a miracle. Christians were eager to see these relics even if it meant traveling hundreds of miles. Their pilgrimages greatly contributed to a town's local economy. No wonder towns tried so hard to get the most important and powerful relics in their churches.

The Empress Helena

The Abbey of Hautvillers in Champagne, France, claims to have the relics of the Empress Helena, the mother of the Roman Emperor Constantine the Great. These objects were taken to the Abbey from Constantinople in A.D. 849. Helena was a very religious woman who searched for relics throughout the Empire.

Bible Lesson

Helena is also said to have brought the bodies of the three wise men, discovered in Persia in the fourth century, to Constantinople. In the fifth century, they were taken to Milan, Italy. Since 1163, they supposedly have been at the Cathedral of Cologne, Germany.

The Roman soldiers cast lots for Jesus' seamless robe at the foot of the cross. Called the *tunica Christi*, the robe was said to have been taken to the Cathedral of St. Peter in Trier, Germany, by the Empress Helena in the fourth century.

Stolen Relics

Strangely enough, the best way to get an authentic relic was to steal one. Stolen relics were included in the collections of the most famous European pilgrimage sites. If the thief claimed that a saint, appearing to him in a dream, told him to take a relic, then the theft was justified. Or if miracles occurred at the relic's new home, it meant the saint approved. Unhappy saints supposedly punished thieves.

Even if a town secretly bought a relic, they often claimed they stole it. These thefts were carefully orchestrated and the successful thieves were local heroes. The Italian town of Bari, in 1087, commissioned the theft of the remains of Saint Nicholas from the Turkish town of Myra. The successful expedition meant that the citizens of Bari basked in the glory of possessing the bones of Santa Claus.

chapter 19

The Founders of Modern Science

Beginning about 1,000 years ago, modern science, through the work of intelligent and talented individuals, began to replace superstition. The natural world was observed, explored, and explained a little at a time. This chapter examines the beliefs of a few of those credited with founding modern science. Did they embrace the evolutionary worldview? Or did their Christian beliefs guide their experiments? Read on—the answers to these questions may surprise you.

Scientists of the Late Middle Ages

"How did God do it?" was the question that puzzled the early founders of modern science. They began with the assumption that God created the universe and they wanted to discover the mysteries of his creation. Embedded in the assumption of creation is the belief that God created the universe within a plan. He was no mere wizard pointing a wand here and there, poofing trees and gazelles and planets into existence. The early scientists recognized patterns and a quality of interrelationship among the many aspects of creation. They sought to discover the key to God's creative work.

Robert Grosseteste (1175–1253), a Franciscan at Oxford University, was a minister dedicated to reforming the church. He practiced hermeneutics: insisting on studying the original texts whenever possible, he sought the author's intended meaning. He translated ancient documents and wrote a physics of Aristotle. Because of his love for learning, he invented a scientific method that involved using step-by-step procedures for testing his hypotheses. He found mathematics to be the key for investigating natural phenomena.

Timeless Truth

The ancient Greek philosopher Aristotle believed that the sun moved around the earth. This was a common misconception based on observation. Still today, people talk about the sun rising and the sun setting even though it is known that the earth revolves around the sun. Nicholas Oresme (1330–1382) determined this scientific fact. He had to argue for his position against the accepted view of his day.

Grosseteste's student Roger Bacon (1214–1294) was also a Franciscan. Like Grosseteste, he believed that evidence for God's existence was found in nature. Through science, people would be so inspired by God's intricate and artistic creativity that they would yearn for a personal relationship with him. With this as his motive and utilizing his mentor's experimental methods, Bacon studied mathematics, physics, optics, and philosophy. He examined both rainbows and solar eclipses in his search for explanations of "how God did it." Through his experiments, Bacon concluded that the earth was a sphere and that a ship could sail all the way around it. He also estimated the distance from the earth to the stars. He made predictions about modern eyeglasses, ships, and vehicles.

The Christian Humanists

The years from 1494 to 1564 are known as the High Renaissance. This was a time when idealism and rationalism were especially valued. The educated people of this time period studied the Bible and the classical literature of the Greco-Roman world. They believed that these texts contained important information that was relevant to their lives. The Christian Humanists shared these views even as they focused on issues pertaining to the church.

The Christian Humanists believed that they could restore Christianity to its original purpose and meaning. The most famous Christian Humanist was Desiderius Erasmus (1466–1536) who promoted education in the humanities and the study of the Bible in its ancient languages, something not done in the Middle Ages. This educational pursuit brought liberation to many scholars, which led to understanding and obeying the Bible's command to subdue and have dominion over the earth (Genesis 1:28). This was the beginning of modern science.

The Scientific Revolution (1600–1715)

Aristotle's view that the sun revolved around the earth is known as a geocentric (earth-centered) view of the universe. The philosopher taught that the earth was a stationary object—not a planet—that was fixed in space. He asserted that not only the sun but also the moon and the five known planets (Mercury, Venus, Mars, Jupiter, and Saturn) revolved around the earth. These were thought to be held in their orbits by crystalline spheres.

The Egyptian ruler Ptolemy (second century B.C.) used his influence and knowledge to advance the geocentric view. Because it fit snugly to the church's belief that the earth was the centerpiece of God's creation, religious leaders also taught that the sun, moon, and planets revolved around our terrestrial home.

Nicholas Copernicus (1473–1543)

Copernicus held the office of canon in the cathedral of Frauenburg and was a staunch believer in the Bible's account of creation. He was also among the first to discard Aristotle and Ptolemy's geocentric view in favor of a heliocentric, or sun-centered, view. In his book *Revolutions of the Heavenly Bodies* (1543), he argued that the earth and the other planets revolved around the sun. Copernicus included two radical ideas in his book, which are now elementary facts:

- It takes one year for the earth to revolve around the sun.
- It takes twenty-four hours for the earth to rotate one time on its axis.

To the Western world, which widely accepted the Ptolemaic theory that the universe was a closed space, Copernicus's work was tantamount to heresy. It defied what they could see with their own eyes (the rising and setting of the sun, the appearing and disappearing of the stars, etc.).

John Napier (1550–1617)

Napier hailed from Scotland and was the first prominent scientist from the British Isles. David Hume, the renowned skeptic, said that he was the greatest Scot who ever lived. A devout Christian, Napier was an ardent biblical scholar who wrote a commentary on the book of Revelation titled *A Plaine Discourse on the Whole Revelation of St. John*.

However, Napier is best known as the inventor of every algebra student's nemesis—the logarithm. In 1614, he developed these calculating shortcuts. He is also the man behind the concept of negative numbers and the decimal notations for fractions. His work laid the foundation for calculators and computers, two items used regularly today. Napier is also the father of the modern tank, death ray (laser), and submarine.

Johannes Kepler (1571–1630)

Known as the father of celestial mechanics and modern optics, Kepler was a brilliant German mathematician and astronomer. He was assisted in his work by the precise astronomical observations of the great astronomer Tycho Brahe (1546–1601). Kepler's *On the Motion of Mars*, published in 1609, announced two planetary laws that supported Copernicus' heliocentric universe. His third planetary law was discovered in 1619. The three laws are as follows:

- The orbits of the planet are not circles but ellipses, with the sun at one end (foci).
- The motion of a body is not constant, but speeds up closer to the sun (a line connecting the sun and the planet sweeps out equal areas in equal times).
- The farther away a planet is, the more slowly it moves.

Kepler believed that his purpose was to use mathematics and astronomy to reveal God to others. "Let also my name perish," he said, "if only the name of God the Father is elevated." Among his many accomplishments, Kepler was the first to explain planetary motion, predicted that the distances to stars could be measured by trigonometric parallax, and taught that the moon caused the ocean tides to ebb and flow. He also improved lenses for eyeglasses and telescopes, and invented a gear-driven calculating machine and a pinhole camera. His book *The Dream* is about a trip to the moon and is considered the first science-fiction story.

Galileo Galilei (1564–1642)

Galileo didn't invent the telescope, but he was the first to turn it skyward. Through his observations and record-keeping, he realized that there were craters on the moon and discovered four of Jupiter's moons. He also studied sunspots, the phases of Venus, and the stars of the Milky Way.

Fantastic Find

Through his experiments, Galileo recognized and demonstrated the law of inertia. This is the scientific precept that a moving mass will continue to move until a force acts to stop it.

Galileo said: "I have two sources of perpetual comfort: first, that in my writings there cannot be found the faintest shadow of irreverence toward the Holy Church; and second, the testimony of my own conscience, which I and God in Heaven thoroughly know. And He knows that in this cause for which I suffer, though many might have spoken with more learning, none, not even the ancient Fathers, have spoken with more piety or with greater zeal for the Church than I."

A devout Christian, Galileo did not hold to the geocentric view of the universe. He held fast to his heliocentric belief, which was validated by his observations, despite immense pressure from the Church. He said, "Holy Scripture and Nature are both emanations from the divine word: the former dictated by the Holy Spirit, the latter the observant executrix of God's commands." He also said, "I render infinite thanks to God for being so kind as to make me alone the first observer of marvels kept hidden in obscurity for all previous centuries."

Sir Francis Bacon (1561–1626)

Sir Francis Bacon believed that the Scriptures predicted an increase in knowledge (Daniel 12:4). This motivated him to invent a *Novum organum*— a new tool—that would fulfill the Bible's prediction.

Known as the founder of modern science, Bacon advocated examining details, gathering evidence, and then interpreting the results. He was also a poet, and while his scientific observations were, to him, acts of worship, his poetry praised God and his handiwork. He believed that humans had a duty and an obligation to use their intellect to explore God's creation rather than depend on Aristotle's views of the universe.

Isaac Newton (1642–1727)

As most every schoolchild knows, Newton "discovered" gravity when an apple fell on his head. That may not have been exactly what happened, but Newton did establish that gravity keeps people on their planet and the planets in their orbits. He said he stood upon the shoulders of those who went before him, thus attributing his success to Copernicus, Kepler, and Galileo. And like his scientific predecessors, Newton was a Christian who believed that God created the universe. He wrote many works on the Bible.

Newton's work *Mathematical Principles of Natural Philosophy*, also known as the *Principia*, details the three laws demonstrating the motions of objects on the earth. He incorporated Kepler's laws into his own principles by naming Kepler's force as gravity, a force that exists between all objects with mass. Newton is also recognized for inventing a form of calculus.

William Harvey (1578–1657)

An English scientist and pious Christian from the University of Padua, Harvey is credited for his work in anatomy. He studied the human circulatory system and how the heart pumps blood through the arteries, lungs, and veins. His work was the foundation for another scientist, Marcello Malpighi (1628–1694), who looked through a microscope and found capillaries. Modern embryology is traced to Harvey's work.

Blaise Pascal (1623–1662)

Pascal was a mathematician who invented an early mechanical calculator. He described the first systematic theory of hydrostatics in his work *Treatise on the Equilibrium of Liquids*, in which he formulated the law of pressure. Following his observations and experiments, Pascal invented the syringe and the hydraulic press. Without his contributions to scientific knowledge, the modern world would be without submarines, scuba gear, and many other pneumatic devices.

Timeless Truth

Pascal's Wager is the famous challenge that encourages individuals to consider that if one chooses to believe in Christianity and it is false, nothing is lost. But if one chooses to disbelieve in Christianity and it is true, then everything is lost. Pascal believed that Christianity was a positive and true choice by which he found peace.

Robert Boyle (1627–1691)

Considered the father of modern chemistry, Boyle was a devout Bible-believing Christian who wrote *The Christian Virtuoso*, *Style of the Scriptures*,

Occasional Reflections, Ethics, and *Some Motives and Incentives to the Love of God.* He not only believed that science was a means to loving God, but he also believed in miracles. Accepting the book of Genesis as literal, historical truth, Boyle was known to study the Scriptures in their original languages.

"I am not a Christian," said Boyle, "because it is the religion of my country, and my friends, when I chuse to travel in the beaten road, it is not, because I find it is the road, but because I judge it is the way."

In addition to his scientific work, Boyle supported missionaries and Bible translations. Of him it was said, "His great thought of God, and his contemplation of his works, were to him sources of continual joy, which he never could be exhausted."

Antony van Leeuwenhoek (1632–1723)

Leeuwenhoek made the invisible visible through his perfection of a technique that increased the power of the microscopic lens. His lenses, no bigger than a pinhead, had a power as high as 270 × and a 1.4 micron resolution. This was the prototype for the electron microscope. Thanks to his dedication to seeking out the invisible, we know about such things as bacteria, sperm cells, and blood cells. He made over 500 microscopes, which were really powerful magnifying glasses.

Investigating the mysteries of the natural world was Leeuwenhoek's passion. His faith in God and love for his creation undergirded his science. Along with others, he exposed the fallacy of spontaneous generation, the superstitious belief that life sprung from material objects, such as raw meat "birthing" maggots.

Scientists of the Enlightenment

During the period known as the Enlightenment, biblical principles began to be questioned. But the scientists of the time who continued their devotion to God as the Creator made incredible discoveries and vital contributions to the world's knowledge. They introduced the world to what is now considered modern science.

Carolus Linnaeus (1707–1778)

Known as the father of taxonomy, Linnaeus classified organisms into recognizable groups. His principles of hierarchical organization aid scientists in the classifying and naming of previously undiscovered species. He was a creationist who believed that the Genesis writer meant what he said when he wrote that God created plants and animals to reproduce "after their kind."

Look in the Book

In the preface to a late edition of his work titled *Systema Naturae: Creationis telluris est glaria Dei ex opere Naturae per Homonem solum*, Linnaeus stated, "The Earth's creation is the glory of God, as seen from the works of Nature by man alone. The study of nature would reveal the Divine Order of God's creation, and it was the naturalist's task to construct a 'natural classification' that would reveal this Order in the universe."

Linnaeus traveled over 4,000 miles, on foot, in "God's garden" in order to classify as many species as possible. In his masterpiece *Species Plantarum*, he quotes Psalm 104:24: "O Lord, how ample are your works! How wisely you have fashioned them! How full the earth is of your possessions!"

William Herschel (1738–1822)

The father of stellar astronomy, Herschel built the largest telescopes of his time. His astronomical discoveries include binary stars, the nature of nebulae (especially the Orion nebula), comets, two of Saturn's moons (Mimas and Enceladus), and the planet Uranus. Herschel mapped out the stars and the earth's relationship to them in the universe. He catalogued over 90,000 stars. Through his observations, the number of nebulae increased from 103 to 2,500. Incredibly, he proved that the laws that govern the earth are the same throughout the universe. Herschel's sister Caroline, his assistant, discovered six comets.

Herschel's pioneering work in astronomy was motivated by his belief in God as the Creator and author of all natural laws. He was a devout Christian devoted to prayer who believed that God could be worshiped through knowledge of his creation.

Scientists of the Nineteenth Century

During this time, Darwin's theories of evolution were taking hold. Many scientists didn't embrace his ideas and continued a belief in a Creator God. These scientists, like those who came before, made significant scientific achievements.

John Herschel (1792–1871)

William's son continued in his father's comet tracks, though the elder Herschel wanted his son to become a preacher. John catalogued 1,200 double stars (a total of 70,000 celestial objects) and he observed nebulae, the Magellanic Clouds, Halley's comet, star clusters, sunspots, and the moons of Saturn. A talented chemist, John learned about Daguerre's discovery in photography and a week later had reproduced it. Like his father, John believed in divine creation and was a regular churchgoer. He was remembered as a humble man of integrity.

Samuel F. B. Morse (1791–1872)

The inventor of the first binary code, the Morse code, Morse gave God all the credit for inventions. His code made it possible for communication to occur over great distances through the telegraph. Annie Ellsworth, daughter of Henry Ellsworth (the first patent commissioner and Morse's friend), chose the first message sent across the wires. It was Numbers 23:23—"What hath God wrought"—and was sent from the Supreme Court room in the Capitol to the Baltimore railroad department on May 24, 1844. "It is His work," Morse said when the message was sent. He then said, "Not unto us, but to name, O Lord, be all the praise" (Psalms 115:1).

Timeless Truth

Samuel F. B. Morse once said, "The nearer I approach the end of my pilgrimage, the clearer is the evidence of the divine origin of the Bible, the grandeur and sublimity of God's remedy for fallen man are more appreciated, and the future is illuminated with hope and joy."

A painter of landscapes, Morse was also the father of modern American photography. He enthusiastically supported both education and the value of Sunday school. "Education without religion," he said, "is in danger of substituting wild theories for the simple commonsense rules of Christianity."

Michael Faraday (1791–1867)

Though a renowned physicist, Faraday preferred studying the Bible and praying above receiving praise for his scientific accomplishments. Among these were the invention of the first electric motor and dynamo, the discovery of new organic compounds, and the technique for liquefying a permanent gas. He also demonstrated the relationship between electricity and chemical bonding.

Because of Faraday's extensive accomplishments, we have cars to park in our garages, planes to take us across the country, and clocks to wake us up in the morning. Pumps, fans, vacuum cleaners, generators, transformers, and many other devices came about due to Faraday's work.

Fantastic Find

A unit of electrical quantity is called a faraday after the physicist. A unit of capacitance is called a farad in his honor. He is the only physicist to have two international units named after him. In addition, the Faraday effect describes the influence of magnetism on polarized light.

Faraday called his scientific work his holy calling. He often met with others in small Bible study groups that were part of the back-to-the-Bible movement. These Christians were intent on following the teachings of the apostles rather than following the traditions of various denominations.

James Prescott Joule (1818–1889)

Joule is credited with recognizing what is now known as the first law of thermodynamics. This scientific law states that neither matter nor energy can be created or destroyed. This proof is one of the greatest achievements of any scientist in history. Through an experiment conducted in 1843, Joule was convinced that all forms of energy were equivalent. He had discovered the mechanical equivalent of heat.

Timeless Truth

"I shall lose no time in repeating and extending these experiments," said Joule, "being satisfied that the grand agents of nature are by the Creator's fiat, *indestructible*; and that wherever mechanical force is expended, an exact equivalent of heat is *always* obtained."

Joule and Lord Kelvin (William Thomson) worked together to discover the Joule-Thomson effect. Their collaboration is the reason for the existence of refrigerators. Joule's work also led to the liquid air production and invention of toasters, hair dryers, space heaters, irons, and other modern appliances.

A man of sincere faith, Joule glorified God for his many accomplishments. "After the knowledge of, and obedience to, the will of God," said Joule, "the next aim must be to know something of his attributes of wisdom, power and goodness as evidenced by His handiwork. It is evident that an acquaintance with natural laws means no less than an acquaintance with the mind of God therein expressed."

William Thomson, Lord Kelvin (1824–1907)

Lord Kelvin had accomplishments of his own in addition to his work with Joule. He came up with the temperature scale bearing his name, the Kelvin temperature scale, which begins at absolute zero. He also supervised the first transatlantic cable across the ocean and predicted the heat death of the universe by applying the second law of thermodynamics. Like Joule, he was a faithful Christian. A promoter of Christian education, he studied the Bible, history, and the geography of the ancient world.

James Clerk Maxwell (1831–1879)

As the father of electrodynamics, Maxwell utilized four differential equations to sum up all electromagnetic phenomena. Through his study of light, electricity, and magnetism, he realized that light was an electromagnetic wave transmitted through empty space. To Maxwell, we owe gratitude for televisions, radios, cell phones, pagers, radar, satellites, and spacecraft and aircraft communications. As if this wasn't enough, Maxwell is also recognized for his work in statistical thermodynamics, the nature of Saturn's rings, and color vision.

Fantastic Find

Maxwell put his faith in Jesus and opposed Darwinian evolutionary theories. He gave God the credit for his scientific achievements. "I have been thinking how very gently I have been always dealt with," he said. "I have never had a violent shove in all of my life. The only desire which I can have is like David to serve my own generation by the will of God, and then fall asleep."

Both the largest, tallest mountain on Venus and a crater on the moon are named after Maxwell. The James Clerk Maxwell telescope, located on the summit of Mauna Kea, Hawaii, explores the universe.

Gregor Mendel (1822–1884)

An Augustinian monk, Mendel was a Christian who believed in creationism. He is remembered for his pioneering work in genetics. Through his experiments and observations, he demonstrated that species are resistant to change. This is precisely because of characteristics that are inherited throughout generations. "Species do not transform one into the other," he said. "They show stability from generation to generation, and my experiments demonstrate that fact." He also said, "[N]atural selection can explain the survival of the fittest, but not the arrival of the fittest."

In his work "Experiments with Plant Hybrids," Mendel showed how traits were inherited. His experiments with green peas aided the development of his theories on heredity. His systematic study of the genes is the foundation for modern genetics and biomathematics.

Bernhard Riemann (1826–1866)

Until Riemann came along, mathematics was trapped in the constraints of Euclidean geometry. Riemann created a "new curved space" that was the foundation for Albert Einstein's theories of relativity. Because of Riemann, math students get to struggle with calculus. A devout Christian, Riemann's tombstone reads, "All things work together for good to them that love God" (Romans 8:29).

Louis Pasteur (1822–1895)

Pasteur is remembered as a great chemist and biologist who revolutionized medicine and public health. His motivation came from the Old Testament teachings that uncleanness causes disease. He also believed the Genesis account that created life reproduces its own kind. He worked to demonstrate the fallacy of spontaneous generation, which many continued to believe despite the work of Leeuwenhoek in the previous century. Pasteur proved the scientific law of biogenesis ("like reproducing like"), invented pasteurization, and revolutionized food processing. He is also lauded for his work on germ theory and disease.

Timeless Truth

"No—there is today no circumstance known in which it can be confirmed that microscopic beings have come into the world without germs, without parents similar to them," said Pasteur. "Those who maintain this view are the victims of illusions, of ill-conducted experiments, blighted with errors that they have either been unable to perceive or unable to avoid."

A stickler for scientific proof and integrity, Pasteur said, "If I have at times disturbed the tranquility of your academics by somewhat stormy discussions, it was only because I am a passionate defender of the truth."

Pasteur discovered cures for rabies, anthrax, chicken cholera, and silkworm disease. He contributed to the development of the first vaccines and set the stage for modern biology, biochemistry, stereochemistry, microbiology, virology, bacteriology, molecular biology. He was also instrumental in both winemaking and antiseptic operations.

Joseph Lister (1827–1912)

After studying Pasteur's work on bacteria, Lister concluded that surgical infections occurred because of the little beasties. His name may be more familiar as part of the brand name of a certain mouthwash touted to kill bacteria. Lister once stated, "I am a believer in the fundamental doctrines of Christianity."

The Bible and Darwin's Theory of Evolution

Charles Darwin (1809–1882) is possibly the scientist most pertinent to the discussion of the Bible. His theory of evolution, which states that change in the genetic composition of a population over time results in the development of a new species, challenges the theory of creationism. Many Christians believe the Bible is in clear opposition to an evolutionary view of the origins of life. Psalm 8:4 asks the question, "What is man?" The answer is found in Psalm 9:5: "a little lower than the angels." The Bible teaches that a human being is a dichotomy, a duality, a twofold creature with both a spiritual and a physical aspect.

Timeless Truth

Noted evolutionist Sir Julian Huxley said, "The whole of reality *is* evolution—a single process of self-transformation." Pierre Teilhard de Chardin, renowned anthropologist and evolutionist, stated, "Evolution is a general postulate to which all theories, all hypotheses, all systems must henceforth bow and which they must satisfy in order to be thinkable and true. Evolution is a light which illuminates all facts, a trajectory which all lines of thought must follow."

Furthermore, the Bible says that first, a human being is a physical body. This body is part of a person's nature and is inherently good (Genesis 1:31). Second, a human being is a spirit or soul (the words are interchangeable). The spiritual aspect has no physical substance but is a created spiritual substance. It is not divine, but it does survive physical death (Matthew 10:28; Hebrews 12:23; Revelation 6:9; 20:4). The soul is considered the essence of personhood and the source of one's ability to have communion and fellowship with God. Both the physical and spiritual aspects are necessary for the human's whole, authentic existence.

Humans and Animals

Genesis 1:1 states that God created all of the elements as the fundamental components of all that exists. All the celestial bodies are made of combinations of these elements. Genesis 2:19 says that animals were formed out of the ground by God. Adam was made out of the dust of the ground (Genesis 2:7) and Eve was made out of Adam's rib (Genesis 2:22). Of course, some take the biblical account of Adam and Eve literally, while others consider it simply an allegory.

Look in the Book

The references in Genesis 2 to the ground or the dust of the earth refers to the ninety-six natural elements, such as hydrogen, carbon, and oxygen, plus the heavier elements made in accelerators. These make up all of God's physical creation (Genesis 2:17; 3:19; 1 Corinthians 15:47). In other words, all of creation is supposedly composed of some combination of these elements.

In Genesis 1:27, Jesus said, "From the beginning of the creation God made them male and female" (Mark 10:6). This asserts that Adam and Eve were the first humans and they came into existence at the very beginning of creation, not from a past ancestor, as Darwin's theory holds.

In Genesis 1:28, God told Adam to subdue the earth and to have dominion over every living thing that moves upon the earth. Christians take this passage to mean that human beings are not in the same category as animals. Furthermore, when Adam was naming all the animals he did not find one like himself that could be a helper fit for him. This is another popular point of resistance taken by Christians against Darwinian evolution.

The apostle Paul made a clear-cut distinction between animals and human beings when he said, "All flesh is not the same flesh: but there is one kind of flesh of men, another flesh of beasts. Another of fishes, and another of birds" (1 Corinthians 15:39).

Macro- and Microevolution

Many believe that the Bible refutes the teachings of macroevolution, the evolutionary theory that one species can become or evolve into an entirely different kind of species. However, many also maintain that it doesn't refute microevolution. This is when a change occurs within a species.

Those that believe the Bible supports microevolution recognize that there are multiple breeds of dogs and cats, birds and fish. There are even varying characteristics among humans (blonde and brunette, tall and short, etc.).

However, Genesis 1:11–12 states that grass, herbs, and trees produce after their own kind. The living aquatic creatures, creatures that live upon the land, and birds all produce after their own kind (Genesis 1:21). Those who believe that the Bible supports micro- but not macroevolution hold that each kind was designed by God to produce after its own kind—not to become some other kind.

Timeless Truth

> The Hopeful Monster theory, as proposed by evolutionist Stephen Jay Gould of Harvard University, states that a radical change in the genes or chromosomes of an individual member of a species causes that member to produce a completely different species.

What about Theistic Evolution?

Theistic evolution is the belief that God exists and created the heavens and the earth, but that he used the process of evolution to accomplish his creative work. This compromise allows one to straddle the fence separating a Christian worldview from an evolutionary worldview. However, some believe the Hebrew language doesn't allow such a compromise. When the Genesis writer says that God created the world in six days and rested on the seventh, some believe he is referring literally to six twenty-four hour days.

Timeless Truth

> Colin Patterson, noted evolutionist with the British Museum of Natural History, said, "Just as pre-Darwinian biology was carried out by people whose faith was in the Creator and His plan, post-Darwinian biology is being carried out by people whose faith is in, almost, the deity of Darwin."

God is considered supernatural by definition. It follows then, for Christians, that God created the universe in a supernatural way. Evolution excludes a supernatural power (though its opponents believe it often requires leaps of blind faith). Evolutionist and Harvard professor George Simpson stated, "Evolution is a fully natural process, inherent in the physical properties of the universe, divergently and progressively." Sir Julian Huxley said, "Darwin pointed out that no supernatural designer was needed; since natural selection could account for any known form of life, there was no room for a supernatural agency in its evolution." As Simpson and Huxley explained, the belief in a supernatural God participating in the creation process violates the basic belief of evolution.

Look in the Book

Hebrews states, "In the beginning, O Lord, you laid the foundations of the earth, and the heavens are the work of your hands. They will perish, but you remain; they will all wear out like a garment. You will roll them up like a robe; like a garment they will be changed. But you remain the same, and your years will never end" (Hebrews 1:10–12).

Jesus said, "Have you not read, that he who made them at the beginning, made them male and female" (Matthew 19:3–6; Mark 10:6; Genesis 1:27; 2:24). From this statement, many Christians hold that Jesus believed Adam and Eve to be historical people—the first created human beings on the earth. This stance does not support evolutionary theory.

Scientists of the Twentieth Century

Many scientists who adhered to the Christian faith also contributed to the scientific knowledge of the twentieth century; in fact, there are enough for a separate book. Read on to discover the accomplishments of a few of the more well-known twentieth-century scientists.

George Washington Carver (1864–1943)

In an interview, Carver said he prayed to God and first asked God why he created the universe. God told him it was too big a question for him to ask. Carver then asked why God created man and received the same response. Finally, Carver asked why God created the peanut; he later discovered over 300 uses for the adaptable legume. Because of his extensive work, Carver is known as the father of chemurgy, or agricultural chemistry. Besides his creativity with the simple peanut, Carver invented thirty-five products from the velvet bean and 118 from the sweet potato. "There's no more important work than what you are doing right here," Teddy Roosevelt said of Carver's efforts when he visited Carver's Institute of Higher Education. In fact, numerous products are derived from plants, including bleach, adhesive, paper, paint, pavement, synthetic rubber, wood stain, metal polish, tenderizer, and talcum powder.

Fantastic Find

"Without my Savior, I am nothing," Carver said. Each day he prayed, "Lord what do you want me to do today?" He said, "I love to think of nature as an unlimited broadcasting station, through which God speaks to us every hour, if we will only tune in."

Carver believed the Genesis mandate where God told Adam and Eve to "be fruitful and multiply, and fill the earth, and subdue it; and have dominion over the fish of the sea and the fowl of the air and over every living thing that moves on the earth" (Genesis 1:28). Carver saw himself as an environmental steward, responsible for the dominion of the earth through science.

Wernher von Braun (1912–1977)

On October 3, 1942, von Braun's A-4 rocket was launched. An ecstatic von Braun said, "Do you realize what we accomplished today? Today the spaceship has been born!" Because of von Braun, the American space program included his Redstone rocket, Mercury, Gemini, Apollo, Mariner 2 and Mariner 4, the Saturn V rocket, Skylab, and Apollo-Soyuz.

The United States was embarrassed in 1957 when the Soviets launched Sputnik. President Kennedy gave the green light to von Braun to redeem the United States in the space race.

Opposing the one-sided teaching of evolution in the public schools, von Braun said, "To be forced to believe only one conclusion—that everything in the universe happened by chance—would violate the very objectivity of science itself. Certainly there are those who argue that the universe evolved out of a random process, but what random process could produce the brain of a man or the system of the human eye? Some people say that science has been unable to prove the existence of a Designer . . . They challenge science to prove the existence of God. But, must we really light a candle to see the sun?"

After von Braun's death, Major General John Medaris commented, "His imagination strolled easily among the stars, yet the farther out into the unknown and unknowable vastness of Creation his thoughts went, the more he was certain that the universe, and this small garden spot within it, came from no cosmic accident, but from the thought and purpose of an all-knowing God."

Neil Armstrong (1930–)

The first man to place a foot on the moon's surface, Armstrong spent twenty-one hours and thirty-seven minutes exploring earth's lunar satellite. Before a joint session of Congress on September 16, 1969, Armstrong said, "To those of you who advocated looking high we owe our sincere gratitude, for you have granted us the opportunity to see some of the grandest views of the Creator."

Timeless Truth

Archaeologists have excavated the steps leading to the Temple in Jerusalem—the very steps Christians believe Jesus walked on to enter the Temple. Neil Armstrong visited the Holy Land in 1988 and stood on these very steps. "It means more to me to stand on these steps," Armstrong said, "than to stand on the moon."

Armstrong conducted seventy-eight combat missions in the Korean War. He became an astronaut in 1962. As the command pilot for Gemini 8 in 1966, he performed the first successful docking of two vehicles in space. From 1971 to 1979, he was professor of aerospace engineering at the University of Cincinnati. Throughout his career, he flew over 200 different kinds of aircraft. He deserves his place in the history of scientific exploration.

chapter 20

Exploring *The Da Vinci Code*

In a modern discussion of the history of the Bible it's worth-while to investigate Dan Brown's historical novel *The Da Vinci Code*. On the inside cover of the book, the following statement appears: "All descriptions of artwork, architecture, documents, and secret rituals in this novel are accurate." Using knowledge of the biblical canon, ancient languages, and archaeological discoveries, this chapter will delve into the bestseller's claims and get to the bottom of such topics as Jesus' relationship with Mary Magdalene and the purpose of the Priory of Sion.

The Author's Claims

The *New York Times* bestseller, *The Da Vinci Code*, has been wildly successful and has been one of the major reasons for the general public's revived interest in all things biblical. The book is considered a historical novel, and the author has declared on several occasions that the occurrences in the book are historically factual. For example, on NBC's *Today* show, interviewer Matt Lauer asked Brown, "How much of this is based on reality in terms of things that actually occurred?" Brown's response was, "Absolutely all of it. Obviously [the main character] Robert Langdon is fictional, but all of the art, architecture, secret rituals, secret societies—all of that is historical fact" (interview aired June 9, 2003). Furthermore, ABC News aired a special entitled *Jesus, Mary, and Da Vinci* in which Brown said that he believed what he wrote in his book (November 3, 2003).

Biblical scholars cannot accept a claim that something is "fact" without examining the evidence provided by history, the Bible, art, architecture, archaeology, and the ancient languages. Keeping in mind what you've read thus far, continue on to review a few of *The Da Vinci Code*'s claims.

The Priory of Sion

The Priory of Sion, according to Brown's book, was a secret European society founded in Jerusalem in 1099 by the crusading French king, Godefroi de Bouillon. The Priory's purpose, as depicted in the book, is to keep Jesus' marriage to Mary Magdalene, and the birth of their daughter Sarah, a secret. It is asserted that Mary, as Jesus' wife, should have been the true leader of the Christian Church. The secret of the marriage, the book claims, has been handed down from generation to generation of the Godefroi family since the first century A.D. The ancient documents confirming the marriage were supposedly buried beneath the ruins of the Temple in Jerusalem.

Parchments known as *Les Dossiers Secrets* (The Secret Papers) that identified numerous members of the Priory were discovered in the Paris Bibliotheque Nationale in 1975. According to Brown, these documents prove his claims about the Priory of Sion and, indeed, the parchments do exist. However, it was discovered that an anti-Semite, pro-Nazi embezzler named Pierre Plantard fabricated the documents and hid them in the Bibliotheque Nationale in the 1960s. It is known that Plantard was convicted and jailed for fraud in 1953. Obsessed with a desire to be an occult master and the descendant of kings, he created the Priory of Sion in 1956. The secret society was named after a mountain in Geneva.

Look in the Book

In *The Da Vinci Code*, among those named as members of the Priory of Sion were Sir Isaac Newton, artist and sculptor Sandro Botticelli, the author Victor Hugo, and the ultimate Renaissance man, Leonardo da Vinci. The idea that these men owed allegiance to the Priory's secret has drawn much criticism.

Plantard made a grave error when he named Roger Patrice Pelat, a close friend of then-President Francois Mitterand, as one of the Priory's Grand Masters. Plantard was brought before a French court in 1993, where he confessed his forgery of *Les Dossiers Secrets* under oath. When his home was searched, investigators found documents, obviously forged, that claimed Plantard was the true and rightful king of France. He was warned by the judge to cease his forgeries and was dismissed as a crank.

Additionally, one of Plantard's accomplices admitted that the *Les Dossiers Secrets* were fabricated, including the genealogical tables and the lists of the Priory's so-called grand masters. The French journalist Jean-Luc Chaumeil exposed Plantard as a fraud and published a series of books about him and his bogus Priory of Sion. He also worked with the British television station BBC2 on a program aired in 1996. Given all of this historical background, *The Da Vinci Code*'s claims about the Priory of Sion appear to be unfounded.

The Knights Templar

The Priory of Sion, according to Brown, established the oldest of the church's military-religious orders: the Knights Templar. They were to guard the secret of Jesus' supposed marriage and retrieve the documents buried beneath the Temple. However, history shows that the Knights were founded in A.D. 1118, during the Crusades, to protect pilgrims traveling to and from the Holy Land.

The last Crusader fortress at Acre fell in A.D. 1291. The Knights were no longer needed, but by this time, they had become extremely wealthy and a medieval financial institution.

The Da Vinci Code declares that Pope Clement V suppressed the Knights Templar because they were blackmailing him with the secret of the Holy Grail. Brown divides the medieval French term for Holy Grail, which is *sangreal*, into *sang* (blood) and *real* (royal). From this, he concludes that the sangreal, or royal blood, that begins with Jesus and Mary Magdalene flows through the Merovingian dynasty. In Brown's theory, Mary is the Holy Grail, "the chalice that bore the royal bloodline of Jesus Christ." Instead of submitting to their blackmail, Pope Clement arrested the Knights and burned them as heretics. With the Knights out of the way, it was left to the Priory of Sion to preserve the secret.

The historical account is not quite as dramatic as Brown's story. King Philip IV ("The Fair") of France was a greedy man who coveted the Knights' wealth. After forcing Pope Clement to suppress their order, the king arrested and burned some of the Knights, including their Grand Master Jacques de Molay, who was burned at the stake in A.D. 1314.

Allegations about Constantine

In Brown's book, religious goddesses were sacred. The Roman emperor Constantine and his male successors obliterated this matriarchal paganism and substituted Christianity, a patriarchal religion. The book claims that the emperor financed the acceptance of a new biblical canon that omitted the documents that emphasized Jesus' human nature and included the gospels that emphasized his godly nature. For his own financial gain, the emperor wanted Jesus to be made into a god and, Brown writes, even went so far as to move the Christian day of worship from Saturday to Sunday.

Is there any truth to these claims about the emperor Constantine? Look at what you already know. The canon, as discussed earlier in the book, was established in the first century A.D., some 200 years before Constantine was born. It's also clear from Acts 20:7 that the Christians met to worship on the first day of the week, Sunday, to commemorate both the day of Jesus'

Resurrection and the Day of Pentecost (Acts 2:1). The church officially began on the Day of Pentecost, fifty days after Jesus ascended to heaven.

Bible Lesson

First Corinthians 16:2 says that on the first day of the week, Sunday, the Corinthians were to take up a collection for the poor in Jerusalem as part of their worship. Revelation 1:10 notes that on the Lord's Day (Sunday) the apostle John, exiled on the island of Patmos, heard Jesus speak to him. So, according to the Bible, Sunday was established as the day of worship more than 200 years before Constantine was born.

Brown bases his claims on two books that were written centuries after the New Testament was written. One of these documents claims to have been written by the apostle Philip, who died in the first century A.D., but that would be possible only if Philip lived to be over 200 years old. The other is the Gospel of Magdalene. Again, Mary Magdalene is known to have died in the first century A.D. and could not possibly have written the work 200 years later. These books were never considered part of the biblical canon. In fact, they were rejected as heretical. *The Da Vinci Code* asserts that the apostle Philip and Mary (who lived and died in the first century A.D.) were a couple hundred years old when they wrote these two gospels.

Here's another issue to investigate: Brown's book claims that in a relatively close vote, the Council of Nicaea passed a resolution that Jesus was a god. But history shows that the Council of Nicaea (A.D. 325) never debated Jesus' divinity. It seems they didn't need to—all the early Church Fathers testified to the deity of Jesus. The Council's vote was on whether Jesus was co-eternal with the Father. That resolution passed by an overwhelming vote of 300 to 2.

Allegations about Mary Magdalene

Mary Magdalene is first introduced in Luke's Gospel. She became part of a group of women who financially supported and traveled with Jesus after he cast out the demons that enslaved her (Luke 8:1–3). Brown interprets Mary's presence with Jesus as proof that they were married. However, it is known that Jewish men and women always traveled together in the ancient world, though they traveled in separate caravans.

A prime example of traveling in separate caravans is found in Luke 2:41–52. Jesus was taken to the Temple in Jerusalem when he was twelve years old to celebrate the Passover and to become "a son of the law" (similar to a modern day *bar mitzvah*). When Mary and Joseph arrived back home in Nazareth, they discovered that Jesus was missing. He was in Jerusalem teaching the rabbis. Men and women traveled in separate caravans. Boys under the age of twelve traveled with their mothers. Boys of twelve ("sons of the law") and older could stay with their mothers or travel with their fathers. Mary and Joseph each thought Jesus was with the other parent.

Look in the Book

The writers of three of the biblical Gospels explain that Mary Magdalene was present at Jesus' crucifixion (Matthew 27:55–56; Mark 15:40–41; John 19:25), yet they don't identify Mary as Jesus' wife. Christians believe that John, a member of Jesus' inner circle, certainly would have known about a marriage even if Matthew and Mark didn't.

Magdalene was not Mary's surname, but indicated that she lived in the town of Magdala. Other women were with Mary Magdalene at the crucifixion, including Jesus' mother, Mary. Mary Magdalene was the first person Jesus appeared to after his resurrection (Matthew 28:1; Luke 24:10; John 20:11–18). When she saw that Jesus was alive, she fell at his feet and clung to them. Then, following his instructions, she ran to tell the apostles about Jesus' resurrection. Brown rewrites this scene with details of a sexual encounter. Read the Gospel accounts and see what you think. "I shan't bore you with the countless references to Jesus and Magdalene's union," writes Brown—perhaps because there are no such references. Examine the evidence and determine your own conclusions.

The Gospel of Philip

According to Brown, the Gospel of Philip states that Jesus kissed Mary on her mouth as his "spouse or wife". However, the truth is that words are omitted from this text. Here is how the passage, Philip 63:32–64:10, reads: "And the companion of the [_____] Mary Magdalene [_____ loved] her more than [all] the disciples [and used to] kiss her [often] on her [_____]."

Because of damage to the manuscript, no one really knows what words belong within the empty brackets. Who loved Mary? It's hard to say. Did her mystery lover kiss her on the mouth, as Brown suggests? This is also difficult to determine. Filling in the blanks can yield all sorts of interesting scenarios.

Fantastic Find

In his book, Brown states that the writer of the Gospel of Philip used the Aramaic word for spouse or wife. However, this third-century book was written in Coptic, not Aramaic. Regardless, the document is considered by many to be a forgery and condemned as heretical.

In the previous verse, the word *companion* is translated from the Greek word *koinonos*, which means "companion or friend." It cannot be translated as "wife," which is *gyne* in the Greek. That said, it's seemingly impossible to prove with any credibility that even this false Gospel writer claimed that Jesus and Mary were married.

The Gospel of Mary Magdala

Brown's second reference to a union between Jesus and Mary Magdalene is found in the Gospel of Mary Magdala 17:10–18:21. In this passage, the apostle Peter challenged Mary's supposed role in receiving special revelation from Jesus. Brown finds in the text that Peter spoke against Mary as Jesus' wife, but the word *wife* doesn't appear in this text. Suppose for a moment that Jesus and Mary were married. Not even the impetuous, hot-tempered Peter would have dared say anything against her. According to first-century Jewish custom and protocol, such a thing just wasn't done. In light of all this evidence, it is highly unlikely that Jesus and Mary Magdalene were ever married.

Evidence That Jesus Was Not Married

Now that you've examined Brown's claims about Jesus and Mary Magdalene, it's time to search for biblical evidence that Jesus was not married.

The first question that comes to mind is this: If Jesus had been married, wouldn't Paul have mentioned it? Since Peter, the other apostles, and Jesus' half-brothers had wives, Paul says he could also marry if he wanted to (1 Corinthians 9:5). If Jesus had been married, Paul would probably have named him in this list of married men before Peter and the others.

Look in the Book

The writers of all four of the Gospels named women who traveled with Jesus. Often their husbands' names were also given (Matthew 27:55–56; Mark 15:40–41; Luke 8:2–3; John 19:25). But no Gospel writer named Mary Magdalene, or any other woman, as the wife of Jesus.

Was Jesus a Rabbi?

Brown asserts that because Jesus was a rabbi, he would have been married. It's true: The disciples called Jesus *Rabbi*, the word for teacher. But the Bible shows that Jesus was not, and never claimed to be, an official Jewish rabbi. A man had to graduate from rabbinical school to earn that distinguished title. According to the Bible, Jesus attended no such school. Furthermore, Jesus calls himself *teacher* (*didasklos*) rather than *rabbi* (*hrabbi*) in Matthew 10:24; Luke 6:40; and John 13:14.

After Jesus threw the moneychangers out of the Temple, his enemies demanded to know "'By what authority are you doing these things? And who gave you authority to do this?'" (Mark 11:28). Jesus' enemies probably would have known if he were an official rabbi, and if he were, they would not have questioned the source of his authority or credentials. Brown apparently attempts to give Jesus both an official rabbinical status and a marital status that are not supported by Scripture or any other document.

Bible Lesson

The Gospel of Matthew says that Jesus exhorted the people in his kingdom to commit to full-time ministry by becoming eunuchs, or remaining unmarried (Matthew 19:10–12). Some of the book's critics say that it seems odd that a married man would encourage his followers to stay single. Conversely, Christians see marriage as a holy and sacred institution. In that regard, many think it would be odd for Jesus to keep his marriage a secret.

Queen Mary?

Brown says that it was Jesus' intention for Mary Magdalene to lead the church because she was descended from the royal House of Benjamin. But historical documents do not record Mary's tribal affiliation. Nor is there any indication that Jesus intended anyone other than his apostles to lead the young church. Furthermore, the "royal House of Benjamin" was pretty much obliterated when its sole king (Saul) and most of his descendants were killed in battle (1 Samuel 31:7–8).

The Status of Women

In Jesus' culture, women were not considered trustworthy. They were not even allowed to testify in a court. In their prayers, Jewish religious leaders thanked God that they were not made slaves, animals, or women. The Pharisaic host commented on Jesus' acceptance of the woman (who is not Mary Magdalene) who washed his feet with her tears (Luke 7:36–50). His apostles were amazed that he spoke to the Samaritan woman at the well (John 4:1–42). If Jesus was married, or if he had elevated Mary to lead his church, his enemies would not be silent. But no such records exist.

More Allegations

At this point, you have probably begun to question the validity of the events presented in *The Da Vinci Code*. Now consider some more allegations Brown makes in his book and judge for yourself whether some liberties have been taken on a variety of topics. A few of the most interesting controversies follow:

- **Sex:** Brown seems to have a preoccupation with the goddess Venus and supports a matriarchal paganism, a consort goddess who is more worthy of worship than God. The church has demonized sex, he writes, and should instead participate in what he calls a "holy marriage" of the sacred feminine. In the biblical records, however, sex is God's wedding gift to the newly married couple—a beautiful and holy intimacy within the confines of marriage.

- **The Olympic Games:** Brown says that the Olympic Games were a tribute to the goddess Venus and were organized to correspond with her eight-year cycle. Also, according to Brown, the five rings of the Olympics represent the Egyptian goddess Ishtar's pentagram. These notions are easily refuted. The Greeks never would have paid tribute to a Roman goddess, nor called their goddess, Aphrodite, by a Roman name. Also, the Olympic Games were dedicated to Zeus, not Venus, and were held every four years, not every eight. The five modern Olympic rings represent the five inhabited continents.

- **Architecture:** In his novel, Brown compares a cathedral's long hollow nave to a woman's womb. However, the architects and builders of the great European cathedrals would probably disagree with this description. Their designs did not symbolize feminine sexuality, but the Greek cross.

- **Leonardo da Vinci:** *The Last Supper*, one of Da Vinci's most well-known paintings, "practically shouts at the viewer that Jesus and Magdalene were a pair," writes Brown. Brown states that it isn't the apostle John sitting to Jesus' right—it's Mary. But then where is John? It is unlikely that Da Vinci would omit the favored apostle. The Bible states that John was present at the Last Supper and that he had a place of honor beside Jesus (John 13:1–30; esp. 13:23).

- **The Bible:** Brown's character Teabring says that "more than eighty gospels" were prime candidates for the canon, but only four were chosen. However, you've already learned how the biblical Gospels were accepted into the canon in the first century A.D. The false gospels were written a few hundred years later, long after the apostles and prophets had died. *The Nag Hammadi Library,* published in English in 1977, contained forty-five separate titles, but most were not gospels. If this document is Brown's source for his "more than eighty gospels," he has exaggerated the number.

- **Noah:** According to Brown, Noah was an albino, but it's unclear how he could know that. There is no evidence that Noah was anything other than an olive-skinned Middle Eastern shipbuilder in a place where there were no ships. An albino monk, according to Brown, was a member of Opus Dei, a global Roman Catholic organization. It's strange to imagine that an albino monk had perfect eyesight, since albinos seldom do. Furthermore, it is believed that Opus Dei doesn't have an order of monks or a bishop.

- **The Temple:** In Brown's book, ritualistic sex was practiced in the Old Testament Temple in Jerusalem to worship the goddess Shekinah. However, history shows that the Israelites were monotheistic; there is no Hebrew word for goddess. Monotheism is the worship of only one God, a radical concept in the ancient world. The fact that there is no Hebrew word for goddess demonstrates that the Hebrews did not recognize such a concept.

chapter 21
A Modern Perspective

Your literary journey into the ancient world is coming to a close. You have explored divine inspiration and the biblical canon, ancient culture and languages, and the scientific and archaeological discoveries that confirm or deny individual events recorded in both the Old and New Testaments. But what does that have to do with the twenty-first-century postmodern world? How does the Bible influence the culture and lives of present-day people? In this chapter, you'll gain a biblical perspective of the present and take a look at where things might be headed.

The Jesus Seminar

About 200 people of assorted religious beliefs, including some atheists, joined Robert Funk in establishing the Jesus Seminar in 1985. Their objectives were to discover what history says about the historical Jesus and to make the public aware of their scholarly research. As Funk said, "It is time for us [scholars] to quit the library and study and speak up. . . The Jesus Seminar is a clarion call to enlightenment. It is for those who prefer facts to fancies, history to histrionics, science to superstition." Through the years, this group has received extensive publicity in major news magazines and from network news organizations.

What Do They Believe?

If the Bible teaches it, you can almost bet that the members of the Jesus Seminar don't believe it. In their view, Jesus' birth and resurrection are myths. Prophecies and miracles are thought impossible. For the most part, Jesus' teachings to his followers are considered legends made up by others. For example, seminar members don't just say that Jesus was not the Messiah. They say he never even claimed to be the Messiah. Not only wasn't Jesus the second person of the Godhead; they say he never claimed to be that either.

Bible Lesson

The Gospels of Matthew, Mark, Luke, and John say Jesus once fed 5,000 people by multiplying a few loaves and fishes. The Jesus Seminar scholars tell a different version. They say that at Jesus' signal, the 5,000 pulled out their lunches from beneath their cloaks so they could all eat together.

Naturally, the Jesus Seminar members believe there's no need to repent or to be concerned about heaven and hell. And even though the seminar says that the resurrection didn't happen, they do celebrate Easter's symbolic message of hope and new life. Funk calls Jesus a "secular sage who satirized the pious and championed the poor." He also says, "Jesus was perhaps the first stand-up Jewish comic."

Given their disdain for the canonical Gospel writers, it seems odd that the seminar praises the Gospel of Thomas. Recall from what you read earlier that this book is thought by many to be a forgery that was written in A.D. 400, long after the apostle Thomas had died. Many believe it was written by Gnostics, certain pre-Christian pagan, Jewish, and early Christian sects. Those in opposition to the Seminar's purpose say that this group believes a fifth-century forgery takes precedence over the authentic first-century Gospels.

Voting

The Jesus Seminar members vote, using different colored beads, on their opinion of whether or not a statement was actually said by Jesus. The bead color scheme is as follows:

Red: Jesus undoubtedly said this or something very like it.
Pink: Jesus probably or might have said something like this.
Gray: Jesus did not say this, but the ideas are close to his own.
Black: Jesus did not say this; it represents a later tradition.

Many believe voting is an unusual method of scholarship. Those who oppose the Jesus Seminar's practices and beliefs ask, where is the historical evidence, the textual research, the hermeneutical approach? According to some, the seminar scholars base their votes on their own presuppositions instead of on objective evidence.

Bible Codes

Michael Drosnin, a former *Wall Street Journal* and *Washington Post* reporter, wrote *The Bible Code* in 1997. Though he is not a biblical scholar, historian, or theologian, Mr. Drosnin claims to find secret messages in the Bible that predict the assassinations of John F. Kennedy, Anwar Sadat, and Yitzhak Rabin. Letters, words, or phrases appear with equal spacing between the letters in a word or the words in a phrase. The so-called messages may be read horizontally, vertically, diagonally, or even backwards.

Secret Biblical Messages?

Is it possible that God inspired secret messages to be written into the Bible? Some say the Bible itself denies this possibility. For example, take a look at Isaiah 45:19: "I have not spoken in secret, from somewhere in a land of darkness; I have not said to Jacob's descendants, 'Seek me in vain.' I, the Lord, speak the truth; I declare what is right." Christians believe that the prophet Isaiah clearly states that God reveals his truth, without keeping secrets. Those in opposition to Drosnin's theories ask, why would God conceal secret messages that can only be found by modern computers? Why should we be given messages denied to our ancestors?

Hidden Codes in Other Books

Different people claim to have found so-called hidden codes in other large books as well. For instance, some people found their names in Charles Darwin's *Origin of the Species*. Others claim to have found hidden messages in the Koran, Herman Melville's *Moby Dick*, and even in Ted Kaczynski's Unabomber Manifesto. Leo Tolstoy's massive tome, *War and Peace*, is supposedly a treasure trove of secrets. The word *Bulls* was found thirty-two times in Book One, as were the words *Jordan*, *Chicago*, *President Clinton*, *Apollo*, and *moon*.

Timeless Truth

Some say hidden codes and messages can be found in any book that has half-a-million words or more. Even Drosnin's book, *The Bible Code*, contains hidden messages, including this one: "the code is evil." According to some, what Mr. Drosnin claims for the Bible can be found in any book.

Strangely, some claim the phrase "God is dead" can be found in the Torah. The phrase, "there is no God" can supposedly be found five times. However, some scholars say it's inconceivable that such phrases would be hidden messages in a text that establishes God's existence, creation work, and the first redemptive prophecies.

Cryptograms

A cryptogram is a type of code, and there are some cryptograms in the Bible. For example, the prophet Jeremiah writes *Sheshach* in Jeremiah 25:26 as code for Babylon (Jeremiah 51:41). Here the Hebrew alphabet is reversed. Additionally, Jeremiah writes *Leb Kamai* (Jeremiah 51:1), which stands for Chaldea, which in turn refers to Babylon. Some believe the existence of such cryptograms supports Drosnin's theories.

Gematria

Probably the most famous and most interpreted code in the Bible is the mark of the beast, the infamous "666" (Revelation 13:18). This is called *gematria*, which is "manipulation with numbers." According to this theory, names have a definite numerical value. For example, "Nero Caesar," in the Greek, adds up to 666. However, in Hebrew, the name only adds up to 616. But none of this is significant. The number seven represents perfection in the Bible, and seven minus one equals six, the number that represents man. The number three represents God (the Father, the Son, and the Holy Spirit). With this information, one can deduce that Revelation's 666 represents the Antichrist. This is the man (6) who makes himself God (3)—i.e., three sixes represents man making himself God.

J. R. R. Tolkien: *The Lord of the Rings*

After the success of his children's book *The Hobbit*, J. R. R. Tolkien's publishers requested a sequel. The author took seventeen years to complete the manuscript of *The Lord of the Rings*, a complex tale of good versus evil. Tolkien set both books in Middle Earth, a mystical land inhabited by men, elves, wizards, and hobbits. A philologist and Oxford professor, Tolkien (1892–1973) longed to uncover a mythology belonging to England. He spent most of his life writing and rewriting *The Silmarillion*, a collection of stories that includes a creation narrative, a rebellion, and judgment. Tolkien's devotion to his project included developing languages for his various cultures and complicated genealogies for many of his characters.

A devout Catholic who influenced C. S. Lewis's decision to become a Christian, Tolkien's writings of Middle Earth explore Christian themes of good and evil, sacrificial redemption, mortality and immortality, without mentioning religion.

Timeless Truth

Both J. R. R. Tolkien and C. S. Lewis were Inklings, a group of writers who met nearly every Thursday night to read and discuss their unfinished literary works. It's known that Tolkien read his *Lord of the Rings* manuscript to his fellow Inklings as he was writing and rewriting.

Tolkien's books and expansive Middle Earth mythology gained millions of new fans with the release of the three *Lord of the Rings* movies directed by New Zealander Peter Jackson. The final movie, *Return of the King* (2003), won a clean sweep of the 2004 Academy Awards, taking home all eleven Oscars for which it was nominated (tying with *Ben Hur* of 1959 and *Titanic* of 1997). It has been said that the dense mythology, didactic story, and character genealogy of *The Lord of the Rings* is highly reminiscent of the Bible, one of the possible reasons behind its popularity.

C. S. Lewis: *The Chronicles of Narnia*

C. S. Lewis (1898–1963), a professor of medieval and Renaissance literature, taught at both Oxford and Cambridge Universities. He was a prolific writer in various genres, but he is perhaps best known for his series of children's stories about four orphaned children who discover a mysterious world through the doors of an old wardrobe. Central to *The Chronicles of Narnia* is the lion Aslan, an allegorical Jesus, who encounters the children during their various adventures in magical Narnia. "I wrote the books I should have liked to read," Lewis once said. "That's always been my reason for writing."

Lewis also wrote the popular *Screwtape Letters* and *Mere Christianity*, a science fiction series known as the *Space Trilogy*, and several other works. He once called himself a most reluctant Christian, but said his intellectual honesty wouldn't allow him not to believe in Jesus. In his view accepting Jesus solely as a great moral teacher just wasn't possible. Because of the claims Jesus made, Lewis insisted only three possibilities existed: Jesus was a lunatic who believed he was God, a liar who claimed to be God, or who he said he was, the Son of God.

Look in the Book

The characters and events in an allegory represent specific ideas and themes. *The Chronicles of Narnia* is often classified as an allegory because of its spiritual parallels to Christianity and church history. For example, the wardrobe is the entryway into a spiritual kingdom and the queen-witch is evil. The siblings battle the wicked queen and Aslan sacrifices himself for one of the brothers.

The *Left Behind* Series

Christian authors Jerry Jenkins and Tim LaHaye teamed up to write a series of books promoting dispensational premillennialism. The final product was the *Left Behind* series, published in 1995. In the books' view of the end times, Christians are taken to heaven (raptured), while the rest of mankind stays on earth. The sensational series begins with Christians throughout the world simply disappearing in the secret rapture. The remaining non-Christians are left to wonder what happened to them.

A Scottish teenager, Margaret MacDonald, claimed she had a vision of a secret rapture in 1830. This supposed aspect of the last times was unknown before then. An early leader of the Plymouth Brethren, John N. Darby, gave credence to the teenager's secret rapture tenet in his writings. Other teachers and preachers embraced this view, which was eventually incorporated into the *Scofield Reference Bible*.

The word *rapture* does not appear in the Bible; however, the concept is worthy of your attention. The Latin word *rapio* means "to be caught up, snatch out, or gather out of." The following three biblical passages pertain to the rapture.

Just as the Tares (Matthew 13:24–43)

First, look at the parable of the wheat and the tares. This parable is about the sowing of wheat and the sowing of tares, or weeds, in a field. Both the wheat and the tares were permitted to grow together in the field until the time of the harvest. At that time, the tares were gathered *first* and *then* the wheat was gathered by the reapers (Matthew 13:30).

The disciples later came to Jesus wanting an explanation of the parable. Jesus explained the parable by correlating its points to the elements of the second coming. Jesus made the following points of comparison:

- The Kingdom of Heaven (13:24) equals a man (Jesus) who sowed good seed (13:37).
- The good seed (13:24) equals sons of the Kingdom or God's people (13:38).
- The field (13:24) equals the world (13:38).
- The enemy (13:25) equals the Devil (13:39).
- The tares (13:25) equal sons of the evil one/unbelievers (13:38).
- The harvest (13:30) equals the end of the age (13:39).
- The reapers (13:30) equal God's angels (13:39).
- The rapture equals the gathering (13:28–30, 40, 41).

In Jesus' explanation of the parable, he gives the order of the rapture. The Gospel of Matthew says that just as the tares are gathered, so it will be at the end of the age (Matthew 13:40). How were the tares gathered (raptured)? This Gospel also says the tares were gathered *first*, and then the wheat was gathered second (Matthew 13:30).

The Bible says that at the second coming of Jesus, he will send the reapers (angels) and gather out (rapture) all who offend and practice lawlessness (the tares/sons of the evil one/non-Christians; Matthew 13:41). This passage teaches a two-phase rapture, one of the wicked or unbelievers and one of believers. It says the wicked will be raptured *before* the believers (Matthew 13:30).

Just as in the Days of Noah (Matthew 24:36–44)

The Bible says no one except the Father knows the day when Jesus will return a second time (Matthew 24:36). The days before the second coming will be just like the days of Noah before the Flood (Matthew 24:37). What were the days of Noah like? They were characterized by people concerned with matters of the world. They were eating, drinking, marrying and giving in marriage until the day Noah entered the ark (Matthew 24:38). They (the unbelievers) did not know of their impending destruction until the Flood came and took them all away (Matthew 24:39), thus leaving only eight righteous people alive on the earth. According to the Bible, this is what will take place at the second coming (Matthew 24:39).

Bible Lesson

According to the Bible, at the time of the rapture, two men will be working in the field. One will be taken and the other will be left (Matthew 24:40). Which one was taken? The answer is the one who didn't know (Matthew 13:39)—i.e., the nonbeliever. Two women will be working at the mill. One will be taken and the other one will be left. The one taken is the one who corresponds to the days of Noah—those who do not know (the wicked). The righteous, as in Noah's case, will be left to be taken in the second phase of the rapture.

The Bible shows that no one knew the time of the impending Flood. But Noah and his family were watching for its coming. They were ready so they were not swept away (raptured) by the Flood. The second coming of Jesus also will come at a time when Christians do not expect it (Matthew 24:44). Those not ready or watching (the nonbelievers) will be raptured (swept away), leaving believers (just like Noah) to be raptured afterwards.

First Thessalonians 4:13–18

In this passage, Paul states that there will be a shout from Jesus, the voice of the archangel Michael, and a trumpet blast. It's hard to keep a secret making that much noise. Paul also says that when Jesus returns again, he will bring those who have fallen asleep (dead Christians) with him

(1 Thessalonians 4:13–14). Christians who are alive when the Lord comes back will not precede those who have died in Christ (1 Thessalonians 4:15). Jesus brings Christians' souls back to reunite with their physical bodies. The dead in Christ will rise first (physical resurrection; 1 Thessalonians 4:16). Second, those Christians who are alive and remain will be caught up in the air (raptured) and all Christians will always be with the Lord (1 Thessalonians 4:17). The contrast or comparison is with two groups of Christians: dead Christians and living Christians.

Look in the Book

Paul does not mention the non-Christian phase of the rapture. He was only concerned with the rapture of Christians, whether dead or alive, at Jesus' second coming. The viewpoint presented in the *Left Behind* series of a secret rapture leaving non-Christians behind on the earth is not supported in the very Bible that Jerry Jenkins and Tim LaHaye use. Their novels are fun to read, but lack biblical support in their main thrust of a "secret rapture."

The Bible teaches that all people, whether wicked or righteous, will be raptured. There are two phases of the rapture: The wicked will be raptured first followed by the rapture of the righteous. The Bible says God is going to clear the earth by rapturing everyone to his throne room. The physical universe will be evacuated for its redemption—the renovation of the universe—while mankind will stand before God in judgment (Romans 8:20–22; 2 Peter 3:10–13).

The Passion of the Christ

Despite tremendous negative publicity, Mel Gibson's movie about the arrest, trials, graphic beatings, and execution of Jesus was an overnight financial success. Its popularity is even more remarkable considering that the movie's dialogue is spoken in Latin and Aramaic (though it has English subtitles). The movie's script was based on the Gnostic Alexandrian manuscripts. Father William Fulco, a Jesuit priest, translated the English script.

Timeless Truth

Gibson reportedly spent $25 million of his own money to finance the film and, despite his personal popularity as an actor, had trouble finding a distributor. The movie opened on Ash Wednesday, February 25, 2004 in over 3,000 North American theaters. It earned an incredible $23.6 million. A month later it was released in the United Kingdom and Ireland. Other countries first got to see it during the Easter season.

Though Gibson said he wanted to be true to the Gospels, several scenes in the film aren't found in the Bible. For example, as Jesus is being beaten, Mary awakens and seems to sense his torment. In Aramaic, she asks, "Why is this night unlike any other night?" This comes from the Jewish liturgy of the Passover and refers to the Angel of Death passing over the homes of the Hebrews the night before Pharaoh freed them from slavery. Jesus was crucified during the Passover season. A few other examples of added material include:

- Satan watches as Jesus prays in the Garden of Gethsemane.
- After Jesus' arrest and while he is in chains, he falls from a wall. As he dangles there, Jesus looks into the eyes of his betrayer, the apostle Judas, who just happens to be sitting near the wall.
- Judas is pursued by demon-children.
- In one scene, Mary, Jesus' mother, and Mary Magdalene are standing with the soldiers. Jewish women would never be in such close company with Roman soldiers.
- Jesus would have been scourged tied to a post or pillar. The Roman soldiers look as if they don't have a clue to what they're doing, instead of being professional executioners.
- Jesus is crucified on the familiar Greek cross—i.e., a cross shaped like the small letter t. However, Jesus was crucified by the Romans on a cross shaped like a capital T.
- Jesus remains stationary on the cross, but he would have to raise himself up to inhale (a T-position) and then sag back down to exhale (a Y-position).
- Birds peck out the eyes of one of the bandits.

- Mary, Jesus' mother, is still at the cross when Jesus died (which conflicts with the biblical accounts).

Scenes that aren't in the Bible are mostly taken from the writings of two Catholic nuns, the mystics St. Anne Catherine Emmerich, an eighteenth-century Augustinian nun, and Mary of Agreda, a seventeenth-century Franciscan nun. Gibson said that St. Anne "supplied me with stuff I never would have thought of" (*The New Yorker*, Sept. 15, 2003).

Timeless Truth

The Dolorous Passion of Our Lord Jesus Christ, written by St. Anne, begins with Satan accusing Jesus of "having spent the price of the property of Mary Magdalen at Magdalum." Her vision is otherwise unexplained. Mary Magdalene stayed at the cross while most of Jesus' apostles deserted him. For this reason, St. Anne exalts her. This Mary also went with Mary, Jesus' mother, and the apostle John and performed the stations of the Cross on the Via Dolorosa.

Though the movie graphically portrays the horrors of Jesus' final twelve hours on earth before his death, it dramatizes events from extrabiblical sources. Students of the Bible are encouraged to know which scenes come from the Bible and which scenes come from the visions of mystic nuns.

The movie also condenses events. The Gospel accounts indicate that Jesus endured six illegal trials, while the movie doesn't show this.

1. Before Annas
2. Before Caiaphas and the Sanhedrin (only twenty-four members had to be present)
3. Before the Sanhedrin
4. Before Pontius Pilate
5. Before Herod
6. Before Pilate for a second time

While celebrated for such aspects as its actors, music score, and cinematography, Gibson's film inspired controversy around the globe. Biblical scholars point out its nonadherence to the Bible, while others enjoy the film's provocative perspective and artistic value.

Church and State

"We have staked the whole future of American Civilization," writes James Madison, chief framer and architect of the U.S. Constitution, "upon the capacity of each and all of us to govern ourselves according to the Ten Commandments of God." It is widely believed that the idea for three separate branches of the government of the United States of America comes from Isaiah 33:22, which says, "For the Lord is our judge, the Lord is our lawgiver, the Lord is our king." From a Christian perspective, the Founding Fathers based America's judicial, legislative, and executive branches on this Scripture. Here are a few more little known facts:

- Of the fifty-five people drafting the Constitution, fifty-two were Christians.
- Of the fifty-six signers of the Declaration of Independence, twenty-seven had Bible seminary degrees.
- Thirty-four percent of documents written between 1760 and 1805 quoted the Bible; no other source was quoted as frequently.
- Ninety-four percent of all quotes by the Founding Fathers were based on the Bible.

This kind of devotion to Scripture as the basis for political thought doesn't dominate today's government leaders as it did the Founding Fathers. Instead, today's American government officials and citizens work to build and maintain a separation between church and state.

Just as you did with the Bible, take some time to reference the document at hand, the Constitution. The First Amendment to the Constitution states, "Congress shall make no law respecting an establishment of religion, or prohibiting the free exercise thereof." The words are simple ones, as is their meaning: Congress absolutely cannot establish a national religion. Keep in mind that many of those who first came to America did so because they didn't want to be members of whatever church the current British monarch favored. This amendment was important because the "people feared one sect might obtain a preeminence, or two combine together," said Madison, "and establish a religion to which they would compel others to conform."

"Wall of Separation"

The phrase "wall of separation," so often bandied around to justify removing any Christian influence from the government sphere, was first written by Thomas Jefferson in a private letter to the Danbury [Connecticut] Baptist Association dated January 1, 1802. They had heard a rumor that the government was planning to establish the First Congregationalists Church. Jefferson reassured them that no one denomination would be favored over another. He didn't use the phrase in any *official* document and certainly never intended for the principles of Christianity to be eliminated from government. The "wall" he spoke of was to protect the church from the state, not the state from the church. No historical document proposes the absolute separation of church and state.

Supreme Court Justice Hugo Black took the opportunity to rewrite the First Amendment in *Everson v. Board of Education of Ewing Township* in 1947. He stated that the "First Amendment has erected a wall between church and state. That wall must be kept high and impregnable. We could not approve the slightest breach." ACLU lawyer Leo Pheffer wrote the decision, which promoted the so-called separation of church and state. No precedents are included in the decision, though the Supreme Court had previously declared America as a Christian nation. The first declaration, *Church of the Holy Trinity v. United States*, was in 1892. The second was *United States v. Macintosh* in 1931.

"Safeguarding the Free Exercise"

The second phrase of the First Amendment forbids the government interfering with a citizen's freedom to worship as he pleases. Nothing in the First Amendment says that Christians aren't allowed to participate in politics or that they have to check their religious views on the way out of the church-building door.

So which is it? Does the First Amendment guarantee that Americans are free *from* Christianity or does it guarantee freedom *of* religion? Alabama judge Roy Moore believes so strongly that it's the latter that he defied a federal order to remove a monument to the Ten Commandments, which weighed

5,300 pounds, from his state courthouse. His belief and defiance cost him his job even though Moses is shown, with his famous Ten Commandments, on federal buildings, including a frieze on the Supreme Court building itself.

Timeless Truth

Writing for the majority in the case of *United States v. Ballard* in 1944, Justice Douglas writes about the dual aspect of the First Amendment. He says that the amendment not only "forestalls compulsion by law of the acceptance of any creed or the practice of any form of worship," but also "safeguards the free exercise of the chosen form of religion."

The Constitution's Tenth Amendment says that the powers that aren't given to the federal government in the Constitution belong to the states. Since, by virtue of the First Amendment, the federal government can't make laws regarding the establishment of religion, what federal laws did Moore break? Did the federal government violate the right of the state of Alabama to make its own decision about the monument? If religious liberty is slowly being eroded away, as many Christians fear, then more is at stake here than a complex legal question and a block of stone.

The Supreme Court Decisions of June 27, 2005

On June 27, 2005, the Supreme Court ruled that displaying the Ten Commandments inside courthouses violates the dogma of separation of church and state (the Kentucky ruling of *McCreary County v. ACLU*, No. 03-1693), but also ruled that the Ten Commandments could be displayed on government land (the Texas ruling of *Van Orden v. Perry*, No. 03-1500).

Chief Justice Rehnquist said, "Simply having religious content or promoting a message consistent with a religious doctrine does not run afoul of the Establishment Clause." Justice Scalia stated that a "dictatorship of a shifting Supreme Court majority" denied the Ten Commandments' religious meaning. He stated, "Nothing stands behind this court's assertion that governmental affirmation of the society's belief in God is unconstitutional except in the court's own say-so."

Just the Beginning

Through reading this book, you have journeyed back in time as a detective and examined the evidence of literature, archaeology, and science. You have investigated wondrous and mysterious artifacts and events, and explored hundreds of Bible passages in pursuit of the truth behind the stories. But the adventures don't end with this book; this is only the beginning. There are so many exciting places to explore and excavate. Even the best-educated, most devoted scholars in the world have only just begun to scratch the surface.

There are so many literary documents to translate and learn from. Seeking them out and uncovering the facts they hold is the only way to discover the truth about the past. The world holds so much knowledge, and it's all out there just waiting to be found! Keep a lookout for new archaeological finds and discoveries. Look at all the evidence, be logical, and, most importantly, think for yourself.

Timeless Truth

Sincerity is an admirable trait, but keep in mind that Saul of Tarsus was sincere in his persecution of the early Christians—and was also sincerely wrong. Don't accept anything without investigating it for yourself. Don't be afraid to look at alternatives to your own positions and to expand your own horizons.

The Bible is an ancient text that many deem largely impossible to confirm or deny. Think of it as a great mystery to be solved, though it may not be solved in this lifetime, or the next, or ever. As time passes, more and more historical and archaeological evidence is uncovered, but time also serves to bring ancient documents and artifacts further wear and tear. For this reason, it's important to be diligent and consistent in your continued study of the history of the Bible. Beware of those who seek to completely assert or discount any one hypothesis without providing evidence to back up their claims. Keep an open mind and let the facts guide you as you move forward on your biblical journey of discovery!

Appendix A
Glossary of Terms

Abraham

Abraham is known as the father of the Israelite nation and the father of all believers. God told Abraham to leave his homeland in Ur and go to the promised land of Canaan. There, God entered a covenant with him (Genesis 12:1–3; 15:12–21). The Jewish people regard themselves as Abraham's descendants and as a special people chosen by God (Isaiah 51:1–2). From a spiritual standpoint, God promised Abraham, "all peoples on earth will be blessed through you" (Genesis 12:3).

Adam

Adam, the first human ever created by God, was made in God's own image (Genesis 1:26). After naming all of the animals, Adam fell into a deep sleep. God took his rib and created Eve (Genesis 2:19–22). They were commanded to "be fruitful and increase in number; fill the earth and subdue it" (Genesis 1:28). Because of their later disobedience, eating fruit from the Tree of Life, Adam and Eve were expelled from the Garden of Eden (Genesis 3:23).

Adoptionism

The heretical theory that Jesus was in nature a man who became God by adoption.

Allegory

A literary narrative in which persons, places, and events are given symbolic meanings.

Annas

A former Jewish high priest who was present at Jesus' trial (John 18:13). Annas was the father-in-law of Caiaphas, who was the high priest at that time.

Antilegomena

The early church historian Eusebius used this term for the disputed writings that were neither universally accepted (homologoumena) in the biblical canon nor universally rejected as authoritative.

Apocalyptic

Of or pertaining to a religious world view that anticipates the imminent end of the world.

Apocalyptic literature

A branch of prophetic writing that flourished in Judaism from about 200 B.C. to A.D. 140.

Apocrypha

A body of Jewish religious writings published under the names of apostolic writers that dated from about 200 B.C. to A.D. 100. These books were not included in the official Hebrew Bible canon. The term *apocrypha* is from the Greek ta *apokrypha*, meaning "the hidden things." These texts were deliberate fabrications and never had any serious claim to be in the Bible canon.

Aramaic

The West Semitic language of the Arameans (ancient Syrians) that was spoken in parts of Mesopotamia from about 1000 B.C. After the Babylonian captivity (538 B.C.), it became the common language of the Israelites and was the language Jesus spoke on a daily basis.

Athanasius

Athanasius (A.D. 296–373) was the Bishop of Alexandria from A.D. 328–373. He is considered the greatest theologian of his time.

Augustus Caesar

Octavian, known as Augustus Caesar, was the first emperor of Rome (31 B.C.–A.D. 14). His leadership brought peace, the Pax Romana, to the Roman world, which had endured centuries of civil war. According to Luke 2, Octavian's decree ordering a census of "the whole world" was the reason Joseph and Mary were in Bethlehem when Jesus was born.

Baptism

The Greek word *baptidzo* means "to immerse." This ceremony was first associated with John the Baptist, who baptized the Jewish people and Jesus (Mark 1:4; 11:30; Luke 7:29). On the Day of Pentecost, Christian baptism was commanded for the forgiveness of sins and the gift of the Holy Spirit (Acts 2:38).

Bar Kochba

This name means "son of the star" and refers to the leader of the Second Jewish Revolt against Rome (A.D. 132–135).

Beatification

Through this legal process, the Roman Catholic Church determines whether a deceased servant of God is worthy of special recognition in a particular church, diocese, or region. A beatified person is called "blessed."

Bethlehem

This small town located about five miles south of Jerusalem was the birthplace of both King David (1 Samuel 17:12) and Jesus (Micah 5:2; Matthew 2:5–6; Luke 2; John 7:42).

Bible

The English word *Bible* is derived from the Greek *biblion*, which means "roll" or "book." A biblion was a roll of papyrus or byblus, a reedlike plant. It was widely used as a writing material in the ancient world. The sixty-six books of the Bible are divided into the Old and New Testaments.

Bishop

The title of "bishop" describes the function of a presbyter or elder in the church. In Acts 20:17–28 and Titus 1:5–7, these terms are used interchangeably. The qualifications for becoming a bishop or elder are found in 1 Timothy 3 and Titus 1.

Black, Hugo

Hugo Black (1886–1971) was the Supreme Court Justice credited for rewriting the First Amendment in the 1947 *Everson v. Board of Education* case. In his youth, Black was a member of the Ku Klux Klan. He was anti-Catholic and feared religious influence in public life.

Caesar

A hereditary name used by the Roman emperors to commemorate Gaius Julius Caesar, the great-uncle and adopted son of Octavian (Caesar Augustus), Rome's first emperor (Luke 2:1; 3:1; Mark 12:14; Acts 11:28; 25:11).

Caiaphas

Joseph Caiaphas was the High Priest of Jerusalem during the reign of the emperor Tiberius Caesar and condemned Jesus in an illegal trial (Matthew 26:3; 57–66; John 9:49; 18:13–28; Acts 4:6).

Calvary

The place outside Jerusalem's walls where Jesus was crucified (Luke 23:33). *Calvary* derives from the Latin word *calveria*, a translation that means "skull" (Matthew 27:33; John 19:17). Its location is best attested to being inside the Church of the Holy Sepulcher.

Canon

Generally, a standard by which religious beliefs, sculpture, architecture, or documents are judged acceptable. The word, from the Greek *kanon*, specifically refers to the books of the Bible, which are considered sacred and authoritative by the apostles and prophets of God and recognized by Christians.

Canonization

A legal process in the Roman Catholic Church in which a deceased servant of God, who has already been beatified, is declared a saint. Such persons are entered into the canon or catalog of saints invoked at the celebration of Mass.

Capernaum

A town located on the northwest shore of the Sea of Galilee. Jesus stayed there during his Galilean ministry (Matthew 9:1, 9–11; Mark 1:21–29; 2:3–11; Luke 7; John 4:46–54).

Cardinal

A senior official in the hierarchy of the Roman Catholic Church.

A prospective cardinal is nominated by the pope and, since 1962, is raised to the office of bishop if it's not already held. Cardinals are required to reside in Rome unless they are diocesan bishops. They wear a special cassock and red skull cap and have the title of "Eminence."

Catholic

A transliteration of the Greek *katholikos*, which means "throughout the whole" or "general." This term has been used in a variety of ways during the history of the church.

Centurion

An officer in the Roman army who was in charge of a century, a division of eighty soldiers.

Chalcedon, Council of (A.D. 451)

The fourth council of the church was summoned by the Eastern Emperor Marcion. This council safeguarded both the divine and human natures of Christ existing in one person (*prosopon*) and one substance (*hypostasis*).

Christ

Christ is a title, from the Greek word *Christos*, which, in turn, is a translation of the Aramaic *meshiha* and the Hebrew *mashiah* or *messiah*, which means "the anointed One." It is not a proper name and is definitely not Jesus' surname.

Christian

This name refers to Jesus' followers. In Acts 11:26, Luke tells us that the name originated in Antioch. Here, believers in Jesus were first called (divinely called) Christians. Acts 26:28 records King Agrippa using the word *Christian*. The only other passage in the Bible where the word *Christian* is used is 1 Peter 4:16.

Church, the

In the New Testament, the word *church* translates from the Greek word *ekklesia*, which designates a public assembly of people (Acts 19:32, 39, 41). The Church is not the building where Christians gather to worship, but Christians themselves.

Church and state

The phrase refers to an ancient differentiation between two institutions that both structure and define the lives of human beings. Despite what many believe, America's founding fathers didn't segregate religion from the national life.

Cicero

Cicero (106–43 B.C.) was one of Rome's most famous citizens. He was an exceptional orator, politician, lawyer, and philosopher. Marc Antony ordered his execution. His head and hands were cut off and nailed to the speaker's podium in the Senate.

Claudius

As the fourth Roman emperor (A.D. 41–54), Claudius expelled the Jews from Rome (Acts 11:28; 18:2).

Codex

A manuscript book of an ancient biblical text. Christians pioneered this process to replace the scrolls on which the Scriptures were originally written.

Cornelius

Cornelius was a Roman centurion associated with the Jewish synagogue in Caesarea. He became the first gentile convert to Christianity in A.D. 40 (Acts 10–11).

Councils, church

A council is a conference called by the leaders of the church to give guidance to the church. A council may be either ecumenical and thus represent the entire church, or it may be local, having regional or local representation.

Cross; crucifixion

In the method of execution known as crucifixion, the victim was nailed to a cross. Nails were driven into both wrists of the victim and one large nail was driven through both feet (the right foot on top of the left). It is one of the most painful, cruel, and barbaric forms of execution. Jesus was nailed to a T-shaped cross, called a St. Anthony's cross (*crux commissa*).

Crucifragium

Roman soldiers smashed the crucified victims' leg bones from their knees to their ankles with a small hammer to hasten death. This procedure was called crucifragium. Once the leg bones were broken, the victim could no longer push up to inhale and died of asphyxiation.

Darby, John Nelson (1800–1882)

The most influential British leader of the separatist Plymouth Brethren movement, Darby believed in a new idea called the secret rapture. By this, he meant that Jesus would come back to earth secretly and rapture (snatch) Christians from the earth and leave the non-Christians behind.

David

The youngest son of Jesse, David was a shepherd who became the second king of Israel (1000 B.C.). He created an Israelite empire (1 Samuel 16; 2 Kings 2) and was succeeded by his son Solomon.

Dead Sea Scrolls

These scrolls are a collection of ancient documents preserved in caves near Qumran on the northeast shore of the Dead Sea. The first scrolls were found by a young Bedouin boy who was herding his goats.

Death

In Christianity, death is separation. Physical death is the separation of the soul or spirit from the physical body. Spiritual death is when the soul, the image of God, is separated from God (the soul is dead). Eternal death is the eternal separation of an individual from God and everything else in a place called hell.

Docetism

This belief, associated with the Gnostic community, held that Jesus was pure spirit and only appeared to be physically human. It comes from the Greek verb meaning "to seem."

Ebionites

The Ebionites were ascetics who chose poverty as a way of life. They were heretical in their teachings about Jesus because they denied his divinity. They rejected the Pauline letters, and saw Christianity only as obedience to a moral code.

Emmaus

A town near Jerusalem. The resurrected Jesus appeared to two disciples who were walking from Jerusalem to Emmaus on the Sunday after the crucifixion (Luke 24:13–32).

Ephesus, Council of

The Council of Ephesus met to discuss whether the Virgin Mary should be called *Theotokos* ("mother of God").

Essenes

According to Josephus, the Essenes were one of the three major sects of Judaism in the first century A.D. They are usually associated with the Qumran area and with the Dead Sea Scrolls, but there is no evidence that they were ever at Qumran.

Eve

The name of the first woman, created by God from one of Adam's ribs, who "would become the mother of all the living" (Genesis 3:20). Eve was created because it was "not good for the man to be alone," so God made "a helper suitable for him" (Genesis 2:18). This means that Eve was equal to Adam and that they were complementary to each other.

Evolution, organic

Organic evolution teaches that life comes from sterile nonlife and increases complexity and at some point in time generates successive replication—all by itself. This is called *spontaneous generation*, and also called *abiogenesis*.

Exegesis

The analysis and interpretation of a written text to discover the author's intended meaning.

Fathers, Church

The Church Fathers were the first Christian writers of acknowledged eminence from the second century through the sixth century A.D.

Flood, Noah's

The Flood described in Genesis is a genuine historical event of catastrophic proportion that involved the "fountains of the deep" erupting and the canopy of water that surrounded the earth collapsing (Genesis 7:11). During the Flood, the mountains of the earth were submerged (Genesis 7:19–20). The Flood was a punishment for mankind's unrepentant wickedness (Genesis 6:5).

Galilee, Sea of

The major body of fresh water in northern Israel and the source of livelihood for many Galilean fishermen (Luke 23:5–7).

Gallio

Gallio was a proconsul of Asia (the Roman province of Greece) who dismissed the charges brought against Paul by the Corinthian Jews (Acts 18:12–17).

Gentile

A non-Jewish person, a member of the nations that are not in a covenant relationship with God (Yahweh). Jewish writers commonly refer to gentiles as "the uncircumcised" because they didn't bear this ritual mark of the covenant people.

Gnosis

The Greek word for "knowledge."

Gnosticism

This extremely diverse and heretical group was totally devoted to the destruction of Christianity. The followers believed that salvation is gained through a special knowledge (gnosis).

Gospels, Apocryphal

These false and heretical books were attributed to the apostles. They were recognized by the early church as false because they were written hundreds of years after the apostles died.

Hebrew Bible

A collection of sacred writings written in Hebrew with some Aramaic. The Hebrew Bible was divided into three parts: the Torah or Law; the Prophets; and the Other Writings.

Heresy

A theological statement that is contrary to the sacred writings of the Old and New Testaments.

Herod the Great

Herod the Great, also known as Herod I, was the Idumean Roman-appointed king of Judea (40–4 B.C.). He was the ruler when Jesus was born (Matthew 2:1).

Herodias

The granddaughter of Herod the Great and the daughter of Aristobulus. She was the half-sister of Herod Agrippa I. John the Baptist condemned her for deserting her first husband and marrying Herod Antipas, who had divorced his wife to marry Herodias. Through her conniving, John the Baptist was beheaded (Matthew 14:1–12; Mark 6:17–29; Luke 2:19–20).

Hittites
The Hittite Empire dominated Mesopotamia, Syria, and Israel from 1600–1200 B.C. The Hittites invented iron to make weaponry. They invaded Egypt and controlled the Egyptian people until about 1552 B.C., when Ahmose drove them out of Egypt.

Holy Spirit, The
The third person in the Holy Trinity or Godhead, which includes God the Father, God the Son, and God the Holy Spirit. All three are the one God, but they are distinct persons.

Homologoumena
This refers to the writings of the New Testament, which are universally recognized in the church as canonical.

Incarnation
The incarnation refers to the conception of God the Son (the pre-incarnate Christ) in a young virgin girl named Mary. Jesus didn't cease to be God when he took on a human nature.

Inspiration
A supernatural guidance exerted on chosen individuals (prophets and apostles) by God to ensure that they made

no mistakes in what they said or wrote. The message, whether spoken or written, was free of error and included all that God deemed necessary for salvation and service.

Interpretation of the Bible
The biblical documents were written in Hebrew, Greek, and Aramaic at various times between 1450 B.C. to A.D. 96. A proper interpretation of these documents requires an understanding of their different historical and cultural settings to determine the writer's intended meaning.

Irenaeus
Irenaeus (A.D. 130–200) was a Greek father of the early church. He was the bishop of Lyons in Gaul.

James
The eldest of Jesus' half-brothers named in the Gospels (Matthew 13:55; Mark 6:3), James did not believe that Jesus was God the Son (Matthew 12:46–50; Mark 3:31–35; Luke 8:19–21; John 7:3–5). He became a Christian after Jesus appeared to him after his resurrection (1 Corinthians 15:7). A leader in the Jerusalem Church, James wrote the New Testament book bearing his name (Acts 15:13–34; 21:18–26).

Jamnia, Academy of
An assembly of rabbis and Pharisees who met in A.D. 90 to define Judaism after

it had been devastated by the Romans in the destruction of Jerusalem.

Jerome

Jerome (A.D. 347–419) was a biblical scholar and translator who aspired to introduce the best Greek learning to Western Christianity. Working from the Hebrew Old Testament and the Greek New Testament, he produced the Latin Vulgate. It took him twenty-three years.

Jesus

The name given to God the Son when he was born to the virgin girl named Mary. The name is the English form of a Latin name which is derived from the Greek *Iesous*. This comes from the Hebrew name *Yahoshua*, or Joshua, which means "Yahweh saves."

Jew

The name given to a descendant of the man Abraham and a member of the tribe or kingdom of Judah (2 Kings 16:6; 25:25).

John the Apostle

A Galilean fisherman, John was the son of Zebedee. Both he and his brother James were called by Jesus to be among his twelve apostles (Matthew 4:21–22; Mark 1:19–20).

John the Baptist

John (the Baptist) was the son of the priest Zechariah and Elizabeth (Luke 1:5–24, 56–80). John preached a message of repentance to Israel (Matthew 3:7–12) and baptized (immersed) Jews in water (Matthew 3:6). He was the herald or forerunner of the Messiah. John pointed at Jesus and proclaimed him to be the long-awaited Messiah (John 1:29).

Joseph

The husband of Mary and a legal father of Jesus, Joseph was a descendent of the Bethlehemite David (Matthew 1:20). However, he lived in Nazareth (Luke 2:4), where he was a carpenter (Matthew 13:55).

Josephus, Flavius

An important Jewish historian (A.D. 37–100), Josephus wrote two major works, *Antiquities of the Jews* and *The Jewish War*. The latter covered the revolt and destruction of Jerusalem in A.D. 66–70. These texts provide valuable background material for first-century Judaism and the early Christian first century.

Judaism

The religion and culture of the Jewish people. Jewish civilization includes historical, social, and political dimensions in addition to the religious. The word *Judaism* derives from the Greek *Ioudaismos*, a term first used in the intertestamental period by Greek-speaking Jews to distinguish their religion from

Hellenism. In the New Testament, the word appears twice (Galatians 1:13–14) in reference to Paul's prior consuming devotion to Jewish faith and life.

Jupiter

The Latin name of the chief Roman deity and counterpart of the Greek Zeus, king of the Olympian gods. Some men of Lycaonia mistook Paul's friend Barnabas for Jupiter.

Koine

The common Greek language in which the New Testament was written and was the everyday language of the Hellenistic world.

Kustodian

A kustodian was a Roman military unit of sixteen soldiers and the deadliest fighting force in the ancient world. Their job was solely to guard, protect, and/or bring back to the Roman Emperor whatever belonged to the Emperor. Jesus' body was guarded by a Roman kustodian.

Lamb of God

Twice in the New Testament, Jesus is called the Lamb of God (John 1:29, 35). Jesus is the sacrificial lamb who bears the world's sins and removes it by taking it on himself. He bears on himself alone the iniquity of all mankind and is led as a lamb to the slaughter (Isaiah 53).

Law

The Law refers to the Torah ("teaching; instruction") or Pentateuch, the first five books of the legal material written by Moses. Namely, this is Genesis, Exodus, Leviticus, Numbers, and Deuteronomy.

Left Behind Series, The

A collection of novels written by Tim LaHaye and Jerry Jenkins. These novels deal with the events following a secret rapture. The authors base their works on a relatively new (nineteenth century) theory of how Jesus will return at the second coming. The novels have sold over 75 million copies since first being published in 1995.

Luke

A medical doctor by profession and traveling missionary with Paul (Colossians 4:14; Philemon 24; 2 Timothy 4:11). Many believe that Luke wrote the Gospel of Luke and the book of Acts.

LXX

A common abbreviation for the Septuagint, the Greek translation of the Hebrew Bible made in Alexandria, Egypt in 286 B.C.

Macroevolution

The theory that, through random processes over time, a kind of life (a species) changes into another totally different kind of life (species). For example, the single-celled creature became a multi-cellular marine organism, with fish evolving into amphibians, then into reptiles, and then into birds and mammals.

Magdala

This town on the northwest shore of the Sea of Galilee is the home of Mary Magdalene ("of Magdala"; Matthew 15:39).

Mark

Mark was a Jew from Jerusalem who accompanied his cousin Barnabas and Paul on an early missionary journey (Acts 12:12–25; 13:5, 13; 15:37).

Martyr

A witness for Jesus who dies for his or her faith. The first Christian martyr, Stephen, was stoned to death while Saul of Tarsus held the cloaks of those throwing the stones (Acts 22:20; Revelation 2:13; 17:6).

Martyr, Justin

Justin Martyr (A.D. 100–165) was a defender of the faith who attacked false doctrine. He wrote the *Apology* and the *Dialogue*.

Mary

The young virgin girl who gave birth to Jesus. She was betrothed to and later married Joseph the carpenter. Her name is from the Latin and Greek *Maria*, from the Hebrew *Miryam* (Miriam). The angel Gabriel told her that she had been chosen by God to be the earthly mother of God the Son (Matthew 1:18–25; Luke 1:26–56; 2:1–18, 21). Her sister Salome was the wife of Zebedee and mother of the apostles James and John (John 18:25; Matthew 27:56). She was also related to Elizabeth, the mother of John the Baptist (Luke 1:36).

Masada

This stronghold was built by Herod the Great on a fortified plateau 800 feet above the Dead Sea. Masada was captured by Zealots during the revolt against Rome (A.D. 66). When the attacking Romans finally entered Masada (A.D. 73), they found only seven women and children alive. The others, 953 people, died in a homicide/suicide pact.

Masoretes

Medieval Jewish scholars who copied, annotated, and added vowels to the written text of the Hebrew Bible.

Masoretic Text (MT)

The standard text of the Hebrew Bible as given final form by the Masoretes in the seventh through ninth centuries A.D.

Mesopotamia

The territory between the Euphrates and Tigris rivers at the head of the Persian Gulf (modern Iraq). It was the cradle of civilization of the Sumerians, Akkadians, Assyrians, and Neo-Babylonian civilizations (Genesis 24:10; Judges 3;8–10; 1 Chronicles 19:6; Acts 2:9; 7:2).

Messiah

This Hebrew term means "anointed one." Jesus was the Messiah or "Christ" as expressed in Peter's confession that Jesus is the Christ (Messiah), the Son of the living God (Matthew 16:13–20; Mark 8:27–30; Luke 9:18–22).

Microevolution

The theory of change within pre-existing kinds of life, which deals with heredity and variation. For example, there are changes with dogs, there are changes with cats, etc. There is no crossing over from one species to another—i.e., a dog will not produce a cat, a fish will not evolve into a reptile, a reptile will not become a bird, an apelike creature will not evolve into a human being.

Mid-Oceanic Ridge

The longest continuous mountain system on the earth. It is located on the ocean floors and stretches around the world for a distance of 40,000 miles. It is a place where plate divergence and volcanic and earthquake activity occur.

Mishnah

A collection of Pharisaic oral interpretations (Halakah) of the Torah compiled and edited about A.D. 200.

Monroe, James

James Monroe (A.D. 1758–1831) was president of the United States from 1817 to 1825. He is known for the Monroe Doctrine, which became a major tenet of U.S. foreign policy in the Western Hemisphere.

Moses

The great Hebrew lawgiver and reformer, Moses was the son of Amram, a Levite, and Jochebed, and brother to Aaron and Miriam (Exodus 2:1–4). Adopted by Pharaoh's daughter and raised at the Egyptian royal court (Exodus 2:5–10; Acts 7:2), Moses delivered the Israelites from Egyptian bondage (Exodus 14–15).

Nag Hammadi Library

The Nag Hammadi Library was discovered in 1945 in Egypt. The library is a collection of ancient codices, many of which are primary Gnostic Scriptures that were written hundreds of years after the New Testament was written. The Gnostics were heretical in their teachings and forged documents by signing the names of persons from the first-century world to their documents.

Nazareth

A town in Lower Galilee above the Plain of Esdrelon (Megiddo) where Jesus spent his youth and began his ministry (Matthew 2:23; Luke 1:26; 4:16; John 1:46).

Nebuchadnezzar

Nebuchadnezzar was the second king of the Neo-Babylonian Empire from

605–562 B.C. He conquered Jerusalem and rebuilt Babylon.

Nicaea, Council of

The first ecumenical council in the history of the church was convened by the Emperor Constantine in A.D. 325. The council met to heal the church, which had been ravaged by false teaching.

Nicodemus

A leading Pharisee and member of the Jewish Supreme Court, the Sanhedrin. He visited Jesus at night and was taught about the "new birth" (John 3:1–21). He also defended Jesus against other Pharisees (John 7:45–52) and helped Joseph of Arimathea to bury Jesus' dead body (John 19:38–42).

Pantibulum

The pantibulum was the cross-beam that was fastened to a larger vertical wooden beam to form the Roman T-shaped cross.

Papacy

The pope is the head of the Roman Catholic Church and considered the successor of Peter and the vicar of Christ. He is first of all the bishop of Rome. The word *pope* is derived from the word *pappa*. In the eleventh century A.D., Pope Gregory VII made official the title of pope.

Paradise

Literally a "park" or walled garden, the name referred to the Garden of Eden (Genesis 2:8–17).

Passion

This word is commonly used to refer to Jesus' suffering and death.

Passover

An annual Jewish observance commemorating Israel's last night of bondage in Egypt. On this night, the Angel of Death passed over Israelite homes marked with the blood of a sacrificial lamb to destroy the firstborn of every Egyptian household (Exodus 12:1–5). Beginning the seven-day Feast of Unleavened Bread, the Passover is a ritual meal eaten on the date of Nisan 14 (sometime in March or April) and includes roasted lamb, unleavened bread, and bitter herbs (Exodus 12:15–20; 13:3–10; Leviticus 23:5; Numbers 9:5; 28:16; Deuteronomy 16:1).

Paul

The most influential apostle and missionary and the author of most of the New Testament. First known as Saul of Tarsus, he was a Pharisee and scholar who was also a citizen of Rome. He first persecuted the early church and held the cloaks of those who stoned the first Christian martyr, Stephen. He became a Christian after being blinded by a bright light while on the road to Damascus where he saw the risen Jesus. He was a missionary to the gentiles and may have been martyred in Rome by the Emperor Nero in A.D. 68.

Pentateuch

The first five books of the Hebrew Bible, the Torah. The word comes from a Greek word meaning "five scrolls."

Pentecost

A one-day celebration held fifty days after Passover at the juncture of May and June. It is also called the Feast of Weeks (Exodus 34:22; Deuteronomy 16:10), the Feast of Harvest (Exodus 23:16), and the Day of the First Fruits (Numbers 28:26). On the day of Pentecost, God the Holy Spirit was poured on the apostles assembled in Jerusalem (Acts 2:1–41) signaling the beginning of the Church.

Pesher

This Hebrew word refers to an analysis or interpretation of Scripture and is applied to the commentaries (pesherim) discovered among the Dead Sea Scrolls.

Peter

The most prominent of Jesus' twelve apostles, Peter is also known as Simon, Simeon (Acts 15:14; 2 Peter 1:1), and Cephas (John 1:40–42). He was the son of Jonas or John (Matthew 16:17; John 1:42; 21:15–17), the brother of Andrew, and a native of Bethsaida, a fishing village on the Sea of Galilee (John 1:44). Though he denied knowing Jesus during Jesus' arrest, Peter was a leader of the early Church.

Pharisees

A leading religious group in Judaism during the last two centuries B.C. and the first two centuries A.D. They were the "people's representatives" and were very strict in their observances of the Law. They believed in the physical resurrection and believed in angels. The apostle Paul was a Pharisee (Acts 23:6; 26:5; Philippians 3:5).

Philo Judaeus

The most influential philosopher of Hellenistic Judaism, Philo was a Greek-educated Jew living in Alexandria, Egypt (20 B.C.–A.D. 50).

Pilate, Pontius

Pilate was the Roman prefect (also called a procurator) of Judea from A.D. 26–36. He presided at two of Jesus' trials for sedition against Rome and sentenced him to death by crucifixion (Matthew 27:1–26; Mark 15:1–15; Luke 3:1; 13:1; 23:1–25; John 18:28–19:22; Acts 3:13; 13:28; 1 Timothy 6:13).

Prophet

A prophet is a spokesman and law enforcer for God (Deuteronomy 18:9–22; Amos 3:7–8). The word *prophet* comes from the Greek *prophetes*, from *pro* ("before" or "for") and *phemi* ("to speak").

Prophets, the

This term refers to the second major division of the Hebrew Bible. The Prophets are usually divided into the four major prophets—Isaiah, Jeremiah, Ezekiel, and Daniel—and the twelve minor prophets—Hosea, Joel, Amos, Obadiah, Jonah, Micah, Nahum, Habakkuk, Zephaniah, Haggai, Zechariah, and Malachi—according to the length of their writings.

Pseudepigrapha

Literally, this term refers to books falsely ascribed to important biblical people. It is a collection of religious books outside the Hebrew Bible canon composed from about 200 B.C. to A.D. 200.

Qumran, Khirbet

The Dead Sea Scrolls were discovered close to the ruins of this community near the northwest corner of the Dead Sea.

Rabbi

A Jewish title meaning "teacher." Jesus was frequently addressed by this title (Matthew 23:8; 26:25, 49; Mark 8:5; 10:51; 11:21; 14:45; John 1:38, 49; 3:2; 4:31; 6:25; 9:2; 11:8; 20:16). John the Baptist was also called a rabbi (John 3:26).

Relics

Objects preserved as memorials of the earthly lives of saints, Mary, and Jesus, including their bodies and items that came into contact with them.

Reliquaries

Boxes, caskets, or shrines that house the relics of the saints.

Resurrection

The return from physical death to life (Isaiah 26:19; Daniel 12:2–3, 13). Jesus physically was resurrected from the dead. Because of his resurrection, Christians will rise physically from the dead (1 Thessalonians 4; 1 Corinthians 15).

Revelation, general

The divine disclosure to all persons at all times and places by which one comes to know that God exists and what he is like. General revelation mediates the conviction that God exists and that he is self-sufficient, transcendent, immanent, eternal, powerful, wise, good, and righteous. Christians believe that everyone has an internal innate knowledge that God exists. General revelation also includes the external natural world and providential history.

Revelation, special

The recorded knowledge given by God through his prophets and apostles concerning the specific events of redemption. Specific people, places, and events are provided to mankind, which includes God becoming a man in Jesus of Nazareth. The redemption provided by Jesus' death, burial, resurrection, and appearances is written down for all generations in the Bible.

Sadducees

This Jewish group of the first century B.C. and first century A.D. was composed largely of wealthy and political influential landowners. They denied the physical resurrection, angels, and a judgment in the afterlife.

Salome

There are two biblical women named Salome. One was the daughter of Herodias and Herod (son of Herod the Great). She danced before her uncle, Herod Antipas, and at her mother's urging, she asked him for the head of John the Baptist (Matthew 14:3–11; Mark 6:17–28). The second was the sister of Mary, the mother of Jesus.

Samson

Samson was a judge (military leader) of Israel for twenty years (Judges 13–16; Hebrew 11:32). From the tribe of Dan and known for his great strength, he broke his Nazirite vow. He fought the Philistines and died when he destroyed the Philistine temple of the false god Dagon.

Sanhedrin

The Supreme Jewish judicial council from about the third century B.C. until the Romans destroyed Jerusalem in A.D. 70.

Scroll

A roll of papyrus, leather, or parchment. The rolls were made of sheets measuring about nine to eleven inches high and five or six inches wide. These were sewn together to make a strip up to twenty-five or thirty feet long that was wound around a stick and unrolled when read (Isaiah 34:4; Revelation 6:14; Jeremiah 36). The Hebrew Bible and New Testament were written on scrolls.

Septuagint (LXX)

The Greek translation of the Hebrew Old Testament made by seventy-two Jewish scholars in 286 B.C.

Simon Magus

A Samaritan sorcerer, Simon tried to buy the miraculous power of the apostles from Peter (Acts 8:9–24). The sale of church offices is called *simony* after Simon Magus.

Sodom

Along with Gomorrah, Admah, Zebolim, and Zoar (Genesis 13:10–12; 14:2; Deuteronomy 29:23), Sodom was one of the five cities of the plain. It was destroyed by God because of its wickedness (Genesis 19:1–29).

Stipes

The long vertical piece of a cross that was secured into the ground and used by the Romans in crucifixion. A shorter cross-beam would be fastened to this stipes to form a T-shaped cross.

Synagogue

In Judaism, a gathering of no fewer than ten adult males assembled for worship, scriptural instruction, and administration of local Jewish affairs in a synagogue. The term may have originated with Moses or it may refer to "meeting places" in Psalm 74:8. Synagogues may have begun during the Babylonian exile when the Jerusalem Temple no longer existed (Ezekiel 11:16; 8:1; 14:1; 20:1).

Tacitus, Cornelius

Tacitus (A.D. 55–117) was a Roman historian. He wrote the *Annals*, a history of the Roman emperors from Octavian (Caesar Augustus) through Nero. Tacitus also wrote the *Histories*, a history of the Roman emperors from Nero through Domitian.

Talmud

A huge collection of Jewish traditions consisting of two parts: (1) the Mishnah (written editions of ancient oral interpretations of the Torah) and (2) the Gemara (extensive commentaries on the Mishnah).

Ten Commandments

The basic laws of the covenant formed between God and Israel at Mount Sinai in 1440 B.C. In Hebrew, the commandments are called the "Ten Words." The Ten Commandments are recorded twice in the Old Testament. First they were given to Moses in the Sinai Covenant (Exodus 20:2–17). The second time they appear is in the description of the renewal of the covenant on the plains of Moab (Deuteronomy 6:6–21).

Thaddeus

One of the twelve apostles of Jesus (Matthew 10:3; Mark 3:18).

Thomas

Thomas, also called *Didymus* ("twin"), was another of Jesus' twelve apostles (John 11:26; 20:24; 21:2). He didn't believe that Jesus resurrected from the dead until Jesus personally appeared to him, which is the source of the phrase "Doubting Thomas" (John 20:24–29).

Titulus

A placard or board, fastened to a stick, that had a condemned person's crime written on it. This was carried by a Roman soldier in front of the victim who was carrying part of a cross to the place of execution. The titulus was then nailed to the top of the cross. This was done at Jesus' crucifixion.

Torah

Another name for the Pentateuch, the first five books of the Old Testament.

Turin, Shroud of

A linen cloth bearing the double, head-to-toe image of a man who had been severely scourged, beaten, and crucified in the first century A.D. It is kept in Turin, Italy.

Twelve, the

The twelve apostles of Jesus, who were personally chosen by him with a divine commission (Matthew 10:1–5; Mark 3:16–19; Luke 6:12–16; Acts 1:13–14).

Virgin birth of Jesus

The birth of Jesus resulted from a miraculous conception. Jesus was conceived in the womb of the Virgin Mary by the power of God the Holy Spirit without a human father.

Vulgate

Jerome's Latin translation of the Bible.

Zoroastrianism

A dualistic religion established by the east Iranian prophet Zoroaster in the late sixth century B.C. This religion believed that the universe was a duality of spirit and matter, light and darkness, good and evil.

Appendix B
Sources

Albright, William F. *Archaeology and Palestine*. Baltimore: Penguin, 1960.

———. *Archaeology and the Religion of Palestine*. Baltimore: Johns Hopkins, 1953.

———. *From the Stone Age to Christianity*. 2nd ed. Garden City, NJ: Doubleday, 1957.

———. *Recent Discoveries in Bible Lands*. New York: Funk & Wagnalls, 1956.

Allegro, John M. *The Treasure of the Copper Scroll*. 2nd ed. Garden City, NJ: Doubleday, 1965.

Andrews, Herbert T. *An Introduction to the Apocryphal Books of the Old and New Testaments*, revised and edited by Charles F. Pfeiffer. Grand Rapids, MI: Baker, 1964.

Apocrypha. *Revised Standard Version of the Old Testament*. New York: Thomas, 1957.

Archer, Gleason L., Jr. *A Survey of Old Testament Introduction*. Chicago: Moody, 1974.

Barnstone, Willis, and Marvin Meyer. *The Gnostic Bible*. London: Shambhala, 2003.

Barthelemy, D., and J. T. Milik. *Discoveries in the Judean Desert*. London: Oxford Univ. Press, 1955.

Beckwith, Francis. "History and Miracles." *In Defense of Miracles*, edited by R. Douglas Geivett and Gary R. Habermas. Downers Grove, IL: InterVarsity, 1997.

Beckwith, Roger. *The Old Testament Canon of the New Testament Church and Its Background in Early Judaism*. Grand Rapids, MI: Eerdmans, 1986.

Bermant, Chaim, and Michael Weitzman. *Ebla: An Archaeological Enigma*. London: Weidenfeld and Nicholson, 1979.

Bettenson, Henry, ed. *Documents of the Christian Church*. 2nd ed. London: Oxford Univ. Press, 1963.

———, ed. and trans. *The Early Christian Fathers: A Selection from the Writings of the Fathers from St. Clement of Rome to St. Athanasius*. London: Oxford Univ. Press, 1956.

———, ed. and trans. *The Later Christian Fathers: A Selection from the Writings of the Fathers from St. Cyril of Jerusalem to St. Leo the Great*. London: Oxford Univ. Press, 1970.

Biggs, Robert. "The Ebla Tablets: An Interim Perspective." *Biblical Archaeologist* 43, no. 2 (Spring 1980): 76–86.

Biram, Avaraham. "House of David." *Biblical Archaeology Review*. March/April 1994.

Birdsall, J. N. "The New Testament Text." *The Cambridge History of the Bible*, edited by P. R. Ackroyd. Vol. 1, From the Beginnings to Jerome. Cambridge: Cambridge Univ. Press, 1970.

Black, Matthew. *The Scrolls and Christian Origins*. London: 1961.

Blaiklock, E. M., and R. K. Harrison, eds. *The New International Dictionary of Biblical Archaeology*. Grand Rapids, MI: Zondervan, 1983.

Blomberg, Craig. *The Historical Reliability of the Gospels*. Downers Grove, IL: Inter-Varsity, 1987.

———. *Jesus and the Gospels*. Nashville, TN: Broadman & Holman, 1997.

Bock, Darrell. *Breaking the Da Vinci Code: Answers to the Questions Everyone's Asking*. Nashville, TN: Nelson, 2004.

———. "Was Jesus Married to Mary Magdalene? All the Available Evidence Clearly Points to an Answer of 'No.'" ✑*www.ABCNews.com*, November 12, 2003.

Boer, Harry. *Above the Bible: The Bible and Its Critics*. Grand Rapids, MI: Eerdmans, 1975.

Bowker, John. *The Targums and Rabbinic Literature*. London: Cambridge Univ. Press, 1969.

Brown, Colin. *Miracles and the Critical Mind*. Grand Rapids, MI: Eerdmans, 1984.

Brown, Dan. *The Da Vinci Code: A Novel*. New York: Doubleday, 2003.

Brown, Harold O. J. *Heresies*. Garden City, NJ: Doubleday, 1984.

Brown, Walter. *"In the Beginning . . ."* Phoenix, AZ: Center for Scientific Creation, 1989.

Browne, E. J. *Charles Darwin's Voyaging*. Princeton, NJ: Princeton Univ. Press, 1996.

Bruce, F. F. *The Books and the Parchments*. Rev. ed. Westwood, NJ: Revell, 1963.

———. *The Canon of Scripture*. Downers Grove, IL: InterVarsity, 1988.

———. *The English Bible: A History of Translations*. 3rd ed. New York: Oxford Univ. Press, 1978.

———. *The New Testament Documents: Are They Reliable?* Grand Rapids, MI: Eerdmans, 1965.

———. *Second Thoughts on the Dead Sea Scrolls*. Grand Rapids, MI: Eerdmans, 1956.

Carson, D. A. *Exegetical Fallacies*. Grand Rapids, MI: Baker, 1984.

Carson, D. A., Douglas Moo, and Leon Morris. *An Introduction to the New Testament*. Grand Rapids, MI: Zondervan, 1992.

Charles, Robert H., ed. *The Apocrypha and Pseudepigrapha of the Old Testament*. 2 vols. Oxford: Clarendon, 1913.

Craig, William Lane. *Knowing the Truth about the Resurrection*. Ann Arbor, MI.: Servant, 1988.

Cross, F. M., and E. A. Livingstone, eds. *The Oxford Dictionary of the Christian Church*. 2nd ed. London: Oxford Univ. Press, 1974.

Cross, F. M. "The Contributions of the Qumran Discoveries to the Study of the Biblical Text. *Israel Exploration Journal* 16 (1966): 81–95.

———. "New Directions in Dead Sea Scroll Research." *Bible Review* 1:2 (Summer 1985): 12–25; 1:3 (Fall 1985): 26–35.

Dahood, Mitchell. "Afterward: Ebla, Ugarit, and the Bible." In Giovanni Pettinato, *The Archives at Ebla*: *An Empire Inscribed in Clay*. Garden City, NY: Doubleday, 1981.

Danby, Herbert, trans. *The Mishnah*. Oxford: Oxford Univ. Press, 1933.

Darwin, Charles. *The Origin of Species by Means of Natural Selection or The Preservation of Favored Races in the Struggle for Life and The Descent of Man and Selection in Relation to Sex*. New York: Modern Library, n.d.

Douglas, J. D., ed. *The New International Dictionary of the Christian Church*. Rev. ed. Grand Rapids, MI: Zondervan, 1978.

DuPont-Sommer, Andre. *The Essene Writings from Qumran*. Translated by G. Vermes. Cleveland, OH: World, 1962.

Dyck, Cornelius J. "Ebla Update." Articles in *Biblical Archaeology Review*, 1977ff.

Foster, Lewis. "The Earliest Collection of Paul's Epistles." *Bulletin of the Evangelical Theological Society* 10, no. 1 (Winter 1967).

Funk, Robert, Roy Hoover, and the Jesus Seminar. *The Five Gospels: What Did Jesus Really Say?* New York: Macmillan, 1993.

Gaussen, Louis. *Theopneustia: The Bible, Its Divine Origin and Entire Inspiration, Deduced from Internal Evidence and the Testimonies of Nature, History, and Science.* Translated from the French by David D. Scott. (1841; repr., Grand Rapids, MI: Baker, 1971).

Geisler, Norman. *The Battle for the Resurrection.* Nashville, TN: Thomas Nelson, 1989.

———. "Bible Manuscripts." In *Wycliffe Bible Encyclopedia*. Edited by Charles F. Pfeiffer, Howard F. Vos, and John Rea. 2 vols. Chicago: Moody, 1975.

———, ed. *Decide for Yourself: How History Reviews the Bible.* Grand Rapids, MI: Zondervan, 1982.

———. "The Extent of the Old Testament Canon." In *Current Issues in Biblical and Patristic Interpretation*. Edited by Gerald F. Hawthorne. Grand Rapids, MI: Eerdmans, 1975.

———. *Miracles and Modern Thought.* Grand Rapids, MI: Zondervan, 1982.

Geisler, Norman, and William Nix. *A General Introduction to the Bible.* Chicago: Moody, 1986.

Gelb, Ignace J. "Thoughts About Ebla: A Preliminary Evaluation, March 1977." *Syro-Mesopotamian Studies* 1, no. 1 (May 1977): 1–30.

Golb, Norman. *Who Wrote the Dead Sea Scrolls?: The Search for the Secret of Qumran.* New York: Scribner, 1995.

Goldin, Judah, trans. *The Living Talmud.* Univ. of Chicago Press, 1957.

Greenleaf, Simon. *The Testimony of the Evangelists.* Grand Rapids, MI: Baker, 1984.

Gromachi, Robert. *New Testament Survey.* Grand Rapids, MI: Baker, 1996.

Habermas, Gary. *The Historical Jesus: Ancient Evidence for the Life of Christ.* Joplin, MO: College Press, 1996.

———. *The Verdict of History.* Nashville, TN: Thomas Nelson, 1988.

Hanegraaff, Hank, and Paul Maier. *The Da Vinci Code: Fact or Fiction.* Wheaton, IL: Tyndale, 2004.

Harris, R. Laird. *Inspiration and Canonicity of the Bible.* Grand Rapids, MI: Zondervan, 1957.

Heidel, Alexander. *The Babylonian Genesis.* 2nd ed. Univ. of Chicago Press, 1954.

Hennecke, Edgar, and Wilhelm Schneemelche, eds. *New Testament Apocryphal.* 2 vols. Philadelphia: Westminster, 1963, 1965.

Henry, Carl F. H. *Revelation and the Bible.* Grand Rapids, MI: Baker, 1958.

Hills, Margaret T. *A Ready-Reference History of the English Bible.* Rev. ed. New York: American Bible Society, 1962.

Hoehner, Harold. *Chronological Aspects of the Life of Christ.* Grand Rapids, MI: Zondervan, 1978.

Hofner, Harry. "The Hittites and the Hurrians," *People of the Old Testament.* Ed. by D. J. Wiseman. London: Oxford Univ. Press, 1973.

Irenaeus. *Against Heresies.* In *Library of Christian Classics*, vol. 3, *Christology of the Latin Fathers.* Translated and edited by Edward R. Hardy. Philadelphia: Westminster, 1953.

James, Montague Rhodes. *The Apocryphal New Testament*. Oxford: Clarendon, 1955.

Jefferson, Thomas. *Jefferson Writings*. Edited by Merrill Peterson. New York: Literary Classics, 1984.

Josephus, Flavius. "Against Apion," *The Antiquities of the Jews*. New York: Ward, Lock, Bowden, 1900.

————. *The Life and Works of Flavius Josephus*. Translated by William Whiston. Philadelphia: Winston, 1936.

————. *The Works of Flavius Josephus*. Translated by William Whiston. Grand Rapids, MI: Associated and Authors, 1860.

Kelly, J. N. D. *Early Christian Doctrines*. San Francisco: Harper & Row, 1978.

Kenyon, Sir Frederick G. *Archaeology in the Holy Land*. New York: W. W. Norton, 1979.

Kenyon, Kathleen. *Beginning in Archaeology*. New York: Praegar, 1962.

Kilby, Clyde. *The Christian World of C. S. Lewis*. Grand Rapids, MI: Eerdmans, 1964.

Kittel, Gerhard, ed. *Theological Dictionary of the New Testament*. Translated and edited by Geoffrey W. Bromily. Grand Rapids, MI: Eerdmans, 1964–76.

Kramer, Samuel N. *History Begins at Sumer*. New York: Doubleday, 1959.

Lake, Kirsopp, ed. *The Apostolic Fathers*. 2 vols. *Loeb Classical Library* series. New York: Putnam, 1930.

Leiman, Sid Z. *The Canonization of Hebrew Scripture: The Talmudic and Midrashic Evidence. Hamdon*, CT: Archon, 1976.

Leith, John H., ed. *Creeds of the Churches*. Rev. ed. Atlanta: John Knox, 1973.

Lewis, C. S. *Mere Christianity*. New York: Macmillan, 1952.

————. *Miracles*. New York: Macmillan, 1947.

Lovett, Tim. "Gopher Wood or Go For Wood?" ✐*www.worldwideflood.com/ark/ wood/gopher_wood.htm*. April 22, 2005.

Lutzer, Erwin. *The Da Vinci Deception*. Wheaton, IL: Tyndale, 2004.

MacArthur, John. "Birth of the King: Who Were the Wise Men?" ✐*www.biblebb. com/files/MAC/sg2182.htm*. July 7, 2005.

Maier, Paul. *In the Fullness of Time: A Historian Looks at Christmas, Easter.* Harper San Francisco, 1991.

Matthiae, Paolo. *Ebla: An Empire Rediscovered*. Translated by Christopher Holme. Garden City, NY: Doubleday, 1981.

McCarter, P. Kyle. "The Early Diffusion of the Alphabet." *Biblical Archaeologist* 37, no. 3 (September 1974): 54–58.

McDowell, Josh. *Evidence that Demands a Verdict*. San Bernardino, CA: Campus Crusade, 1985.

McGonigal, Terence P. "'Every Scripture Is Inspired': An Exegesis of 2 Timothy 3:16– 17," *Studia Biblica et Theologica* 8 (April 1978): 53–64.

Meier, John. *A Marginal Jew: Rethinking the Historical Jesus*. Vol. 1. New York: Doubleday, 1991.

Merrill, Eugene. "Ebla and Biblical Historical Inerrancy." *Bibliotheca Sacra* 140, no. 560 (October 1983): 302–21.

Metzger, Bruce. *The Canon of the New Testament: Its Origin, Development, and Significance*. Oxford: Clarendon, 1987.

———. *The Early Versions of the New Testament: Their Origins, Transmission and Limitations*. Oxford: Clarendon, 1977.

———. "The Furniture of the Scriptorium at Qumran." *Revue de Qumran* 1 (1959): 509–515.

———. *An Introduction to the Apocrypha*. New York: Oxford Univ. Press, 1957.

———. *Manuscripts of the Greek Bible: An Introduction to Greek Paleography*. New York: Oxford Univ. Press, 1981.

Millard, A. R. "The Practice of Writing in Ancient Israel." *Biblical Archaeologist* 35, no. 4 (December 1972): 98–111.

Miller, Robert, ed. *The Complete Gospels*. Harper San Francisco, 1994.

Moorehead, A. *Darwin and the Beagle*. Harmondsworth, UK: Penguin, 1971.

Moorland, J., and M. J. Wilkins. *Jesus Under Fire*. Grand Rapids, MI: Zondervan, 1995.

Morris, Henry. *The Bible and Modern Science*. Rev. ed. Chicago: Moody, 1974.

———. *Men of Science, Men of God*. El Cajon, CA: Master, 1982.

Nix, William E. "Theological Presuppositions and Sixteenth-Century English Bible Translations." *Bibliotheca Sacra* 124, no. 493 (January–March 1967): 42–50; 124, no. 494 (April–June 1967): 117–24.

———. "Versions, Ancient and Medieval." In *Wycliffe Bible Encyclopedia*, edited by Charles F. Pfeiffer, Howard F. Vos, and John Rea. Chicago: Moody, 1975.

Packer, J. I. "On the Adequacy of Human Language," In *Inerrancy*, edited by Norman L. Geisler. Grand Rapids, MI: Zondervan, 1980.

Pei, Mario A. "The World's Chief Languages." In *Encyclopedia Britannica*, 4th ed., 1954.

Philo, Judaeus. *The Works of Philo*. Vol. 4. Translated by F. H. Colson. Cambridge: Harvard Univ. Press, 1935.

Pliny the Younger. *Letters*. Translated by W. Melmoth. Quoted in Norman Geisler, Baker's Encyclopedia of Christian Apologetics. Grand Rapids, MI: Baker, 1998.

Pope, Hugh. *English Versions of the Bible*. Revised and amplified by Sebastian Bullough. (1952; repr. Greenwood, CT, 1972).

Ramsey, Sir William. *The Bearing of Recent Discovery on the Trustworthiness of the New Testament*. (1915; repr. Grand Rapids, MI: Baker, 1953).

———. *St. Paul the Traveler and the Roman Citizen*. 3rd ed. Grand Rapids, MI: Baker, 1949.

Roberts, Alexander, and James Donaldson, eds. *The Ante-Nicene Fathers*. 10 vols. (1884–86; repr., Grand Rapids, MI: Eerdmans, 1956).

Robertson, James, ed. *The Facsimile Edition of the Nag Hammadi Codices*. Leiden: Brill, 1972–1984.

———. *The Nag Hammadi Library*. Rev. ed. Harper San Francisco, 1990.

Robinson, John A. T. *Redating the New Testament*. Philadelphia: Westminster, 1976.

Schaff, Philip, ed. *Nicene and Post-Nicene Fathers*. 14 vols. 1st series. (1886–94; repr., Grand Rapids, MI: Eerdmans, 1952).

Schaff, Philip, and Henry Wace, eds. *Nicene and Post-Nicene Fathers*. 12 vols. 2nd series. (1890–95; repr., Grand Rapids, MI: Eerdmans, 1952).

Sproul, R. C. *Reasons to Believe*. Grand Rapids, MI: Zondervan, Lamplighter, 1982.

Stobel, Lee. *The Case for Christ*. Grand Rapids, MI: Zondervan, 1998.

Stuart, Moses. *Critical History and Defense of the Old Testament Canon*. London: Tegg, 1849.

Tacitus. *Annals*. In *Great Books of the Western World*, edited by Robert Maynard Hutchins. Vol. 15, *The Annals and The Histories by Cornelius Tacitus*. Chicago: William Benton, 1952.

Thompson, Edward M. *A Handbook of Greek and Latin Paleography*. Chicago: Argonaut, 1966.

Trever, J. C. "The Discovery of the Scrolls." *Biblical Archaeologist* 11 (September 1948).

Unger, Merrill. *Unger's Bible Handbook*. Chicago: Moody, 1967.

Vermes, Geza, trans. *The Dead Sea Scrolls in English*. New York: Heritage, 1962.

Wernburg-Moller, P., trans. *Dead Sea Manual of Discipline*. Grand Rapids, MI: Eerdmans, 1957.

Wikipedia. "C. S. Lewis." http://en.wikipedia.org/wiki/C._S._Lewis. Accessed May 28, 2005.

Wittgenstein, Ludwig. *Tracticus Logico-Philosophicus*. London: Routledge & Kegan, 1961.

Wolters, Al. "Apocalyptic and the Copper Scroll." *Journal of New Eastern Studies* 49 (1990): 145–154.

Yamauchi, Edwin. "Easter—Myth, Hallucination or History," *Christianity Today*. 2 parts. (March 29, 1974; April 15, 1974).

————. "Jesus Outside the New Testament: What Is the Evidence?" *Jesus Under Fire: Modern Scholarship Reinvents the Historical Jesus*. Edited by Michael J. Wilkins and J. P. Moreland. Grand Rapids, MI: Zondervan, 1995.

————. *Pre-Christian Gnosticism: A Survey of the Proposed Evidences*. Grand Rapids, MI: Eerdmans, 1973.

————. *The Stones and the Scriptures*. Philadelphia: Lippincott, 1972.

————. "Unearthing Ebla's Ancient Secrets." *Christianity Today* (May 1981): 18–21.

————. "The Word from Nag Hammadi." *Christianity Today* (January 1978).

Zimmer, C. *Evolution: The Triumph of an Idea*. New York: Harper Collins, 2001.

Appendix C
Recommended Reading

Allis, Oswald. *Prophecy and the Church*. Grand Rapids, MI: Baker, 1945.

Beasley-Murray, G. R. *Baptism in the New Testament*. Grand Rapids, MI: Eerdmans, 1962.

Borland, James. *Christ in the Old Testament*. Chicago: Moody, 1978.

Bruner, Frederick. *A Theology of the Holy Spirit*. Grand Rapids, MI: Eerdmans, 1970.

Clark, Gordon H., et al. *Can I Trust My Bible?* Chicago: Moody, 1963.

Clark, Robert. *Darwin: Before and After*. Chicago: Moody, 1967.

Cottrell, Jack. *Baptism: A Biblical Study*. Joplin, MO: College Press, 1989.

————. *The Faith Once For All*. Joplin, MO: College Press, 2002.

————. *Faith's Fundamentals: Seven Essentials of Christian Belief*. Cincinnati, OH: Standard, 1995.

————. *His Truth*. Cincinnati, OH: Standard, 1980.

————. *What the Bible Says about God the Creator*. Joplin, MO: College Press, 1983.

————. *What the Bible Says about God the Redeemer*. Joplin, MO: College Press, 1987.

————. *What the Bible Says about God the Ruler*. Joplin, MO: College Press, 1984.

Cosgrove, Mark. *Psychology Gone Awry*. Grand Rapids, MI: Zondervan, 1979.

Craig, William. *The Existence of God and the Beginning of the Universe.* San Bernardino, CA: Here's Life, 1979.

———. *The Son Rises: The Historical Evidence for the Resurrection of Jesus.* Chicago: Moody, 1981.

Crossley, Robert. *The Trinity.* Downers Grove, IL: InterVarsity, 1977.

Dickason, Curtis. *Angels, Elect and Evil.* Chicago: Moody, 1975.

———. *Demon Possession and the Christian.* Chicago: Moody, 1987.

Duty, Guy. *If You Continue.* Minneapolis, MN: Bethany, 1966.

Ensign, Grayson, and Edward Howe. *Bothered? Bewildered? Bewitched?* Cincinnati, OH: Recovery, 1984.

———. *Counseling and Demonization: The Missing Link.* Amarillo, TX: Recovery, 1989.

Fudge, Edward W. *The Fire that Consumes: A Biblical and Historical Study of Final Punishment.* Fallbrook, CA: Verdict, 1982.

Gaffin, Richard. *Perspectives on Pentecost.* Grand Rapids, MI; Bake, 1979.

Gardner, Lynn. *Christianity Stands True: A Common Sense Look at the Evidence.* Joplin, MO: College Press, 1994.

Geisler, Norman. *Creating God in the Image of Man? The New "Open" View of God: Neothism's Dangerous Drift.* Minneapolis, MN: Bethany House, 1997.

———. *Is Man the Measure: An Evolution of Contemporary Humanism.* Grand Rapids, MI: Baker, 1983.

Gish, Duane. *Evolution: The Fossils Say No.* 2nd ed. San Diego: Institute for Creation Research, 1973.

Gromacki, Robert. *The Modern Tongues Movement.* Phillipsburg, NJ: Presbyterian & Reformed, 1967.

————. *The Virgin Birth: Doctrine of Deity.* Grand Rapids, MI: Baker, 1974.

Habermas, Gary. *Ancient Evidence for the Life of Jesus.* Nashville, TN: Thomas Nelson, 1984.

Habermas, Gary R., and J. P. Moreland. *Immortality: The Other Side of Death.* Nashville, TN: Thomas Nelson, 1992.

Hendriksen, William. *More than Conquerors: An Interpretation of the Book of Revelation.* Grand Rapids, MI: 1977.

Henry, Carl R. H. *God, Revelation and Authority.* Vol. 1: *God Who Speaks and Shows. Preliminary Considerations.* Waco, TX: Word, 1976.

Hoekema, Anthony. *The Bible and the Future.* Grand Rapids, MI: Eerdmans, 1979.

Horn, Robert. *Go Free!: The Meaning of Justification.* London: InterVarsity, 1976.

Jastrow, Robert. *God and the Astronomers.* New York: Warner Books, 1980.

Joppie, A. S. *The Ministry of Angels.* Grand Rapids, MI: Baker, 1953.

Koch, Kurt. *Demonology, Past and Present.* Grand Rapids, MI: Moody, 1973.

Laidle, John. *The Bible Doctrine of Man, or the Anthropology and Psychology of Scripture.* Edinburg: Clark, 1905.

Lawlor, George. *When God Became Man.* Chicago: Moody, 1978.

Lewis, C. S. *The Problem of Pain.* New York: Macmillan, 1943.

Lewis, Gordon. *Testing Christianity's Truth Claims.* Chicago: Moody, 1976.

Lightner, Robert. *The Savior and the Scriptures*. Grand Rapids, MI: Baker, 1981.

Lindsell, Harold. *Battle for the Bible*. Grand Rapids, MI: Zondervan, 1976.

MacPherson, Dave. *The Incredible Cover-Up*. Medford, OR: Omega, 1980.

McDonald, H. D. *Jesus: Human and Divine*. Grand Rapids, MI: Baker, 1968.

McDowell, Josh, and Bart Larson. *Jesus: A Biblical Defense of His Deity*. San Bernardino, CA: Here's Life, 1983.

Minear, Paul. *Images of the Church in the New Testament*. Philadelphia: Westminster, 1960.

Montgomery, John W., ed. *Demon Possession*. Minneapolis, MN: Bethany, 1976.

————. *God's Inerrant Word*. Minneapolis, MN: Bethany, 1974.

Morris, Leon. *The Apostolic Preaching of the Cross*. Grand Rapids, MI: Eerdmans, 1955.

————. *The Biblical Doctrine of Judgment*. Grand Rapids, MI: Eerdmans, 1961.

————. *I Believe in Revelation*. Grand Rapids, MI: Eerdmans, 1976.

————. *The Wages of Sin*. London: Tyndale, 1954.

Myers, Edward. *The Problem of Evil and Suffering*. West Monroe, LA: Howard, 1978.

Nash, Ronald. *The Word of God and the Mind of Man*. Grand Rapids, MI: Zondervan, 1982.

Packer, J. I. *Knowing God*. Downers Grove, IL: InterVarsity, 1973.

Pentecost, Dwight. *A Harmony of the Words and Works of Jesus Christ*. Grand Rapids, MI: Zondervan, 1981.

Peterson, Robert. *Are Demons for Real?* Chicago: Moody, 1972.

Smith, James. *What the Bible Says about the Promised Messiah*. Joplin, MO: College Press, 1984.

Smith, Wilbur M. *The Biblical Doctrine of Heaven*. Chicago: Moody, 1968.

Staton, Knofel. *How to Know the Will of God*. Grand Rapids, MI: Baker, 1961.

Stott, John. *Baptism and Fullness*. Downers Grove, IL: InterVarsity, 1977.

————. *Understanding Christ*. Grand Rapids, MI: Zondervan, 1979.

Swihart, Phillip. *The Edge of Death*. Downers Grove, IL: InterVarsity Press, 1978.

Too, Peter. *The Ascension of Our Lord*. Nashville, TN: Thomas Nelson, 1984.

Warfield, Benjamin. *Inspiration and Authority of the Bible*. Philadelphia: Presbyterian & Reformed, 1948.

————. *The Person and Work of Christ*. Chicago: Moody, 1969.

Wenham, John. *Easter Enigma: Are the Resurrection Accounts in Conflict?* Grand Rapids, MI: Zondervan, 1984.

Wiersbe, Warren. *Why Us?: When Bad Things Happen to God's People*. Old Tappan, NJ: Fleming H. Revell, 1984.

Wolff, Richard. *The Last Enemy*. Washington, DC: Canon, 1974.

Wysong, R. L. *The Creation-Evolution Controversy: Toward a Rational Solution*. East Lansing, MI: Inquiry, 1976.

Young, Edward. *Thy Word Is Truth*. Grand Rapids, MI: Eerdmans, 1957.

Index

A

B

C

THE EVERYTHING SERIES!

BUSINESS & PERSONAL FINANCE

Everything® Budgeting Book
Everything® Business Planning Book
Everything® Coaching and Mentoring Book
Everything® Fundraising Book
Everything® Get Out of Debt Book
Everything® Grant Writing Book
Everything® Home-Based Business Book, 2nd Ed.
Everything® Homebuying Book, 2nd Ed.
Everything® Homeselling Book, 2nd Ed.
Everything® Investing Book, 2nd Ed.
Everything® Landlording Book
Everything® Leadership Book
Everything® Managing People Book
Everything® Negotiating Book
Everything® Online Business Book
Everything® Personal Finance Book
Everything® Personal Finance in Your 20s and 30s Book
Everything® Project Management Book
Everything® Real Estate Investing Book
Everything® Robert's Rules Book, $7.95
Everything® Selling Book
Everything® Start Your Own Business Book
Everything® Wills & Estate Planning Book

COMPUTERS

Everything® Online Auctions Book
Everything® Blogging Book

COOKING

Everything® Barbecue Cookbook
Everything® Bartender's Book, $9.95
Everything® Chinese Cookbook
Everything® Cocktail Parties and Drinks Book
Everything® College Cookbook
Everything® Cookbook
Everything® Cooking for Two Cookbook
Everything® Diabetes Cookbook
Everything® Easy Gourmet Cookbook
Everything® Fondue Cookbook
Everything® Gluten-Free Cookbook
Everything® Glycemic Index Cookbook
Everything® Grilling Cookbook

Everything® Healthy Meals in Minutes Cookbook
Everything® Holiday Cookbook
Everything® Indian Cookbook
Everything® Italian Cookbook
Everything® Low-Carb Cookbook
Everything® Low-Fat High-Flavor Cookbook
Everything® Low-Salt Cookbook
Everything® Meals for a Month Cookbook
Everything® Mediterranean Cookbook
Everything® Mexican Cookbook
Everything® One-Pot Cookbook
Everything® Pasta Cookbook
Everything® Quick Meals Cookbook
Everything® Slow Cooker Cookbook
Everything® Slow Cooking for a Crowd Cookbook
Everything® Soup Cookbook
Everything® Tex-Mex Cookbook
Everything® Thai Cookbook
Everything® Vegetarian Cookbook
Everything® Wild Game Cookbook
Everything® Wine Book, 2nd Ed.

CRAFT SERIES

Everything® Crafts—Baby Scrapbooking
Everything® Crafts—Bead Your Own Jewelry
Everything® Crafts—Create Your Own Greeting Cards
Everything® Crafts—Easy Projects
Everything® Crafts—Polymer Clay for Beginners
Everything® Crafts—Rubber Stamping Made Easy
Everything® Crafts—Wedding Decorations and Keepsakes

HEALTH

Everything® Alzheimer's Book
Everything® Diabetes Book
Everything® Health Guide to Adult Bipolar Disorder
Everything® Health Guide to Controlling Anxiety
Everything® Health Guide to Fibromyalgia
Everything® Hypnosis Book

Everything® Low Cholesterol Book
Everything® Massage Book
Everything® Menopause Book
Everything® Nutrition Book
Everything® Reflexology Book
Everything® Stress Management Book

HISTORY

Everything® American Government Book
Everything® American History Book
Everything® Civil War Book
Everything® Irish History & Heritage Book
Everything® Middle East Book

GAMES

Everything® 15-Minute Sudoku Book, $9.95
Everything® 30-Minute Sudoku Book, $9.95
Everything® Blackjack Strategy Book
Everything® Brain Strain Book, $9.95
Everything® Bridge Book
Everything® Card Games Book
Everything® Card Tricks Book, $9.95
Everything® Casino Gambling Book, 2nd Ed.
Everything® Chess Basics Book
Everything® Craps Strategy Book
Everything® Crossword and Puzzle Book
Everything® Crossword Challenge Book
Everything® Cryptograms Book, $9.95
Everything® Easy Crosswords Book
Everything® Easy Kakuro Book, $9.95
Everything® Games Book, 2nd Ed.
Everything® Giant Sudoku Book, $9.95
Everything® Kakuro Challenge Book, $9.95
Everything® Large-Print Crosswords Book
Everything® Lateral Thinking Puzzles Book, $9.95
Everything® Pencil Puzzles Book, $9.95
Everything® Poker Strategy Book
Everything® Pool & Billiards Book
Everything® Test Your IQ Book, $9.95
Everything® Texas Hold 'Em Book, $9.95
Everything® Travel Crosswords Book, $9.95
Everything® Word Games Challenge Book
Everything® Word Search Book

Bolded titles are new additions to the series.
All Everything® books are priced at $12.95 or $14.95, unless otherwise stated. Prices subject to change without notice.

HOBBIES

Everything® Candlemaking Book
Everything® Cartooning Book
Everything® Drawing Book
Everything® Family Tree Book, 2nd Ed.
Everything® Knitting Book
Everything® Knots Book
Everything® Photography Book
Everything® Quilting Book
Everything® Scrapbooking Book
Everything® Sewing Book
Everything® Woodworking Book

HOME IMPROVEMENT

Everything® Feng Shui Book
Everything® Feng Shui Decluttering Book, $9.95
Everything® Fix-It Book
Everything® Home Decorating Book
Everything® Homebuilding Book
Everything® Lawn Care Book
Everything® Organize Your Home Book

KIDS' BOOKS

All titles are $7.95
Everything® Kids' Animal Puzzle &
    Activity Book
Everything® Kids' Baseball Book, 4th Ed.
Everything® Kids' Bible Trivia Book
Everything® Kids' Bugs Book
Everything® Kids' Christmas Puzzle
    & Activity Book
Everything® Kids' Cookbook
Everything® Kids' Crazy Puzzles Book
Everything® Kids' Dinosaurs Book
**Everything® Kids' Gross Hidden Pictures
    Book**
Everything® Kids' Gross Jokes Book
Everything® Kids' Gross Mazes Book
Everything® Kids' Gross Puzzle and
    Activity Book
Everything® Kids' Halloween Puzzle
    & Activity Book
Everything® Kids' Hidden Pictures Book
Everything® Kids' Horses Book
Everything® Kids' Joke Book
Everything® Kids' Knock Knock Book
Everything® Kids' Math Puzzles Book
Everything® Kids' Mazes Book
Everything® Kids' Money Book
Everything® Kids' Nature Book

Everything® Kids' Pirates Puzzle and
    Activity Book
Everything® Kids' Puzzle Book
Everything® Kids' Riddles & Brain Teasers Book
Everything® Kids' Science Experiments Book
Everything® Kids' Sharks Book
Everything® Kids' Soccer Book
Everything® Kids' Travel Activity Book

KIDS' STORY BOOKS

Everything® Fairy Tales Book

LANGUAGE

Everything® Conversational Japanese Book
    (with CD), $19.95
Everything® French Grammar Book
Everything® French Phrase Book, $9.95
Everything® French Verb Book, $9.95
**Everything® German Practice Book with
    CD, $19.95**
Everything® Inglés Book
Everything® Learning French Book
Everything® Learning German Book
Everything® Learning Italian Book
Everything® Learning Latin Book
Everything® Learning Spanish Book
Everything® Sign Language Book
Everything® Spanish Grammar Book
Everything® Spanish Phrase Book, $9.95
Everything® Spanish Practice Book
    (with CD), $19.95
Everything® Spanish Verb Book, $9.95

MUSIC

Everything® Drums Book (with CD), $19.95
Everything® Guitar Book
**Everything® Guitar Chords Book with CD,
    $19.95**
Everything® Home Recording Book
Everything® Playing Piano and Keyboards
    Book
Everything® Reading Music Book (with CD),
    $19.95
Everything® Rock & Blues Guitar Book
    (with CD), $19.95
Everything® Songwriting Book

NEW AGE

Everything® Astrology Book, 2nd Ed.
Everything® Dreams Book, 2nd Ed.
Everything® Love Signs Book, $9.95

Everything® Numerology Book
Everything® Paganism Book
Everything® Palmistry Book
Everything® Psychic Book
Everything® Reiki Book
Everything® Tarot Book
Everything® Wicca and Witchcraft Book

PARENTING

Everything® Baby Names Book, 2nd Ed.
Everything® Baby Shower Book
Everything® Baby's First Food Book
Everything® Baby's First Year Book
Everything® Birthing Book
Everything® Breastfeeding Book
Everything® Father-to-Be Book
Everything® Father's First Year Book
Everything® Get Ready for Baby Book
Everything® Get Your Baby to Sleep Book,
    $9.95
Everything® Getting Pregnant Book
Everything® Homeschooling Book
Everything® Mother's First Year Book
Everything® Parent's Guide to Children
    and Divorce
Everything® Parent's Guide to Children
    with ADD/ADHD
Everything® Parent's Guide to Children
    with Asperger's Syndrome
Everything® Parent's Guide to Children
    with Autism
Everything® Parent's Guide to Children with
    Bipolar Disorder
Everything® Parent's Guide to Children
    with Dyslexia
Everything® Parent's Guide to Positive
    Discipline
Everything® Parent's Guide to Raising a
    Successful Child
**Everything® Parent's Guide to Raising
    Boys**
**Everything® Parent's Guide to Raising
    Siblings**
Everything® Parent's Guide to Tantrums
Everything® Parent's Guide to the Overweight
    Child
Everything® Parent's Guide to the Strong-
    Willed Child
Everything® Parenting a Teenager Book
Everything® Potty Training Book, $9.95
Everything® Pregnancy Book, 2nd Ed.

Bolded titles are new additions to the series.
All Everything® books are priced at $12.95 or $14.95, unless otherwise stated. Prices subject to change without notice.

Everything® Pregnancy Fitness Book
Everything® Pregnancy Nutrition Book
Everything® Pregnancy Organizer, $15.00
Everything® Toddler Book
Everything® Toddler Activities Book
Everything® Tween Book
Everything® Twins, Triplets, and More Book

PETS

Everything® Boxer Book
Everything® Cat Book, 2nd Ed.
Everything® Chihuahua Book
Everything® Dachshund Book
Everything® Dog Book   -
Everything® Dog Health Book
Everything® Dog Training and Tricks Book
Everything® German Shepherd Book
Everything® Golden Retriever Book
Everything® Horse Book
Everything® Horse Care Book
Everything® Horseback Riding Book
Everything® Labrador Retriever Book
Everything® Poodle Book
Everything® Pug Book
Everything® Puppy Book
Everything® Rottweiler Book
Everything® Small Dogs Book
Everything® Tropical Fish Book
Everything® Yorkshire Terrier Book

REFERENCE

Everything® Car Care Book
Everything® Classical Mythology Book
Everything® Computer Book
Everything® Divorce Book
Everything® Einstein Book
Everything® Etiquette Book, 2nd Ed.
Everything® Inventions and Patents Book
Everything® Mafia Book
Everything® Mary Magdalene Book
Everything® Philosophy Book
Everything® Psychology Book
Everything® Shakespeare Book

RELIGION

Everything® Angels Book
Everything® Bible Book
Everything® Buddhism Book
Everything® Catholicism Book

Everything® Christianity Book
Everything® Freemasons Book
Everything® History of the Bible Book
Everything® Jewish History & Heritage Book
Everything® Judaism Book
Everything® Kabbalah Book
Everything® Koran Book
Everything® Prayer Book
Everything® Saints Book
Everything® Torah Book
Everything® Understanding Islam Book
Everything® World's Religions Book
Everything® Zen Book

SCHOOL & CAREERS

Everything® Alternative Careers Book
Everything® College Major Test Book
Everything® College Survival Book, 2nd Ed.
Everything® Cover Letter Book, 2nd Ed.
Everything® Get-a-Job Book
Everything® Guide to Being a Paralegal
Everything® Guide to Being a Real Estate
    Agent
Everything® Guide to Starting and Running
    a Restaurant
Everything® Job Interview Book
Everything® New Nurse Book
Everything® New Teacher Book
Everything® Paying for College Book
Everything® Practice Interview Book
Everything® Resume Book, 2nd Ed.
Everything® Study Book
Everything® Teacher's Organizer, $16.95

SELF-HELP

Everything® Dating Book, 2nd Ed.
Everything® Great Sex Book
Everything® Kama Sutra Book
Everything® Self-Esteem Book

SPORTS & FITNESS

Everything® Fishing Book
Everything® Golf Instruction Book
Everything® Pilates Book
Everything® Running Book
Everything® Total Fitness Book
Everything® Weight Training Book
Everything® Yoga Book

TRAVEL

Everything® Family Guide to Hawaii
Everything® Family Guide to Las Vegas,
    2nd Ed.
Everything® Family Guide to New York City,
    2nd Ed.
Everything® Family Guide to RV Travel &
    Campgrounds
Everything® Family Guide to the Walt Disney
    World Resort®, Universal Studios®,
    and Greater Orlando, 4th Ed.
Everything® Family Guide to Cruise Vacations
Everything® Family Guide to the Caribbean
Everything® Family Guide to Washington
    D.C., 2nd Ed.
Everything® Guide to New England
Everything® Travel Guide to the Disneyland
    Resort®, California Adventure®,
    Universal Studios®, and the
    Anaheim Area

WEDDINGS

Everything® Bachelorette Party Book, $9.95
Everything® Bridesmaid Book, $9.95
Everything® Elopement Book, $9.95
Everything® Father of the Bride Book, $9.95
Everything® Groom Book, $9.95
Everything® Mother of the Bride Book, $9.95
Everything® Outdoor Wedding Book
Everything® Wedding Book, 3rd Ed.
Everything® Wedding Checklist, $9.95
Everything® Wedding Etiquette Book, $9.95
Everything® Wedding Organizer, $15.00
Everything® Wedding Shower Book, $9.95
Everything® Wedding Vows Book, $9.95
Everything® Weddings on a Budget Book, $9.95

WRITING

Everything® Creative Writing Book
Everything® Get Published Book, 2nd Ed.
Everything® Grammar and Style Book
Everything® Guide to Writing a Book Proposal
Everything® Guide to Writing a Novel
Everything® Guide to Writing Children's Books
Everything® Guide to Writing Research Papers
Everything® Screenwriting Book
Everything® Writing Poetry Book
Everything® Writing Well Book